Municipal Management Series

Effective
Communication
A Local Government Guide

International
City/County
ICMA
Management
Association

The International City/County Management Association is the professional and educational organization for appointed administrators and assistant administrators in local government. The purposes of ICMA are to enhance the quality of local government and to nurture and assist professional local government administrators in the United States and other countries. To further its mission, ICMA develops and disseminates new approaches to management through training programs, information services, and publications.

Local government managers—carrying a wide range of titles—serve cities, towns, counties, councils of governments, and state/provincial associations of local governments. They serve at the direction of elected councils and governing boards. ICMA serves these managers and local governments through many programs that aim at improving the manager's professional competence and strengthening the quality of all local governments.

The International City/County Management Association was founded in 1914; adopted its City Management Code of Ethics in 1924; and established its Institute for Training in Municipal Administration in 1934. The Institute, in turn, provided the basis for the Municipal Management Series, generally termed the "ICMA Green Books."

ICMA's interests and activities include public management education; standards of ethics for members; the *Municipal Year Book* and other data services; urban research; and newsletters, a monthly magazine, *Public Management*, and other publications. ICMA's efforts toward the improvement of local government management—as represented by this book— are offered for all local governments and educational institutions. ∎

Municipal Management Series

Effective Communication

A Local Government Guide

Published for the
ICMA Training Institute

By the International
City/County Management
Association

Edited by
Kenneth M. Wheeler

Municipal Management Series

Effective Communication: A Local Government Guide

Advanced Supervisory Practices

The Effective Local Government Manager

Effective Supervisory Practices

Emergency Management: Principles and Practice for Local Government

Housing and Local Government

Local Government Police Management

Management of Local Planning

Management of Local Public Works

Management Policies in Local Government Finance

Managing Fire Services

Managing Human Services

Managing Local Government: Cases in Decision Making

Managing Municipal Leisure Services

Managing Small Cities and Counties: A Practical Guide

The Practice of Local Government Planning

The Practice of State and Regional Planning

Service Contracting: A Local Government Guide

Library of Congress Cataloging-in-Publication Data

Effective communication: a local government guide /
   editor, Kenneth M. Wheeler.
      p. cm.—(Municipal management series)
      Rev. ed of: Effective communication: getting the
      message across. ©1983.
      Includes bibliographical references and index.
      ISBN 0-87326-094-5
      1. Public relations—Municipal government. 2.
Government publicity.   I. Wheeler, Kenneth M.
(Kenneth Milton).   II. Series.
JS100.P83E35   1994
659.2'9352—dc20   94-27014
                                            CIP

Printed in the United States of America.
01 00 99 98 97 96 95 94
 8 7 6 5 4 3 2 1

Foreword

Recognizing the need for excellent communication skills in an era of increasing complexity and growing technology, ICMA published *Effective Communication: Getting the Message Across* in 1983. The purpose of the book was to provide local government administrators and employees with clear and succinct guidelines to communicating successfully as they perform the work of local government.

Today, effective communication skills at all levels of the organization are even more indispensable. Citizens are demanding better services, more accountability on the part of their local government, and more participation in that government. Ongoing, two-way communication between local government and citizens is essential; good communication between staff and elected officials and among all local government employees is also essential.

This second edition of *Effective Communication* has been developed to offer local government practitioners information and guidelines on the communication strategies and skills that they need for the 1990s and beyond. Some chapters from the first edition, such as those on communicating with elected officials and the media, have been retained in essence but comprehensively updated to reflect the technological, social, and demographic changes of the 1990s. Four completely new chapters have been added, on communication within the local government organization; planning and developing a communications program; giving effective presentations; and the role of cable television.

A number of people contributed to this book. We would like to thank the following individuals, who made valuable suggestions for updating the first edition: Frank Benest, city manager, Brea, California; Jim Campbell, director of general government services, Greenville, South Carolina; Jim Cavenaugh, management/finance consultant, Pennsylvania Department of Community Affairs; Daniel W. Fitzpatrick, city manager, Oak Park, Michigan; Barbara Johnson, director of public information, Winston-Salem, North Carolina; Leon Johnson, assistant city manager, Suffolk, Virginia; Mark Levin, city administrator, Maryland Heights, Missouri; Pamela Lingle, director, public information, Virginia Beach, Virginia; Jeffrey Luke, associate professor, Department of Planning, Public Policy, and Management and director of the Pacific Program, University of Oregon, Eugene; Virginia Plylar, former training analyst, Appalachian Council of Governments, Greenville, South Carolina; Patrick Svacina, assistant to the city manager, Forth Worth, Texas; Michael Vasu, associate professor of public administration/director, social science computer lab, North Carolina State University, Raleigh; Susan Watkins, president, S. Watkins Communications, Colorado Springs,

Colorado; Sherman Wyman, associate professor, School of Urban and Public Affairs, University of Texas, Arlington.

We also extend special thanks to our editorial advisors, who helped develop the second edition and reviewed early drafts of the chapters: Laurie Cottrell DeVarney, president, Laurel Communications Group, Agoura Hills, California; Robert L. Layton, city manager, Urbandale, Iowa; Lydia Manchester, alderman, Fair Oaks Ranch, Texas (former communications manager, Public Technology, Inc.); and Bill Mascenik, director, CCAN Innovation Group, Long Beach, California.

We are also grateful to Francie Gilman, former business manager, Public Technology, Inc., who assisted with information and advice during the book's development, and to the chapter authors for their contributions and for their patience and cooperation during the book's development.

ICMA staff members who contributed to the project include: Elizabeth K. Kellar, deputy executive director; Barbara H. Moore, director of publications; Verity Weston-Truby, who managed the project; Eileen Hughes, who performed various editorial tasks, including production editing; Dawn M. Leland, who coordinated production; Jane Pellicciotto, who designed the book and its cover; and Phyllis Brown, who performed various administrative tasks and input the manuscript.

We would also like to acknowledge Vincent Ercolano, who helped in the book's development and performed substantive editing; Cary Hoagland, who copyedited the manuscript; and Lynne Hofman, who created the layout.

William H. Hansell, Jr.
Executive Director, ICMA
Washington, D.C.

Table of Contents

PART III Communication Tools and Techniques

Communication
Overview

1 Effective Management Means Effective Communication

As the twentieth century draws to a close, communication technologies and techniques are changing so fast that—in the words of Lewis Carroll—"it takes all the running you can do, to keep in the same place." Local government managers who are determined to keep up (and maybe even gain some ground) realize that to manage is to communicate. They make it part of their job to equip themselves to plan and execute communication programs that are effective.

This revised edition of *Effective Communication* is a tool for public sector managers whose responsibilities include communicating with the public, the media, and government officials, both elected and appointed. Specifically, this book is designed to be helpful to

City and county managers

Assistant managers

Heads of departments and divisions

Directors of communication and public information officers.

The purpose of communication is to achieve results in government and in the community. This introductory chapter sets the tone for the book and sets the stage for the ten chapters that follow by stressing that effective communication is a two-way street. Listening and follow-up play major parts in determining the quality of relationships we develop as public sector communicators. This chapter expands that theme in the following topics:

Why effective communication is important

The changing communication environment

Effective communication: The purpose of this book

The concept of target audiences

Getting results

Communicating through the clutter

The importance of listening.

Why effective communication is important

Because a bond issue fails in California, certain educational, water utility, and fire-protection facilities that are critically needed will not be built. The reason? It was "just a communication problem."

A city council in Texas drastically alters a city manager's carefully balanced budget, resulting in severe problems of morale in the operating of the departments of the city. The reason? It was "just a communication problem."

After what they claim is years of neglect by management, employees of a town in Florida walk off the job, causing operational and legal problems. The reason? It was "just a communication problem."

Despite economic arguments that show clear benefits, a community in Missouri fails to build a new baseball stadium, thus losing a professional team to another city. The reason? It was "just a communication problem."

Today's local government is faced with complex issues that were unknown just a generation ago. Consequently, the organizations that localities have formed to deal with those issues are themselves complex and specialized. The city or county is expected not only to deliver pure

The shorter the message and the more narrowly defined the audience, the better the chances of success.

water, keep the streets crime free, and patch potholes seconds after they develop, but also to keep the local businesses satisfied and productive. The local government is expected to bring in new commerce to generate jobs and tax revenues, stage festivals throughout the year to entertain citizens and attract tourists, provide state-of-the-art computerized access to local services and information, and produce first-class programming for the local government cable channel. Moreover, all these projects are supposed to be run by happy, helpful, empowered, productive, and service-oriented employees.

A matter of life and death

Speaking, writing, reading, listening, gesturing, transmitting data, and other forms of communication so pervade government that they are often taken for granted. And yet communication often makes the difference between government success and failure, sometimes between life and death.

Source: James L. Garnett, *Communicating for Results in Government: A Strategic Approach for Public Managers* (San Francisco: Jossey-Bass, 1992), p. 3.

The increased complexity of the public sector manager's job often serves merely to ratchet expectations up to almost impossible levels. How could any one person or any one organization excel in all of these things all the time? When, as is inevitable, some failure occurs, an objective critique often shows that the management team did a thorough and professional job in most areas. So why the failure? Oh, it was "just a communication problem."

Local government managers are no longer mere "bean counters," responsible only for making sure things don't go wrong. Today's managers are expected to make things go right. If one of the costs of progress is an inevitable clash of ideas, then the manager is expected to be the facilitator, the referee, the motivator—in short, the communicator. Many local government managers spend most of their time filling that role; so do their assistants, department heads, and division heads.

Our time has been dubbed the Information Age. Paper (and recently electronic) transactions have replaced the exchange of hard currency in the marketplace, so that financial institutions are now centers of information in motion. Because of the thousands of messages that bombard all of us every day, some observers have labeled the present period an age of information overload. Most people have learned to cope with the overload by simply tuning out extraneous information. Studies have shown that only fifteen minutes after seeing an advertisement on television, people cannot recall the name of the product.

Communicating effectively through this clutter calls for information programs that are not only well planned and well executed, but also carefully aimed at specific audiences to achieve measurable goals. The shorter the message and the more narrowly defined the audience, the better the chances of success. Successful trial lawyers never make more than three points to a jury. A congressman once asserted that he would never vote for any measure that took more than two minutes to explain.

The changing communication environment

A few decades ago, communication theorist Marshall McLuhan described our world as a "global village." He pointed out that in the time of George Washington, the means of transportation and of communication (they used to be inextricably linked) were essentially the same as they had been in the time of Alexander the Great twenty-two centuries earlier. It took a long time for people—and messages—to move from one place to another. Twenty miles a day was a good pace for both President Washington and Emperor Alexander. In the War of 1812, General Andrew Jackson won a glorious and decisive victory over the British at the Battle of New Orleans. But it was marred by one small difficulty: a peace agreement had been signed two weeks before the battle. Word had not reached either army in Louisiana in time—proving that our ancestors suffered from "just a communication problem" too, only on a different scale from ours.

Later in the nineteenth century, the telegraph revolutionized communication, just as the steam engine forever changed transportation. But although people marveled at the miracles of telegraphy and steam propulsion, they would be awestruck by the commonplace tools of today's communication such as computers, fiber optics, and communication satellites. The ongoing informational revolution is so pervasive a part of life today that few people grasp its impact. In many cities today, the budget for "normal" communications—paper, copying, computers, telephones, modems, fax machines, and staff whose primary job is communicating—may be more than the entire budget for the same community just a few decades ago.

The changes brought about by the communication revolution, though, go far beyond the changes in the technology used to generate and send information. After all, as historian Arnold Toynbee noted, *technology* is just a long Greek word for a bag of tools. From the perspective of city and county governments, the communication revolution has created a new breed of citizens who are better informed—and sooner informed—than ever before.

If knowledge is power, today's citizens are the most powerful in history. Before the election of John F. Kennedy in 1960, U.S. presidential candidates were chosen by a handful of powerful politicians. The "smoke-filled room" was not just a myth. But new forms of communication technology changed all that: Kennedy was the first presidential candidate to make his case directly to the American public. His adept use of mass media—especially television—created a new political world, in which candidates scramble for air time and column inches—and often concern themselves more with images than with substance. For better or worse, presidents are now picked by all the people, not just by politicians.

In view of those far-reaching changes in communication, today's local government manager functions in a world of empowered citizens who are quite ready to take whatever information is at their disposal and mount an informational attack to achieve their goals—or sometimes just to keep others from achieving theirs. This phenomenon of well-informed, empowered citizens is sometimes referred to as "the court of public opinion." But regardless of labels, the fact is that today's local government more than ever needs the consent of the governed in order to govern effectively.

In a nutshell, that requirement means that the manager must be the chief communicator in an organization of very good communicators, constantly taking the pulse of the public and having a keen sense of what people want and what they consider important. It means that the local government needs to understand communication as a two-way, interactive process in which the community is involved in planning and decision making, a process that can build community spirit among citi-

The communication revolution has created a new breed of citizens who are better informed than ever before.

zens and greatly enhance the local quality of life. But such a process requires first a commitment on the part of management and then the communication skills to make the process work.

Great(er) expectations

Government's audiences now expect and demand more of government workers as senders and receivers of communication. The diversity and demands of audiences mean that public managers must consistently communicate at intrapersonal, interpersonal, group, organizational, and public communication levels. This diversity of audiences and levels of communicating requires the ability to analyze audiences and flexibility in communicating with them.

Source: James L. Garnett, *Communicating for Results in Government: A Strategic Approach for Public Managers* (San Francisco: Jossey-Bass, 1992), pp. 15-16.

Even a casual glance at the crystal ball shows that future citizens will be even more copiously informed, thanks to even faster news reporting and more direct communication links with city hall and the county building. As a result, citizens will hold greater expectations of government as an interactive process.

For local public sector supervisors and their staffs, these changes will continue to increase the role that communication plays in management. One of the recent "crystal balls" of special interest to local government managers is the report of ICMA's FutureVisions Consortium, published in 1991. Communication issues are addressed at several points in the Consortium's report, *Future Challenges, Future Opportunities,* and some of the conclusions seem inescapable. The report focuses on the manager's role in building consensus within a community, and offers this succinct advice: "Become a better communicator, analyst, and packager of information."[1]

Effective communication: The purpose of this book

Because communication is more important than ever in local government, ICMA has developed this book to help managers at all levels of local government

1. Acquire a fuller understanding of the communication process in the context of local government
2. Sharpen the communication skills needed to achieve specific results.

The book is organized into three parts: an overview of communication (Chapters 1 and 2), methods of communicating with four important audiences (Chapters 3 through 6), and techniques and tools of communication (Chapters 7 through 11).

The communication overview offered in Chapters 1 and 2 deals with the basic concepts of communication. The topics covered in Chapter 1 include discussions of the importance of effective communication, definitions of communication, and methods of using communication to achieve desired results. Chapter 2 lays further groundwork with a discussion of the importance of organizational identity and image and methods of measuring effectiveness in both of these areas.

The four chapters in Part II cover communication between appointed local government officials and their most important audiences: citizens,

The four most important audiences of appointed local government officials are citizens, elected officials, employees, and the news media.

elected officials, city or county employees, and the news media. Chapter 3 includes a discussion of the various roles played by the citizens of a community—as voters, taxpayers, and customers. The chapter also provides suggestions on gauging community opinion and communicating actively instead of simply reacting. Chapter 4 deals with the importance of effective communication between elected and appointed officials at the local level and methods of keeping the channels of communication open. Chapter 5 covers communication with front-line employees, including pointers on creative management techniques that may challenge the traditional hierarchical approach to organization. Chapter 6 offers local government officials guidance on communicating effectively with the various components of the news media by taking a proactive approach, often anticipating situations in which electronic and print journalists might become involved.

The five chapters that make up Part III focus on various instruments of communication, from the communication program itself to specific media such as newsletters and cable television. Chapter 7 provides guidance on ways of integrating the communication function into the structure of local government organizations. Chapter 8 emphasizes the individual as the starting point of good communication and gives practical advice on how to be a better person-to-person communicator. One of the purposes of Chapter 9 is to help managers determine which situations lend themselves to in-person presentations. Chapter 9 also includes suggestions on preparing and giving personal presentations. Chapter 10 covers the basics of communicating through the written word. It includes a survey of various print media and advice on when and how to use them. Chapter 11 focuses on the increasing importance of cable television as a means of communicating with local government officials' various audiences.

The authors who have contributed to this volume recognize that the thousands of local governments in the United States today are diverse in many ways—in their history, geography, economics, size, politics, ethnic composition, and function. But from New York City to Nome, Alaska, all of them function in a global village where success or failure often hinges on "just a communication problem."

The concept of target audiences

A cornerstone of effective communication is understanding that there is really no such thing as "the general public." Put another way: on most issues, most of the time, most people really don't care. Only a small segment of the population is engaged by any particular community or governmental issue. The trick lies in knowing *which* segment of the population.

In all communities, however large or small, there are typically four broad groups of people—or *target audiences*—with whom local government officials must communicate. Each of these target audiences is the subject of a chapter in Part II (Chapters 3-6) of this book:

Residents of the community

Elected officials of the city or county

Local government employees

Members of the news media.

As the chapters of Part II discuss in more depth, these large groupings, although useful, are often too broad to provide insights into communication situations. For instance, "residents of the community" alone play three roles:

1. As *voters*, they elect their representatives.
2. As *taxpayers*, they put up the money (in the form of taxes and fees) to fund a good portion of the local government's budget.
3. As *customers*, they are regular users of some services of the local government (such as city or county water) and occasional users of others (such as public health clinics).

Sometimes community residents play all three roles during one conversation with a local government employee. In one visit or phone call, a resident might say, "I demand that you get someone out to fix the potholes on my street immediately, because after all, my taxes pay your salary! And if someone doesn't respond, I'll call the mayor and threaten to vote for her opponent next month." Those statements present an interesting challenge to the local government official, who must respond to not just one person, but three in one: a daily user of a city street, a current city taxpayer, and a voter in the upcoming election.

The smaller a group and the more its members have in common, the more effectively local government can communicate with that group. It is generally easier to communicate with all the homeowners living in a single block of a city than with all the people in a neighborhood. Likewise it is generally easier to communicate with one group of city employees working at a single site—a branch library, for example—than with the hundreds and sometimes thousands of diverse individuals who make up an entire local government work force.

Demographics

One method of finding groups of people who have characteristics in common is to use *demographics*. Demographic traits are common, readily recognizable attributes such as age, income level, and even the kind of car a person drives.

At the level of local government, the people developing publicity for an aerobics class to be offered by the recreation department would benefit from finding out some of the demographic traits of potential participants before preparing any communication materials. In a community with a large component of retired people, publicity for the aerobics program would not be couched in the same terms as in an area full of young professionals just out of college.

Sources of demographic information include the U.S. Census Bureau and the Chamber of Commerce. Perhaps much information is available even in your own city or county planning department.

Psychographics

Another method of grouping individuals by shared traits is the use of *psychographics*. Unlike demographics, which focuses primarily on quantifiable physical traits, psychographics concerns people's feelings, values, and lifestyles. Because it explains things about people that demographics cannot, psychographics can be useful to local government officials in dealing with sensitive issues such as the environment, in which people's feelings play a vital role.

Consider a situation in which two families living next door to each other have similar demographic traits. The husbands and wives are the same age and have similar jobs and income. The two families have the same number of children, who are the same ages and attend the same schools. Yet one family enjoys camping, hiking, boating, and other outdoor activities, while the other never ventures any farther than the local mall and likes to attend the opera and symphony. Why? The answer cannot be provided by demographics, but can be explained by psychographics, namely, the families have divergent lifestyles and values.

A pioneering system of psychographic research, VALS (an acronym for *Values and Life Styles*), developed by George Mitchell and others at SRI International in California, categorizes the American public by nine psychographic groups. The groupings are based on three major traits: *need-driven*, *outer-directed*, and *inner-directed*.

There are now many systems, many organizations, and many individuals specializing in psychographic research. An overview of psychographics is given in *Consumer Profiles: An Introduction to Psychographics*, by Barrie Gunter. (For a complete bibliographic citation, see the list of suggested readings at the end of this book.) More information on analyzing audiences for purposes of presentations is provided in Chapter 9.

Getting results

Determining the size, location, and characteristics of a target audience is an important component of effective communication. Because, as noted in the chapter introduction, communicating means getting results, the following questions are crucial:

What results do you want?

What constitutes success?

What is the least you will settle for?

A useful way to decide on the results you want is to ask two questions. The first is *What do you want them to do?* The second is *What's in it for them?*

What do you want them to do?

Once you have identified the target audience for your communication, what action do you expect that audience to take as a result of your communication? Perhaps you want the members of your target audience to make more use of a neighborhood recreation facility, participate in a crime-prevention program, or vote yes on a bond issue.

The desired result can also be stated in negative terms. The question could be: What do you want them *not* to do? You might want that they *not* use a certain traffic route during designated hours, *not* expect solid-waste collection on a certain holiday, or *not* telephone local government facilities during certain hours.

The more clearly the desired result is identified, the greater the likelihood that it will be achieved. Many local government managers lament that they have problems with communication because they have difficulty measuring the effectiveness of communication programs. Most of the time the difficulty is related to a failure to express desired results in simple, measurable terms. In the case of the neighborhood recreation facility, the bottom-line question would be this: Did local residents end up making more use of it? In the case of the traffic-control effort, did area motorists *not* try to use a certain route during designated hours?

What's in it for them?

If you are going to ask people to change their behavior (which is the purpose of your communication program), you are going to have to give

The communicator who keeps the perspective of the intended audience in mind will enjoy the greatest success.

a convincing answer to the second question: What's in it for them? Otherwise, why should they comply with your request? Essentially, many human incentives can be boiled down to a desire for reward and a fear of punishment.

The most effective communication efforts contain both of these motivating forces. Campaigns to get motorists to use seat belts have been effective because they communicated information coupled with both positive and negative reinforcements. The campaigns clearly communicated the message that seat belts save lives and supported that statement with adequate documentation. They also warned people about the penalties for not wearing seat belts, in terms of the risk of personal injury and of having to pay a fine.

The communicator who keeps the perspective of the intended audience in mind will enjoy the greatest success when devising incentives. One person's reward is another's punishment. Some people want a streetlight every ten feet on their block, on the grounds that strong illumination makes a neighborhood safer. Other people will go to great lengths to prevent the installation of streetlights, insisting that the lights keep them awake at night or that they detract from the appearance of the neighborhood. (In Chapter 7, "The communication program in local government," there is further discussion of how to design communication programs to achieve results.)

Communicating through the clutter

Some communication theorists describe a spiraling process in which there are so many messages coming at people from so many directions that they become very adept at tuning out some or all of them. But then organizations and individuals, feeling even more pressure to get their messages out to the public, turn up the volume, in terms of the number of messages they send out and the urgency they infuse into each one.

Surveys of the effectiveness of direct-mail marketing show that most people have no recollection of having received most mailings. Strategists of marketing believe that the attention span of most people receiving direct mail lasts from the time they pick it up to when they drop it into the wastebasket. In that moment, you either get their attention or you don't. Most times you don't. Direct-mail marketers consider themselves fortunate if they get responses to more than one in fifty pieces

Figure 1–1 People tune out messages that are not important to them and receive those that are. (Reprinted with permission of Macmillan College Publishing Company from *Communications: The Transfer of Meaning*, by Don Fabun. ©1968 by Kaiser Aluminum and Chemical Corporation.)

A person needing to cash a check

Someone who is late for an appointment

that they mail. A local government trying to get a message to its constituency through the mail has to compete with this clutter—and most of the competition is operating with superior resources. The same is true of other channels of communication.

There are several ways of narrowing the odds when trying to cut through the clutter:

Be focused

Be brief

Use the appropriate medium or mix of media

Repeat the message without changing the content.

Be focused

Narrowcast, don't broadcast. Use your own knowledge and the information you can derive from demographic or psychographic research to limit the focus of your communication and get a maximum return for a minimum expenditure. Aim for the smallest possible target and the most readily measurable results.

Be brief

In communication, less is more. The message needs to tell the target audience (1) what you want them to do and (2) what's in it for them—as clearly and briefly as possible. A certain salesman was in the habit of folding his order book and departing as soon as he completed a sale. When a colleague asked him why, he explained that more information *after* completion of a sale only tends to talk the customer out of it. Long messages with too much documentation can sound defensive or weak and may have the exact opposite of the desired result. The state of Texas based an effective anti-litter campaign on the slogan "Don't mess with Texas." The message was short, memorable, and well aimed, appealing as it did to the storied pride Texans take in their state.

Use the appropriate medium or mix of media

A smorgasbord of media is available to today's communicator, from face-to-face dialogue to $1-million-a-minute Super Bowl commercials. In media selection, overkill is probably just as bad as overstatement—and maybe worse, since it wastes staff time and communication funds. A phone call is often a better communication medium than a slide show. A one-page letter from a manager to employees is sometimes more effective than an expensive brochure. A public service announcement can often achieve better results than a paid advertisement.

The director of planning in one city government, deciding he needed a videotape or slide show to resolve a vexing community-relations situation, went to the director of communication for assistance. After some discussion focusing on the results the planning director wanted, he and the communication director agreed that several phone calls were in order, perhaps followed by a meeting with two or three leaders of the neighborhood in question. Over time, phone calls achieved the desired results. The videotape or slide show, which would have taken considerable time and money to produce, turned out to be unnecessary.

Repeat the message without changing the content

One of the most effective ways to communicate through the clutter is to take careful aim, determine desired results, distill the message into a few words or symbols that tell people what you want them to do and what's in it for them, choose the appropriate medium or mix of media, and then repeat the message over and over until you are confident that it has been received and understood.

Repetition is important. Because of communication clutter, it is reasonable to assume that people do not hear (or do not comprehend) your message the first time you send it. And they may or may not receive it in a second transmission. Three ought to be a minimum number of times to transmit a message with some kind of assurance that most people in the target audience will actually learn what you want them to do and what's in it for them.

However, this is not to suggest that the same memo or newsletter or phone message ought to be sent to the target audience over and over again. Instead, vary it slightly. Follow-up communication can add something to reinforce the first message—perhaps by including a case history or further facts. The essential message of the communication should not be changed, though, or it is liable to confuse the recipients.

It's also a good idea to conduct some kind of test, on a selective or even random basis, to determine what message (if any) has been received and what kind of understanding the target audience has. This polling might be done in a follow-up phone call asking citizens for feedback:

Did you receive my message?

Do you need any further information?

Are you clear on what I am suggesting or recommending?

Do you understand what's in it for you?

Do you need more or other incentives? If so, what are they?

Are you going to do what I would like you to do?

The questions might not be asked in those words, of course; but the answers constitute the basic information you need to get if you are going to find out whether you are communicating effectively.

The importance of listening

In the world of local government management, an attentive ear is an increasingly prized commodity. City and county managers are trying harder than ever to form working partnerships with people in the community, with the goal of getting civic, neighborhood, and business leaders involved in planning for the future. Listening is an important part of building these important relationships. If people come to believe that they are not being heard or that nothing is being done to accommodate their ideas and suggestions, they will soon drop out of the partnership and try other means of getting their message across—such as forming interest groups, writing letters to the editor of the local newspaper, and contacting elected officials.

Listening is far more than simply not talking. It is actively seeking to hear the speakers' messages (what do they want you to do, and what's in it for you?). Other people may not be effective communicators, though, so actively listening may even involve helping them to get their messages across and to organize their thoughts so that they are able to communicate an idea or a response to you.

Most of the time, however, you'll get plenty of feedback. The problem is hearing the feedback through the communication clutter. A commitment to hear and to understand is the key to being a good listener. (See Chapter 8 for more guidance on the art of listening.)

A final word Next to eating and sleeping, communication is the most-practiced human activity. But good communication does not come naturally. It takes work. The task is hard, but the rewards are great. The chapters that follow will help city and county managers and other local government officials hone their communication skills and turn everyday communication into effective communication.

Checklist

Too often an objective critique shows that the local government manager and his or her team did a thorough and professional job in most areas. So why was there a failure? Oh, it was "just a communication problem."

Local government managers are no longer mere "bean counters," responsible only for making sure things don't go wrong. Today's managers are expected to make things go right. The manager is expected to be facilitator, referee, and motivator—in short, a communicator.

Today's local government manager is working in a world of empowered citizens who are quite ready to take whatever information is at their disposal and mount an informational counterattack to achieve their goals.

This revised edition of *Effective Communication* is a tool for public sector managers whose responsibilities include communicating with the public, the media, and government officials, whether elected or appointed.

The purpose of communication is to achieve results. In fact, the definition can be shortened to a simple equation:

Communicating = Getting results.

The key question in any communication situation, then, is: What results do you want to get?

A useful way to figure out what results you want is to ask yourself two questions. The first is *What do you want them to do?* The second is *What's in it for them?*

A cornerstone of effective communication is to grasp the reality that there is really no such thing as the "general public." On most issues, most of the time, most people really don't care. Only a small segment of the population is interested and involved in any particular public issue. The trick is to know *which* segment of the population.

The key to communicating through the clutter includes five steps:

Be focused

Be brief

Use the appropriate medium or mix of media

Repeat the message

Test to see whether the message was received and understood.

Effective communication involves purposeful listening. Good communicators are almost always good listeners.

Listening is more than just not talking. It is actively seeking to hear other people's messages: What do they want you to do? What's in it for you?

The Identity and Image of Local Government

"**N**ever explain—your friends do not need it and your enemies will not believe you anyway."

Elbert Hubbard, the nineteenth-century entrepreneur and author who made that remark, would have a hard time adjusting to today's business world. Many businesses, and all large corporations, now recognize that good public relations— good communications—are critical to their efforts to keep red ink out of their bottom line. Business schools include corporate communications in their curricula (indeed, the subject is now offered as an undergraduate major at some colleges), and up-and-coming business executives are expected to understand how corporate

identity and image affect profitability. Their bosses also expect them to know what to do to keep their company's identity strong and its image positive.

In government, where there is no clear bottom line by which to measure results, many elected and appointed officials work in ignorance of identity and image and the ways of measuring and improving them. In some localities, elected officials are unseated and appointed executives fired without ever knowing what went wrong.

Given city and county governments' closeness to the "market" they serve and the absence of a profit/loss yardstick, one could argue that good public relations are

more important in local government than anywhere else.

In this chapter, the elements of organizational identity and ways of modifying them to improve public perceptions of an organization are discussed. The chapter addresses the following topics:

Identity and image: Two distinct concepts

Elements of local government identity

Corporate identity

Image: The public perception

Feedback: The public speaks

Active means of measuring image.

Identity and image: Two distinct concepts

Every person in your local government organization—from the top elected official to the most junior clerk—contributes to the identity of the organization and the image projected to the public.

Although the terms are sometimes mistakenly used interchangeably, *identity* and *image* are not the same thing. *Identity* is the sum of what an organization really is—every person, office, telephone conversation, letter, building, uniform, sign, and vehicle.

On the personal level, identity is the way people wear their hair, greet others, respond to stress, and carry themselves. It is how much they know, how well they speak, how hard they work. It is everything they do and say.

On the organizational level, identity is the sum, the aggregate, of all the personal identities of the people who represent the organization, plus all the nonpersonal elements such as signs and vehicles. It also includes intangibles such as cleanliness and pride. Identity is the sum of all the elements that make up an organization. Whether it does so consciously or unconsciously, an organization creates and thus controls its identity.

In the long run, an organization's image can be no better than its identity.

For an organization, *image* is the public's viewpoint. It consists of the perceptions held by all the individuals and groups that come into contact with the organization, whether directly or indirectly. For a city or county government, the contact can range from a ten-second item on the TV news to a six-month negotiation with community groups over the closing of a local high school.

Like beauty, image is in the eye of the beholder. It is entirely possible for one group—say, senior citizens—to perceive the local government as responsive and responsible, while another group—say, people with disabilities—perceives the same government as being indifferent to their needs.

Government officials can sometimes convince themselves that they are projecting a positive identity when, in fact, their image is negative—in the view of at least part of the public. Such a situation invites disaster. Manifestations may include petition drives, demonstrations, and even ousters come election time. An in-house belief that the local government has a positive identity when its public image is actually negative exemplifies the ultimate failure of that government's efforts at communicating and disseminating information.

In the long run, an organization's image can be no better than its true nature, its identity. This point is important, because sometimes a misguided elected official or administrator attempts to create an image that will outshine his or her administration's identity. Although such efforts may succeed briefly, ultimately they are doomed.

There are only two ways to improve an organization's image. The first is to improve the identity of the organization—by hiring more ca-

Everyone contributes to the identity that the organization projects and the image that the public perceives.

pable personnel; training staff members to provide better service; upgrading signs, vehicles, and other physical resources; or (best) by trying a combination of all those actions. If local officials are convinced that their identity is better than it is perceived as being, they can move to the second means of improving image—doing a better job of communicating the city or county's identity to the public.

It has been said that PR (public relations) really stands for *performance reporting*—performing a job well (which creates a positive identity) and reporting the fact that a good job is being done (which builds a positive image).

Elements of local government identity

A local government is the sum of many parts. It is composed of hundreds (sometimes thousands) of employees and volunteers, working in scores of offices in dozens of buildings as well as in the neighborhoods, schools, and marketplaces. A police officer directing traffic in the rain, an inspector of weights and measures in a supermarket, a bus driver for the local school system—all contribute to the identity of the local government. How those workers feel about their jobs and the public they serve, and how they act on the job—and sometimes even off the job—are critical elements of the identity of the organization.

Everything about people communicates, in one way or another. A neat appearance communicates something different from an unkempt appearance. A cheerful "May I help you?" is light-years removed from a grudging "What do you want?"

Appearance

The natural place to start an identity inventory is with appearance. A clean, bright office with well-maintained equipment and personal touches such as plants and wall hangings says a lot about the people who work there and about their attitude toward the members of the public who come there. On the street or highway, a clearly marked work site communicates a message—not only about safety but about the work crew's feelings toward the local residents, whom they serve.

Employees' personal appearance is also important information for an "identity inventory." For instance, a dispirited or angry work crew in worn, ugly uniforms conveys something to passersby that no press release can dispel. No matter how hard they may be working, if the workers' appearance conveys a lack of proper pride, it is unrealistic—and unfair—to expect that they will be able to communicate a message that the local government cares about the community.

Body language also communicates identity. Consider, for instance, the reflection on your local government's identity made by someone who keeps glancing at the clock while working.

Language

Oral language, of course, speaks loudest of all. It reveals the speaker's identity. A person's consistent use of poor grammar discloses more about his or her education than a résumé would. People who use a great deal of jargon or misuse long words may be betraying their need to convince themselves of their superiority; or perhaps they've just been spending too much time around other jargon speakers. Either way, they present a problem. Bureaucratese such as "at this point in time," "priority setting," and "it is the opinion of the office" tends to alienate and confuse. Likewise, technical jargon such as "lane miles," "objectionable use," and "residential density," although it may be a useful form of oral shorthand with colleagues, is gobbledygook to the uninitiated. (See Chapter 8 for further discussion of body language and jargon.)

Two types of encounters are crucial for your city or county government: the person-to-person meeting between the local government employee and members of the public and contacts among employees themselves. In a local government, each of these contacts is important. Cumulatively, they are crucial to the identity of the organization.

Encountering your public

Person-to-person contact brings into play the elements of general appearance, body language, and spoken and written language. City and county employees get used to their surroundings; the office becomes a second home to them. They may not perceive the strangeness that a visitor feels. When the visitor is a citizen and a taxpayer who feels a sense of alienation in an office supported by his or her taxes, the impression is definitely damaging.

A standard joke refers to two glib statements that most people are unlikely to believe: "The check is in the mail" and "I'm from the government and I'm here to help you." This joke (and the invariable response) indicates that a government employee starts at a disadvantage in any face-to-face communication. The twin challenge, therefore, is not just to be pleasant but to be convincing. How many local government employees could look a citizen in the eye and say with a straight face, "My name is——. I work for your local government, and I am here for the sole purpose of serving you"? Perhaps anyone would be embarrassed to use those particular words. Still, unless the sum of general appearance, body language, and spoken and written words conveys that message, the employee is part of a communication problem, not part of the solution.

An image under pressure

In stressful situations, the task of communication becomes especially difficult for the local government employee. Naturally, local government employees continually find themselves in stressful situations—often with little training in how to handle them. Dealing with an angry citizen—often loud, sometimes threatening, occasionally even obscene—takes patience and expertise beyond the ability of many people.

In these times of understaffing in government, it might be impossible to resist the temptation to throw a new employee into the breach when phones are ringing nonstop or lines are long. In the long run, though, if you schedule training as early as possible, your office will be more productive. Of course, supervisors whose staffers must deal with stressful communications should look for attributes such as tact, flexibility, quick thinking, and a firm grasp of language when hiring. But even if you start with employees who have those skills, it is poor economy to delay or stint on their communication training.

It is one of the sad ironies of public service that in many offices it is the least paid, least educated, most recently hired members of the staff who are put forward to deal with the most difficult communication situations. Instead, the opposite should be the case.

Image and identity on the telephone

Ambrose Bierce, author of the delightfully acerbic *Devil's Dictionary*, once said that the telephone is an instrument of the devil. In the wrong hands, it can be just that.

Used properly, though, the telephone can be an extremely useful instrument of communication. First of all, it overcomes distance. And, unlike letters, it offers the advantages of two-way communication, including the opportunity for making immediate corrections and clarifications and for using inflection and tone of voice.

Despite how much everyone uses the telephone, few people are really good at it—especially at work. All too often, the least qualified person in the office is assigned to handle the telephone. The public then gets a message that telephone communications are a trifling matter, beneath the dignity of a seasoned staffer, not to mention the office manager.

Automated systems may create efficient telephone communications, but they may also frustrate citizens.

Many local governments have set up—or, more exactly, have allowed to come gradually into being—telephone systems whose effect is to discourage rather than help. Although the chief executive may have no trouble finding the right office with the right answer, almost no one else has the stamina or the willpower to hazard a call to some local governments. With the proliferation of voice mail and other automated answering systems, the caller may only be able to listen to a series of recorded messages or computerized voices.

Automated systems may create more efficient telephone communications and save money, but they may also frustrate citizens. They may become irate over being unable to talk to local government employees whose salaries—they are quick to point out—they pay. One administrator dealt with this problem with a twist of wry humor in his recorded telephone message: "I'm sorry, but I'm away from my desk right now. If you'll leave your name and number, I promise to call you right back. If you would like to speak to a real human being . . . " Many automated systems include an option for callers who prefer to speak to a person rather than leave a recorded message. To get a good idea of how accessible your phone system is, management expert Robert Townsend advises administrators to try calling some part of their organization and asking for help.[1]

Many city and county governments now routinely communicate with local residents by means of technology such as fax machines and direct computer links. There is every reason to expect even more such connections between government offices and citizens in the future as new technologies become increasingly affordable and cost-effective.

Forms by phone

Oakland [California]'s InfoFax service allows twenty-four-hour-a-day access to government forms and information, thus saving time and money for citizens and businesses dealing with the city on routine matters. The service may be accessed via a local number that allows the user to request a list of reports and forms available. Armed with that information, the caller uses a 900 number to request a specific document, then receives it automatically faxed in mere seconds. One request per call is permitted, for which the user is charged five dollars. Users may obtain permit applications, extracts of ordinances, economic-development data, animal-licensing requirements, and other governmental forms.

Source: Gregg Obuch, "Forms by Phone," *Nation's Cities Weekly,* September 14, 1992, p. 3.

Good telephone communication for any organization begins with the desire to project the best possible organizational identity over the telephone. One of the nation's largest mail-order houses, Lands' End, gives all of its customer-service representatives eighty hours of training before they "solo" on the telephone.[2] A good deal can be accomplished by selecting the right people for the job and giving them the proper training.

Guidelines for telephone etiquette

1. Answer the telephone promptly when it rings.

2. Identify yourself and your department.

3. Speak clearly and naturally.

4. Keep a pencil and paper next to the telephone to note any important information.

5. If the caller is upset, remain calm and use interpersonal skills to calm the person.

6. If a call must be transferred, relate all pertinent information to the person to whom you transfer the call, so that the caller does not have to repeat the information.

7. Do not keep a caller waiting while you look for information. Indicate that you will return the call quickly if more than a few seconds will be needed to locate the information.

8. Return the telephone call within the promised length of time. If it is impossible to do that, call the person back and explain that you are working on the question but need more time.

In Temple Terrace, Florida, the city government has developed *Citizens Are Our Customers—Telephones*, a manual for municipal employees that includes advice on general telephone etiquette, tips for handling complaints, and guidelines and procedures for making personal calls. If your local government does not have the resources to develop appropriate training materials, your area telephone company may be able to help.

Identity and image in the written word

Writing is difficult for most people, perhaps because it is so different from face-to-face communication, in which people use all their senses to send and receive messages. In face-to-face communication, there is immediate correction and feedback—as well as the possibility of communicating without saying anything at all. A parent can restrain a child with a stern look; a listener can reward a storyteller with a smile.

Many statements that make perfectly good sense when spoken seem to lose their meaning when written down. An example of this phenomenon is verbatim transcripts, such as court proceedings and records of town-council meetings.

The best writers rely on several basic techniques to make their messages clear. They write in simple sentences whose subject, verb, and object are easy to pick out. They use the active voice rather than the passive voice most of the time. They use the simplest possible vocabulary without losing meaning or "writing down to" their readers. They summarize their main points at regular intervals, using repetition to ensure clarity. Finally, good writers keep it brief. They tell the reader the point of the communication: what they want the reader to do and what's in it for the reader.

The use of the dictating machine demands special care. Like no other device, it can blur the line between spoken and written communication. Producing a good piece of writing via dictation is not as easy as you'd expect from the TV image of the peripatetic executive hastily dictating crucial correspondence into a small hand-held recorder. That recording later has to be audible and intelligible enough for a transcriptionist to type from. So, if you dictate letters, choose your words carefully, pronounce them clearly, and speak slowly. Take care in proofreading every dictated draft, to make sure it is clear as a piece of written communication.

Many organizations, especially large ones, engage in a good deal more letter writing than necessary. There is also a related tendency to over-use electronic mail (popularly known as *e-mail*) and other forms of internal computerized communication. Although the written word can be a useful communication tool, there are many cases when it is a good idea, before drafting any correspondence, to think about whether some form of spoken communication would serve the purpose better.

If you do have to send a letter, envision its form and content before writing a word. The more important the letter, the more important the preparation. Start by asking yourself what the purpose of the letter is. A simple outline will help with organization. A good conclusion is a must; the goal is to make it clear what you expect the recipient of the letter to do. The language should be simple, clear, and direct, in the style of written—not spoken—English. Always avoid third-person constructions such as "It is the opinion of this office . . ." After finishing the draft, read it over later, with the specific goal of the communication in mind. At that point it is still not too late to ask yourself, Which would serve my purposes best, a letter, a telephone call, or a face-to-face conversation? (See the list of suggested readings at the end of this chapter for specific works on writing letters.)

Face-to-face communication

More and more often, local government officials are communicating directly with local citizens through face-to-face means such as public forums and town-hall meetings. Electronic means, such as radio and TV talk shows and local government cable television, are also becoming popular ways of communicating with citizens. (Forms of direct communication are discussed in more detail in Chapters 9 and 11.) Local government staff members should take public meetings and talk shows seriously, because many citizens base their opinion of government on them.

Allow enough time to plan carefully, and try to control or at least anticipate every possible aspect of the event: the clothing and grooming of the official who will be making the appearance, the appearance of audiovisual materials (remember the vivid charts and graphs that Ross Perot used to such effect during the 1992 presidential campaign?), responses to foreseeable questions, and the composition of the audience, among other factors. The preparation works best when the official who will be making the appearance can delegate logistics (e.g., advance publicity, transportation to and from the hall or studio, the layout of the venue, lighting) to trusted staff members. Then the official can use his or her own preparation time to develop and concentrate on the goals of the appearance and on the best information and strategy to use in achieving those goals.

Corporate identity

The discussion so far has centered on *personal identity*—that is, the identity projected by individuals who work for, or otherwise represent, an organization. The identity projected by an organization as a whole is its *corporate identity*. Corporate identity is generally understood to encompass the collective nonpersonal identity of the organization created by uniforms, vehicles, buildings, letterhead, signs, and other physical objects.

A significant part of corporate identity is the graphic identification of nonpersonal components of the organization—meaning the official logos, seals, banners, lettering styles, and colors used to identify the organization. Coordinating those components is part of the purpose of a *graphics identification program*.

The success or failure of a graphics identification program depends almost entirely on the local government's leaders. The city or county manager or other chief executive must have a personal commitment to the program and see to it that all managers at all levels understand the program and take part in it.

The program should be designed by specialists under the direction of the city or county manager. The designers may be members of the staff, if the organization has a design department. Or they may be engaged as consultants, like other professional contractors such as architects and engineers. Sometimes a local government is fortunate enough to have outside professional people volunteer to help design and implement the program. Although that is an inexpensive (and usually popular) way to develop a graphics identification program, the volunteers have to understand that the manager on staff is in charge and has the final word.

Nonprofessional assistance (e.g., from art students or experienced interns) is sometimes available and can be useful, as long as the work is supervised by competent professionals. The popularity of competitions among high-school or even elementary-school students persists although the results are rarely distinguished. (A notable exception is Alaska's simple and elegant state flag, whose Big Dipper design was submitted by a

---

The graphics identification program

A graphics identification program. What is it? It's a program that uses a consistent combination of colors and visual designs to identify an organization.

Who has one? Pepsi-Cola, Seven-Eleven food stores, Century 21, C & P Telephone . . . and the list goes on. A graphics identification program is important to all those companies for the same reasons that it is important to a city government.

First of all, the program is used so that the company is readily recognized by the people it affects or serves. Second, it creates an impression of a unified group of people working toward a common goal. Finally, the program makes a statement about the company. Benign or aggressive attitudes, impressions of solidity or progressiveness, can all be conveyed through the proper design and use of a graphics identification program.

One city manager had this to say about his city's program: "In addition to providing a symbol of identity, the program has had the value of causing all city officials and employees to review the purpose and tradition of the city; of reorienting departments toward the larger missions of the city; and of reaffirming municipal services as a source of pride."

What's in a graphics identification program? First, there's the symbol—it's the most readily recognized part of the program. Then there's the logotype, the writing used to spell out the name of the company or city. That should be made highly legible and easy to reproduce. The third element is color. Color should enhance legibility and help to make a statement about the company or city.

Application of the elements is the next consideration. Where, how, and on what will the symbol, logotype, and colors be used?

Each use—on stationery, business cards, brochures, signs, uniforms, and vehicles—requires making a model of application.

The graphics manual binds the program into a single organized unit. It explains the purpose of the graphics identification program and sets forth the rules and regulations for the use of the other elements of the program.

Here's an example of how a graphics identification program for the city of Norfolk should work:

We start with the city seal. It establishes the history and the heritage of the city. Next we design a logotype that is strong, legible, and that conveys a progressive image. We choose a combination of colors that enhances the message and will stand out in the community. We apply these constants to the elements of communication that will expose our message to the public. Finally, we set down the rules and regulations for their use in a document that addresses the needs of the city.

Source: A slide script prepared for presentation by the city government of Norfolk, Virginia.

Sometimes outside professional people volunteer to help design and implement a graphics identification program.

twelve-year-old boy.) It is hard to imagine the chief executive of a Fortune 500 company having corporate graphics designed by high-school art students. Out of respect for local residents, your city or county government should likewise hold itself to high standards.

Even with the wholehearted support of top management, though, getting all levels of your local government to participate in a graphics identification program is more easily said than done. Part of the reason is that local government is rarely a simply structured, top-down organization like many private businesses. The organizational charts of some local governments look like bowls of spaghetti, with dozens of semi-autonomous, fully autonomous, elected, and appointed officials, boards, and commissions. All of these people are part of the local government and help make up its corporate identity; but not all of them answer to the appointed manager or consider themselves subject to his or her control. The most effective way of dealing with these people is gentle persuasion. The more professionally designed the graphics identification program and the more accurately it reflects the goals and function of the local government, the more likely everyone is to accept it and use it. People like to be part of a winning team.

To be effective, the graphics program should be applied to all physical objects used by the organization. Those objects can be grouped into several categories: *stationery, vehicles, uniforms, signs,* and *miscellaneous items.*

Figure 2–1 Section on the identification of buildings from *City Logo Style Book: A User's Guide,* city of Kansas City, Missouri.

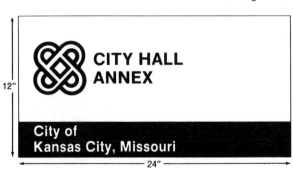

Buildings

Rectangular signs in two sizes — 6″ x 12″ and 12″ x 24″ — are available from the City Hall Office Supply, Mail and Message Center for use on older buildings that didn't incorporate the city logo in their design. These signs are made of 18-gauge steel covered in porcelain enamel, with the upper half displaying the city mark in red and blue on white, and the lower half displaying the "City of Kansas City, Missouri."

The 6″ x 12″ size should be used on most buildings. The larger size should be used on pump stations and outlying buildings.

When a new city building or other structure is being designed, or an older one is being remodeled, the City Seal Committee will work with the city architect to decide on appropriate ways to display the logo. Factors to be considered include size, choice of materials and colors.

City logos in red and blue on a clear, adhesive background are available from the Office Supply, Mail and Message Center to put on glass doors and windows of city buildings.

The corporate graphics should be applied to all general-purpose small vehicles, such as cars, station wagons, and pickup trucks.

Stationery includes letterhead, interdepartmental-memo forms, envelopes, labels, requisition forms, vouchers, invoices, tickets, and many of the other paper forms used by an organization. Even small local governments deal with hundreds of forms daily; all of them should conform to the graphics identification program. When a new program is being introduced, it is often impractical—and certainly unpopular with citizens—to discard all of the old stationery and forms. A better way of making the transition is to introduce the new graphics immediately on business stationery, then gradually start using them on other printed materials as stocks are depleted. Usually a new or revised program can take full effect for all paper materials in a year.

Besides standard sedans, station wagons, and vans, a local government may have dozens of other kinds of *vehicles:* police cars, fire trucks, ambulances, solid-waste packers, bookmobiles, and tow trucks, among others. The corporate graphics should be applied to all general-purpose small vehicles, such as cars, station wagons, and pickup trucks. It might be wise to give emergency vehicles a separate identity, although there may be tie-ins to corporate graphics through the use of symbols, typefaces, or colors. It might also be wise to stipulate that all vehicles of the organization be part of the graphics program unless a convincing reason is offered to exclude them.

Players on sports teams dress alike not only for ease of identification but also to foster a spirit of all members working toward the same goal. Uniforms for use in local government have the same purpose. They must be functional—the type of uniform worn by a solid-waste collector would not be suitable for an usher at the county coliseum, for example—but the need for corporate identification should be considered in their design. Most local governments issue uniforms to their nonoffice employees, but often little attention is given to design and care. Given a choice, taxpayers probably would prefer not to have workers in ill-fitting or filthy uniforms working on their streets, bridges, water mains, and other public property.

Figure 2–2 The recycling trucks in Phoenix, Arizona, are clearly identified.

Signs come in all shapes and sizes and have a variety of uses. Applying the graphics program to all of those uses may be difficult. Clearly, some flexibility is necessary; many parks departments like wood-toned signs with an unfinished look suggestive of the outdoors, whereas police departments sometimes prefer a formal or even a martial look.

The city's or county's logo should be used consistently on everything that is printed.

Every locality has *miscellaneous items* to which the graphics program should be applied that do not fall into the foregoing categories. Those items include newsletters, fliers, brochures, billboards, public service announcements, inserts in bills, and advertisements. Flexibility must be maintained in applying the graphics program to those uses. A slavish application of corporate graphics can undermine the effectiveness of a newsletter. For some uses, such as display advertisements announcing street-repair schedules, holiday pickup of solid wastes, and the like, a standard form with corporate graphics can be designed for all departments that need one. For other uses, such as a brochure about a new neighborhood recreation center, an original and eye-catching design may be needed. The elements of corporate graphics should be applied to each of these uses to illuminate, rather than detract from, the purpose of the use. The logo itself, however, should be used consistently on everything that is printed. In effect, it serves as the city's or county's trademark. (See Chapter 10 for more information on graphic design.)

Every letter, every telephone conversation, every face-to-face meeting, and every glimpse of a local government vehicle, sign, or newsletter is a moment of contact that projects the organization's identity. The sum of all those contacts is, in fact, the identity of the city or county government. Like it or not, the organization is responsible not only for creating its identity but also for re-creating it and projecting it, as a public image.

Image: The public perception

As the organization creates and projects its identity, the impressions people receive form their opinions and attitudes. Those impressions taken together constitute an organization's *image*. Because local government serves a large number of individuals and groups, many images are formed. An individual citizen may have different images of the local government in terms of its police protection, its street repair, its health services, its public education, its parks, or its fire protection. Next-door neighbors might have widely divergent images of a certain service because of individual experiences, coverage in newspapers and on television, gossip, and various other sources.

Individuals and groups can be categorized by demographic variables such as geography, age, income, education, gender, and race. Everyone resorts to generalization as one way of making sense of the world, of course, but demographic categorization is a more scientific and systematic form of that process. (See Chapter 1 for a discussion of demographics.)

Evaluating the local government's image on the basis of demographic groupings can be useful, as long as the dangers of oversimplification are kept in mind. As the French proverb enjoins, "Every generalization is false, including this one." When you hear a comment such as "The police department [or school system, or roads department] has a poor image among certain people," ask yourself, What is the evidence? We are in a period when talk radio, instant TV phone-in polls, and special-interest lobbying can make it hard to distinguish between vociferous, short-term reactions and enduring, deeply felt beliefs. Consequently, it is harder than before to measure the breadth and depth of public attitudes. But measuring attitudes accurately has become more important than ever to an appointed official's ability to serve and work effectively.

Many forms of measurement are available, from listening to feedback to costly attitudinal surveys. More important than the methods or the form is the need for local officials to be constantly aware of people's attitudes toward, and opinions about, the government so that they have a sound basis for informed decision making.

Feedback: The public speaks

Every organization receives responses, or "feedback," from the people it serves. The public sends a variety of messages, in the form of complaints, thanks, requests, and suggestions, through many channels of communication—telephone calls, letters to the organization, comments to news reporters, letters to the editor. All of those messages tell the organization something about its image. Receiving and understanding those messages and reacting to them (without overreacting) is a difficult—but important—job.

The first phase of the task is to monitor and measure any feedback that comes to the organization directly. One irate phone call from a known malcontent to a branch library may not call for corrective action, but a thoughtful letter to the mayor might. One complaint to the water department is unlikely to lead to a change in policy, but a hundred letters to the city or county manager's office might.

To receive and respond to complaints, some localities have established special response personnel in referral offices. Significant advantages to the organization come from providing competent, well-trained, and dedicated staff and a reliable means of dealing with complaints. Referral offices can serve a dual purpose: as early-warning systems to help officials nip problems in the bud, and as containment systems for handling unjustified or crank complaints without undue strain on the organization. The referral office is most effective when it has the support and the ear of the local government manager and when it serves as a supplement or circuit breaker for the organization.

One note of caution, however: referral offices should avoid fostering the impression that they alone handle complaints. Ideally, every office in the organization should be sensitive to negative feedback and be prepared to handle it, within certain limits. The existence of a central office to which all complaints are referred does not reflect favorably on the responsiveness of operating offices of the organization.

Some local governments in the United States employ an *ombudsman,* an autonomous government employee who resolves disputes between citizens and the government, frequently by taking the side of the citizen. In some systems, the ombudsman even can guide the citizen through the legal process in seeking redress from the government. The ombudsman concept enjoys its greatest popularity in Scandinavia and the nations of the British Commonwealth. One of the first local governments in the United States to appoint an ombudsman was Nassau County, New York, when its county executive created the position in 1966.

The local news media are another good source of feedback. Often people will complain to reporters, either before calling the local government or when they feel they have exhausted all possibilities of getting the government's attention directly. Public officials who have good working relations with local journalists can hear a negative comment or a com-

Every office in the organization should be sensitive to negative feedback and be prepared to handle it.

It is helpful to monitor the news reporting of newspapers, radio, and TV as a source of information on local attitudes.

plaint personally before having to read it in the newspaper or see it on television.

Even if a problem discovered and reported by the news media is then dealt with and fixed, it is often hard to persuade journalists to report the corrective action. As a result, local citizens can be left with the impression that the problem is continuing. Because many people form their impressions of local government on the basis of information obtained from the media, it is helpful to monitor the news reporting of newspapers, radio, and TV as a rich source of information on local attitudes. (See Chapter 6 for a more detailed discussion of media relations.)

Radio and television talk shows and call-in programs are another means of learning what's on people's minds. For officials who are willing to go on the air, the increasingly common and popular live programs provide an opportunity to have a dialogue with local citizens and to give them timely information on topical issues. But be forewarned: keep in mind that callers and audience members on such a program will probably express their opinions far more forcefully than other citizens. Few will call to give kudos to the local government for doing a fairly good job; more likely, you and your colleagues will either be hailed as geniuses or condemned as venal and inept. (For guidance on how to prepare for appearances on talk shows and call-in programs, see Chapter 9.)

The elected officials you work for are another important source of feedback. Many people feel more comfortable complaining to the mayor

---

Listening more, listening better

Richard C. Harwood, president of the Harwood Group, a research firm concerned with public issues and innovations, offers the following tips to local government officials interested in "listening intently" to citizens:

Explore the whys and hows. Public officials need to move beyond focusing on just *what* people think, and learn *why* they believe what they do and *how* they formed their views. Then it will be possible to understand what truly concerns people.

Discover connections. In discussions of policy, we tend to compartmentalize public concerns into neat, bite-size issues. Citizens, though, draw connections between issues—seeing a mosaic that resembles their experience of public concerns in their daily lives. Recognizing the connections makes it possible for officials to understand citizens' perspectives on public concerns.

Discern public language. To talk with citizens, officials must listen for the public's language—the words, terms, and phrases citizens use. An obvious point, perhaps, but we have created a professional jargon that is meaningless to most citizens. Listening to the public requires understanding a public language.

Understand emotions. We tend to dismiss emotions as getting in the way of making good policy decisions. They often do. But by listening for the emotions citizens bring with them to debates on public concerns, it is possible to understand their fears, aspirations, and what they may be ambivalent about—all key elements in understanding what motivates people.

Push citizens. Listening must not be a passive endeavor. Public officials must take the initiative in finding out how people deal with contradictions in their own thinking, consider the choices for action, weigh trade-offs and costs, and consider their personal interests along

with those of the community. The resultant insights can provide a sense of the depth of feeling and belief that is key in understanding citizens' voices. Without those insights, only shallow opinions will drive public debate.

Give feedback. Citizens need to know that their concerns have been heard and understood. Public officials need to give citizens feedback; what they have heard, how they understand it, and how it relates to their decision making. So listening means talking too. . .

The challenge facing public officials is not to listen more, it is to listen *differently.* When that happens, citizens will be able to believe that the depth and meaning of their concerns, hopes, and beliefs have been understood *and* that their voices have been heard.

Source: Richard C. Harwood, "Listening More, Listening Better," *Western City,* July 1993, p. 15.

or a council member than to a staffer (for many reasons, the ability to threaten reprisal in the voting booth not least among them). Some elected officials tend to overreact to feedback; council members have been known to be ready to reform an entire department on the basis of a few phone calls. Staff members should encourage elected officials to pass along complaints, as specifically as possible, together with complainants' names and addresses. The elected official should be informed of what the staff did to help and what the outcome was. Always resist the temptation—and the pressure—to overreact yourself.

If you listen to a variety of sources of feedback over a long period, you will grow more confident of your "feel" for the community's state of mind and even find yourself sensing unfavorable trends before serious trouble develops. The main point is always to take the time to listen.

Active means of measuring image

Monitoring various sources of feedback is a *passive* means of measuring an organization's image among the publics it serves. There are also *active* means of measuring image, varying from informal, cost-free techniques to formal and sometimes expensive surveys by professional research firms. Be aware, as the saying goes, that you get what you pay for.

Surveys

Conducting surveys has become a highly exact science. Research specialists have a wide variety of tools at their disposal, with impressively predictable degrees of reliability. Much work can go into every aspect of a survey, from formulating and testing questions (devising the *survey instrument*) to displaying results in various cross-tabulations.

Some cities have in-house organizations dedicated to conducting formal research. The city of Boulder, Colorado, has had a Department of Research and Evaluation for years. Communities may turn to private research firms capable of conducting professional surveys; colleges and universities may also be good sources of information and assistance. For example, an annual survey of citizens formulated by the city government of Auburn, Alabama, is conducted by students from Auburn University.[3] Sometimes business leaders are willing to "loan" members of their research staffs to the local government. Or it may be possible to conduct a survey in cooperation with some local business or industry, to the general benefit of both parties.

The key to making a worthwhile and productive survey is to set clear goals at the outset. The survey team should ask themselves two questions: What kind of information are we looking for? What will we do with it once we have it? It is often useful to get proposals from two or more research sources. A meeting with principals of the research staffs to discuss specific objectives and applications is likewise useful. Proposals should provide information on the budget, methodology, schedule, and expertise of the people who are going to do the work. Proposals often can be modified to meet the schedule, budget, or other conditions of your local government while still furnishing useful information. Conducted properly, surveys can yield information that cannot be obtained in any other way.

Focus groups

Local governments are increasingly using focus groups to find out more about how people feel about certain issues. Focus groups are an excellent means of collecting *qualitative* rather than *quantitative* data.

Gathering quantitative information would be the purpose of a telephone survey in which citizens were asked to rate the police department on a scale of 5 (highly effective) to 1 (very ineffective). In some situations, such as coming up with relative rankings of departments, that type of numerical information can be very useful.

A focus group yields quite different information. In a focus-group discussion, people talk about how they feel about subjects such as police protection, street crime, and traffic control; they also explore various ideas and suggested solutions as a group. Three keys to effective focus-group discussions are

1. Careful selection of participants
2. A purposeful agenda
3. An experienced moderator.

A final word about image

Whether it is formal or informal, passive or active, carried out by staff or contracted out, research puts a tool in your hands that enables you to manage—rather than simply react.

Evaluating the image of your local government can give early warning signals of trouble and valuable information on changes needed in services or programs. By assessing the corporate image, you can also find out where communication could be improved. To provide effective service to citizens, a local government must learn to see itself as its various publics do.

Checklist

Identity and image are not the same thing. *Identity* is what an entity really is. *Image* is the public's perception of it, what people think it is.

For an organization, *identity* is the sum of every employee, every letter, every building. An organization can control its identity because it creates its identity.

Image, on the other hand, is an outward reputation. It consists of all the perceptions of all the individuals and groups that come into contact with an organization, whether directly or indirectly.

In the long run, an organization's image can be no better than its identity.

Assessing the organization's identity and image, and working to improve both, should be twin major objectives for administrators at every level of local government.

The appearance, body language, and spoken and written language of its

members all make up part of the identity of an organization.

The most important point of contact for an organization is the face-to-face contact of its employees with the public.

If used properly, the telephone offers perhaps the most advantageous form of communication, especially in work situations.

Many local governments have set up telephone systems that have the effect of discouraging citizens from seeking services rather than helping them get what they need.

The more important a letter, the more important its preparation. Knowing the purpose of the letter, making a simple outline, and stating a definite conclusion can pave the way for clear communication.

The identity projected by an organization as a whole is its *corporate identity.* Corporate identity generally encompasses

the collective nonpersonal identity of the organization created by uniforms, vehicles, buildings, letterhead, signs, and other physical objects.

A significant part of corporate identity is the graphic identification of nonpersonal components of the organization—meaning the logos, seals, banners, lettering styles, and colors used to identify the organization. Coordinating these components is part of the purpose of a *graphics identification program.*

Monitoring feedback is a good way to measure the effectiveness of an image.

Although central complaint bureaus and ombudsmen can help take pressure off other city or county government offices, all local government offices still have a responsibility to be sensitive to complaints and prepared to handle them.

The key to conducting any type of survey is to know what information is desired and what will be done with it.

PART II

Communicating with Four Important Publics

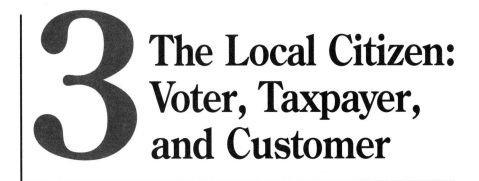

3 The Local Citizen: Voter, Taxpayer, and Customer

To the city or county residents you serve today, the term *local citizen* means something quite different from what it meant to the people served by your predecessors. Today's local citizen is more likely than before to have moved to your area from another state, or even another country, and to retain loyalties (or even hopes of returning someday) to that old home. Citizens' commitment to their city or county of residence is also lessened by technological advances that have made it easier for people to work, learn, shop, and entertain themselves in ways that make the local community seem less relevant and necessary than it used to be.

Instead of thinking of themselves as citizens with a general, wide-ranging interest in how their city or county is governed, people in your community are apt to become active only intermittently and in their individual roles as—among other things—parents of school-age children, victims of crime, homeowners, or business operators. For the manager at any level of local government, perhaps the most useful way of understanding this new kind of citizen is not solely as a taxpayer or a voter, but also as a *customer* for the many services local government provides. The management theory that originated this attitudinal approach is discussed in some detail below.

Just as managers in local government can get a clearer sense of the scope of their jobs by viewing citizens in terms of their many individual roles, they can also benefit from taking stock of the diverse ways local government comes into contact with citizens. From press releases to zoning hearings, and even to street maintenance and garbage collections, all public contacts give local government managers an opportunity to interact with the citizen as a customer. The effort that the local government needs to make to find and serve the citizen as a customer amid the competing demands of contemporary life is the subject of this chapter. Specific topics covered are:

The concept of the citizen as customer

How to take an inventory of local services

How to find the citizen-customer

Developing community support for and involvement with local government

How to meet with citizens

Cultural diversity

The monopoly on certain services that local government has traditionally held has been a mixed blessing. On one hand, for services such as law enforcement, water, and roads, the city or county has essentially had a "captive market." On the other hand, the connection between taxes paid and services delivered is not always clear to the taxpayer—or, for that matter, to the public servant, especially as services provided by local government—and the recipients of those services—become more diverse.

Although the movement toward entrepreneurial government that began in the 1980s has helped bring the concepts of price, competition, and choice more directly to bear on the delivery of services, no one should hold his or her breath waiting for the day when the local police department goes door to door selling subscriptions to its services (although in

1992, the Baltimore city government won the consent of the state government—and just as important, city businesses—to charge owners of downtown commercial property a small surcharge on their property taxes in exchange for increased sanitation and security services[1]). At certain trying moments it must seem a tempting concept, however; it would tend to put government face to face with its customers and customers face to face with the cost/service equation.

Citizens as customers

One of the best-known approaches to customer-driven government has been the concept of TQM (total quality management). This model for industrial management, designed by W. Edwards Deming for a manufacturing environment and used to revive Japanese industry after World War II, has gradually been adapted to service environments in both the private and public sectors. By the early 1990s, jurisdictions as diverse as Dallas (Texas), Madison (Wisconsin), Palm Beach County (Florida), and Wilmington (North Carolina) had incorporated TQM into their management and customer-service practices.[2] The widely reprinted "Fourteen Commandments" of TQM stress, among other things, "constancy of purpose," continuous efforts to improve the product, and cooperation instead of hierarchy.[3]

A 1980 study by Citibank of eighteen large service firms resulted in a list of practices and approaches intended to help translate a TQM-style approach to a service environment. The characteristics and approaches the companies used to develop and sustain a high quality of service included the following points to remember:

Continually monitor levels of service by means of service audits.

Make sure senior management is actively, visibly committed to excellence of service.

Measure performance of service against explicit standards.

Actively seek feedback from customers on service, and use it in making decisions.[4]

Focusing on continuous improvement and on the point of interaction with customers upgrades the role of front-line workers. The tone of routine correspondence, the way a parking ticket is presented, the way a zoning hearing is conducted—all are encounters that become defining moments for the organization in the citizens' view.

The service inventory

A proven way to begin the process of identifying customers, determining what they want, and improving the delivery capacity of a local government organization is a comprehensive *service inventory*.

Service inventories can be used at multiple levels of government. At the *policymaking level,* the inventory can be organized on the basis of broad categories such as police patrol, fire investigation, and land-use regulation. The specifics will depend on how the particular city or county government is organized.

In Charlotte, North Carolina, for example, the mayor and city council developed an inventory in which the major services provided directly to the public were grouped into forty-one categories. Elected officials, city staffers, and citizens then worked through a system of "forced-choice" comparisons that resulted in a priority ranking for each of the forty-one services. Included in the 820 paired comparisons evaluated by each of the participants were comparisons between services such as police patrol and housing rehabilitation. Participants also compared the effectiveness with which services were provided. This exercise presented an opportunity to evaluate the allocation of resources for each service on the basis of its relative importance and how effectively it was performed. The evaluations were summarized in a report comparing each of the forty-one services to every one of the others on the scales of importance and effectiveness. (See Tables 3–1 and 3–2 on pages 36 and 37.) The report showed that the categories of service rated the most important were not always rated among the most effective. For example, police patrol, ranked first in relative importance of services, only ranked tenth in relative effectiveness.

At the *operations level,* the service inventory should be much more detailed. For example, for a local government utility the policy inventory might only include broad aspects such as water treatment quality, capacity, comparative rates, and capital improvement. An operations-level inventory would focus more narrowly, on matters such as meter reading, service connections, complaints about low pressure, and installation schedules.

Breaking democracy's deadlock

Like the nation as a whole, Fontana, California, seems to many local leaders and residents to have lost its sense of identity and of purpose. Once a quiet farm town, later a blue-collar steel-producing city, it now has become home to thousands of commuters who make the long haul to jobs in Orange and Los Angeles counties in order to enjoy the relatively cheap housing here.

In the 1980s, Fontana more than doubled its population, with minorities outpacing whites. Fewer than one-sixth of the residents are over 45, and many of the commuters have little time to meet their neighbors, let alone join in civic life.

In such a setting, local officials have a hard time figuring out what voters want. Residents complain that "the city has run with blinders on and switched from doing what one special interest group wanted to another, satisfying no one." And officials agree that "the city wasn't listening to people."

Turnout at local elections was poor, and the citizens who showed up at council meetings were often a vocal minority, pushing a particular cause of their own. In desperation, the city council resorted to social science opinion-sampling techniques to tap into voters' desires.

At the council's orders, community development director Greg Hulsizer enlisted two faculty members from the Cal State-San Bernardino school of business and public administration, Dean David Porter and Professor J. Peter Graves, to help determine what Fontanans really want.

Graves has been developing an alternative to the dead-end politics of "single-issue candidates, single-issue interest groups, and single-issue referenda." He calls his technique "Community Consensus."

The process started with a citizens' brainstorming session, where Graves got a good sense of what Fontanans liked and disliked about the city and what they hoped it would become. From that, he developed a questionnaire that, unlike most standard polls, is designed to measure priorities, not simply opinions.

Options come in matched pairs, one tested against the other. For example, citizens are asked to rate fire protection/paramedic service against youth programs on a five-point scale, allowing them to say which is more important—and by how much.

One page of the questionnaire lists 36 such service choices, randomly arranged, so no two questionnaires are identical. Another page does the same thing with goals—low crime rate versus accessible hospitals/health care, for example. The final page puts it into budget and planning terms, asking, for instance, whether it would be better for Fontana to limit residential growth or go for a voter-approved local sales-tax increase.

By the time voters have made 252 such choices, they have a pretty good idea of the tough trade-offs the local government faces.

Once tabulated, the results will be given a "reality check" of residents' reactions at an open town meeting, and then, Graves hopes, the council will have a clearer sense of citizens' priorities. Council members hope that the results "will help us make some of the hard choices without getting clobbered by a citizens' backlash."

Graves is optimistic. "Politicians really do want to listen," he said, "but there are so many voices, each pleading its own cause, they don't know who to listen to. This may give them a way of listening to the community's voice."

At both the policy and the operations levels, the service inventory creates a framework for understanding the range of services the local government provides and ranking them by priority.

This process of clarification at the policy and operations levels sets the stage for the next step in developing a customer orientation: a "checklist for transformation" that includes the following nine questions:

Whom do you serve? Identify your customers. Governmental services often have multiple customers. If you are on the planning commission, developers view themselves as your customers. But homeowners next door to the proposed development are your customers too. And remem-

Table 3–1 City of Charlotte service inventory: Overall rankings, relative importance of services.

Rank	Service	Service Number	Score
1	Police patrol	20	65.31
2	Fire fighting and rescue	11	63.80
3	Criminal investigations	22	61.01
4	Police street drug interdiction	24	60.79
5	Pick up household waste and recyclables	29	57.62
6	Crime lab	26	57.34
7	Crime prevention	21	56.85
8	Transit system	34	56.02
9	Youth services (police)	25	54.35
10	Move traffic	35	54.27
11	Maintain streets and ROWs	38	53.42
12	Fire investigations	12	53.15
13	City Within a City	41	52.86
14	Stormwater services	4	52.40
15	Neighborhood development	7	52.27
16	Transportation planning	37	52.11
17	Land development and regulation	5	52.00
18	Fire prevention	13	51.97
19	Job training, development, placement	17	51.15
20	Community improvement	31	51.07
21	Long-range community/land-use planning	19	50.56
22	Engineering capital projects	3	50.40
23	Street lights	36	49.82
24	Neighborhood-based client assistance	18	49.79
25	Housing preservation	6	49.54
26	Economic development	10	49.52
27	Street cleaning	32	47.21
28	Maintain central business district	33	46.74
29	Animal control	1	45.85
30	Collection of miscellaneous items	30	45.75
31	Emergency management	14	45.33
32	Landscape maintenance	15	44.72
33	Funding to community agencies	40	44.56
34	Community relations	8	44.52
35	Urban forestry	16	42.14
36	Funding cultural facilities/agencies	39	41.52
37	Customer-service center	9	39.73
38	Noise control (police)	23	39.04
39	Taxicab ordinance (police)	27	39.00
40	Public information	28	38.99
41	Cable franchise	2	35.55

ber the internal customers in the engineering, transportation, and utility agencies of your local government.

What do your customers expect? Learn what they want. Survey people as they are served. Do follow-up surveys. Survey the community to find out who does not feel like a customer. Find out how other local governments are providing the same service.

What do you provide? Define your products. If the product is information, do all of your customers have the same needs? The land developer probably does not need the same type of information the neighboring homeowners need.

Table 3–2 City of Charlotte service inventory: Overall rankings, relative effectiveness of services.

Rank	Service	Service Number	Score
1	Fire fighting and rescue	11	62.50
2	Pick up household waste and recyclables	29	61.83
3	Maintain central business district	33	58.82
4	Fire investigations	12	57.04
5	Engineering capital projects	3	55.80
6	Fire prevention	13	54.92
7	Street cleaning	32	54.86
8	Maintain streets and ROWs	38	54.04
9	Street lights	36	53.76
10	Police patrol	20	53.15
11	Animal control	1	53.04
12	Collection of miscellaneous items	30	52.55
13	Crime lab	26	51.70
14	Land development and regulation	5	51.60
15	Funding cultural facilities/agencies	39	51.57
16	Landscape maintenance	15	50.90
17	Long-range community/land-use planning	19	50.10
18	Public information	28	49.66
19	Emergency management	14	49.43
20	Criminal investigations	22	49.37
21	Urban forestry	16	49.25
22	Economic development	10	49.11
23	Funding to community agencies	40	48.28
24	Move traffic	35	47.39
25	City Within a City	41	47.38
26	Transportation planning	37	47.33
27	Stormwater services	4	47.27
28	Community relations	8	47.23
29	Transit system	34	47.05
30	Community improvement	31	46.98
31	Police street drug interdiction	24	46.96
32	Customer-service center	9	46.24
33	Youth services (police)	25	46.12
34	Cable franchise	2	46.03
35	Crime prevention	21	45.49
36	Taxicab ordinance	27	44.54
37	Noise control (police)	23	44.36
38	Job training, development, placement	17	44.33
39	Housing preservation	6	44.31
40	Neighborhood development	7	44.21
41	Neighborhood-based client assistance	18	43.80

What benefits do customers get from you? Are new residents or citizens in newly annexed areas satisfied? Can you make a convincing case for the services these new customers will get in exchange for the new taxes they will be paying?

Know Your City

After an annexation added almost 30 square miles to Danville, Virginia (44,000), the city realized that it had a need to provide information concerning city services to its new citizens and to remind current residents of existing services. With the help of the local League of Women Voters, it prepared a booklet called *Know Your City.* It contains a history of Danville, an explanation of the city's form of government, an outline of the local branches of government, a list of boards and commissions, and information on voter registration and institutional services available, as well as information on economic development, cultural organizations, and tourist attractions. It cost the city $20,000 to print 35,000 copies of the booklet. Each household received one booklet from sanitation crews making their scheduled rounds. The residents appreciate the booklet, and the volume of phone calls from citizens requesting information has decreased. As a result of the success of the booklet, the city has instituted a citizen information service, which gives citizens information on 200 topics.

Source: *The Guide to Management Improvement Projects in Local Government,* vol. 14, no. 4 (Washington, D.C.: ICMA, 1990) CCR-5.

Do you know the cost of the service? Citizens usually know what they pay in taxes but often do not know how much each of the specific services costs. You should be familiar with the revenue/cost equation for every service in your inventory.

Can you define your competition? Who else can provide what you do? What do they do better or worse than you do? What alternatives do your customers have? Many governments have developed the attitude that local residents are "captive customers." But citizens can vote "no" on bond issues, initiate revenue-cutting ballot initiatives, or even vote with their feet by moving to a neighboring county. In those ways the local government discovers the costs of failing to appreciate every citizen-customer. Even comparable private providers of services should be evaluated. Do you treat the city or county residents whom you bill for water as well as the private electric company treats *its* customers?

> *Citizens know what they pay in taxes but often do not know how much each service costs.*

By what means are you held accountable? Whom do you answer to? Customers should be able to identify and influence how responsibility for services is distributed.

How is your service measured? Every operation should have a customer-service standard to follow.

Can you define your service cycles? How long did it take from the day the developer asked for a rezoning until the groundbreaking? How much time and opportunity did owners of adjacent homes have for input before the property to be developed was rezoned?

In thinking about the citizen as customer, it is important to develop a checklist for each service. The best checklist will reflect the needs of the variety of customers affected by the service. Work on serving the most obvious customers first—the ones standing in line, waiting on the phone, and driving over potholes. But remember, too, the indirect customers, including those yet to be born or yet to move to your community, when making decisions that will have enduring effects on the physical environment and array of services in your community.

Finding the citizen-customer

Focus groups, which the private sector has long been using to identify customers for a particular product or service, are becoming accepted in the public sector as a means of determining the needs and desires of local citizens. In selecting participants for these guided discussion sessions, demographic data can be used to ensure proper representation of various segments of the community—i.e., retired people, homeowners, bus riders, people with disabilities, or other relevant target groups. The list of questions in the accompanying sidebar is a representative sample. It was developed for a series of focus groups conducted in Charlotte, North Carolina, by Castleberry & Company, a communications consulting firm based in that city.

Some typical focus-group questions

General Questions

What are your recent experiences with city governments?

How could city government services be improved?

What services do you want from city government?

What services do you need from city government?

Do you have questions about the honesty of city government?

Specific Questions

Have you called the city for service in the last year? What were your experiences?

Are there any services you would like from city government that you would be willing to pay higher taxes to get? How much higher?

Are there any services the city currently provides that you would be willing to have reduced or eliminated in order to reduce your taxes?

In the past few years, are there any services or facilities that you think the city government has promised to provide that it has not provided?

How do you get your information about city government?

What would be a good way to get information about city government to you?

Source: Castleberry & Company, Marketing Communications, Charlotte, N.C.

Another way to locate the citizen-customer is to establish a customer-service center like the one in Charlotte. By transferring key customer-service employees from operating departments, Charlotte has been able to establish a central location where customers of all kinds can call for various services. The center assists an average of nearly 11,000 customers monthly. Inquiries pertain primarily to local government services, but often the calls involve state, federal, or nonprofit agencies.

Callers' questions usually involve how to get access to a service: for example, "How do I get large items like appliances collected from my house?" or "Where do I pay a traffic ticket?" In a day's work, too, there are times when employees must go beyond their customary duties to

There are times when employees must go beyond their customary duties to help a caller.

help a caller. A representative once received a call from a woman in Florida whose mother had just died and who needed to notify her sister in Charlotte. But the sister had no telephone. The service-center agent took the address and had the police department personally notify and assist the caller's sister.

Other local governments are contacting their customers by means of multimedia kiosks—some completely automated, some staffed—in shopping malls and other public places. At the kiosks, citizens can ask questions, obtain information, and file complaints. They may even pay utility bills, register to vote, and fill out Medicaid eligibility forms there. Among the many local governments that use a "city hall in the mall" technology are Orlando, Florida; St. Petersburg, Florida; Tulare County, California; and Mercer Island, Washington (a city of about 20,000, which partially defrayed the cost of its kiosk by situating it in a grocery store). Many of the kiosks use 24-Hour City Hall, an IBM-trademarked system developed by the computer giant and Public Technology, Inc., a nonprofit association of local governments.[5]

City Hall in the Mall

To improve city communications and make city services conveniently accessible, St. Petersburg, Florida (243,000), established the City Hall in the Mall/Pinellas County Services Center. The city established an information and services booth at the area's largest shopping center, which attracts more than 15,000 shoppers per day. The county later joined the booth operation for a fee of $10,000 per year. The shopping center management donated free space for the booth, which is staffed 48 hours per week by four part-time employees and volunteers. The booth serves as a drop-off point for city utility bills, county water bills, and electric company bills; a distribution point for informational brochures; a voter registration office; a viewing area for taped city council meetings; a clearinghouse of city job openings; and an information resource about city and county programs and attractions.

Source: Adapted from *The Guide to Management Improvement Projects in Local Government*, vol. 16, no. 2 (Washington, D.C.: ICMA, 1992) CCR-13.

Figure 3–1 The City Hall in the Mall/Pinellas County Services Center in St. Petersburg, Florida.

Developing community support and involvement

Linked with the challenge to identify customers and determine their wants and needs is the dilemma of how to build support in the community. Customers tend to behave and respond according to their individual preferences and circumstances. For many people, government is something to be ignored except when their school, street, or home is directly affected.

Any effort to encourage a community-wide perspective among local residents who may not be inclined to think in terms of the "big picture" requires seven essential ingredients:

Participation. The plan must be inclusive enough to ensure that all points of view are represented.

Information. The material disseminated must be clear and comprehensive to ensure that a full range of options is understood and developed.

Definition of problem. The problem at hand must be explained clearly, to ensure that people share a common understanding.

Education. Participants in any effort to generate community awareness must be willing to educate—and be educated by—one another.

Options. Develop multiple viable choices for the participants to consider.

Consensus. To be meaningful, a group decision must reflect general agreement.

Implementation. All the participants should have a stake—and a role—in carrying out plans.

Those ingredients are found to varying degrees in the neighborhood-based strategies for delivering services that are increasingly becoming models of effectiveness in local government. One such undertaking is Free the Children, an intergovernmental effort initiated in Memphis, Tennessee, to ease the effects of poverty. Another example is Project Atlanta, an initiative spearheaded by former president Jimmy Carter to focus local resources on the problems of the urban core that lead to "capital flight": low-quality housing, crime, and illiteracy.

The innovative City Within a City, a program in Charlotte, North Carolina, developed out of a community self-assessment. Leaders in government, business, and the community take an annual comparison tour of a city considered comparable to Charlotte to learn new ideas and share information on successful programs. In 1990 the group stayed home and toured their own city's central neighborhoods. What they found was an area of sixty square miles and 140,000 residents where crime and poverty were plentiful while education, income, and employment were all in short supply.

The result of the eye-opening 1990 tour was the development of a strategy to end Charlotte's "Tale of Two Cities." The process began with an assessment of all seventy-three of what came to be known as Charlotte's "City within a City" neighborhoods. The assessment emphasized not only the needs and weaknesses of the problem neighborhoods but their capabilities and assets as well.

The components of the City Within a City strategy, although they varied with the characteristics and needs of each neighborhood, included combinations of the following elements:

The assessment emphasized not only the needs and weaknesses of problem neighborhoods but their capabilities and assets as well.

Neighborhood associations, to develop, strengthen, or build upon the neighborhood groups

Matching grants, to ensure successful projects in neighborhoods by providing small sums (generally $3,000) to match residents' labor

Community policing, in which two police officers would be assigned as coordinators in each neighborhood to become protectors, facilitators, advocates, and team members of neighborhood associations

Neighborhood-based service delivery, which, depending on each neighborhood's need, assigned permanent teams of government and social-service workers in such fields as code enforcement, job training, health, solid-waste disposal, and recreation.

In one neighborhood, residents formed a community development corporation that worked with a local bank and the city to buy and rehabilitate dilapidated housing, which was subsequently rented to residents of the neighborhood. In another, the neighborhood association acquired property and rehabilitated a structure for a community center; the association stayed self-supporting by buying and renting adjacent property.

Promoting the neighborhood organization

The City of Southfield encourages the development and strengthening of neighborhood associations to achieve the common goals of all its citizens—maintaining Southfield as an outstanding community in which to live, work, and raise a family.

This Neighborhood Association Handbook is designed to be helpful in achieving common neighborhood goals. The City is prepared to help you establish your own neighborhood association so that every resident becomes an integral part of the community. Don't wait for some crisis or need to occur before your neighborhood organizes.

There is no single formula to tell you what to do. The limits of your neighborhood, the issues, problems, and personalities of the residents, and their lifestyles contribute to the character of your neighborhood. *Organize* and talk about your neighborhood advantages and mutual problems.

Source: Excerpted from city of Southfield, Michigan, *Handbook for Neighborhood Organizations.*

The more successful initiatives viewed problems from the perspective of a citizen-customer rather than from an organizational or therapeutic perspective. Successful approaches shared certain features: they were inclusive, provided information, used common definitions of local problems, included choices, developed consensus, and shared responsibility for implementation. The guiding principle of City Within a City was articulated by Mildred Taylor, president of one of the neighborhood associations, who said, "I don't care what you want to do, if people don't want to get involved, it won't get done."

Meeting with citizens　The interactions of government with its citizens fall roughly into three categories: *routine, positive,* or *external.* Within each category, the contacts made may be formal or informal. Routine transactions include the contacts that result from the everyday business of the government—for example, water bills, licensing inspections, and public hearings. Positive transactions involve using the function of authority to educate, to honor, or to reinforce citizenship. Examples of such transactions include fire-prevention demonstrations and awards to outstanding citizens. External relationships involve inviting people with relevant and respected private positions or expertise to participate in or advise their government. Such relations often involve participation on advisory boards or ad hoc task forces.

> **Planning *with* citizens, not *for* them**
> We cannot plan for the citizenry unless we plan with them, unless we are willing to give to individuals, to neighborhoods, and to communities the power to be heard and the power to challenge, the power most of all to actually decide as much as possible what their communities will look like and how they will work.
>
> Source: John V. Lindsay, mayor of New York City, 1965-1973.

Succeeding in each of the three categories of transactions calls for a citizen-oriented transaction plan, or perhaps even a strategic plan. Every day, government employees have opportunities to communicate with citizens and to leave a positive impression behind. From public hearings to collecting water bills, we need to do a better job of connecting the citizen-customer with the purpose of the transaction.

Meetings and public hearings

For all their shortcomings, meetings and public hearings are important forums for communication between the government and its citizenry. If meetings, traditionally the backbone of citizen participation, are to be productive and effective, it is imperative for participants to receive the agenda and any supporting materials as far in advance as possible. To argue that time and workloads make that impossible is to argue that the meeting is not important, that participation is expected to be of low quality, and that perhaps the meeting should not be held as scheduled (or at all).

The participants as well as the audience need to clearly understand the rules of procedure. Anyone who has seen the look on the face of a citizen just after he or she has been gaveled out of order at a public hearing understands that need. There is also a problem if citizens who wish to speak are not recognized until after the vote has been taken on an issue. In these cases, of course, it is the news reporter who has the first opportunity to talk with the disgruntled citizen.

Because meetings and public hearings are basic to the citizen-participation process, it is helpful to keep those thoughts in mind, along with consideration of how to advertise and how to evaluate a public event after it is over.

Meetings and public hearings are basic to the citizen-participation process.

In regard to encouraging a large *attendance,* general notices in a daily newspaper do little to generate participation. Announcements are more effective in the newsletters of associations and community organizations. Now that computers, publication software, and high-quality printers have become less expensive, newsletters are easy to produce and consequently more common than ever. When choosing newsletters for placing publicity, it is best to think inclusively. Instead of publicizing only in the same group of community newsletters over and over, it is a good use of time to visit a few church lobbies, laundromats, and convenience stores to see who is distributing free publications these days. Two other effective avenues are word of mouth and neighborhood postings; they work quite well for yard sales. These humble but effective forms of promotion will likewise help generate a strong turnout for public hearings—especially those concerning local issues.

After a meeting or public hearing, the outcome must be assessed. Concerning the *decision* that will result from the hearing, several questions need to be answered. Was it in fact made before the hearing? Can those who attend influence the decision? Can those who attend make the decision? Most important of all, were the answers to each of the first three questions made clear to the audience beforehand? If the council or local government staff know in advance that choices are limited or that financing will predetermine the outcome, this must be made clear at the start of the hearing.

Alternative means of meeting the citizens

The obvious disadvantage of the traditional means of reaching citizens—meetings and public hearings—is that the majority of citizens never come to them. This majority, nevertheless, pays taxes, receives services, and, most important, votes. Numerous alternatives are available to involve those citizens who cannot or will not attend public meetings. These methods include the following:

Referenda and surveys

"Welcome" packets offering "discounts" on city or county services

Annual reports, newsletters, and other governmental publications

Interactive cable or computerized complaint systems

Awards, given to or received from citizen groups

A liaison from city or county to neighborhood associations

Opportunities for citizens to participate on boards and commissions

Organized activities in city or county parks

Cultural events organized by local government

Volunteer organizations such as "Friends of the Library"

Community partnerships with local government on collection of recyclable materials

A liaison to community business associations.

Citizens who find the thought of themselves participating in a public hearing impractical, frightening, or otherwise disagreeable can be engaged in whichever of the many types of public roles they would find comfortable: computer user, volunteer serving the local library, member of a team managing a community recycling center, or participant on an ad hoc committee on shopping-district security, to name only a few.

Cultural diversity

The job of providing more effective services to a culturally diverse population is being eased by technology. For example, AT&T's Language Line service provides over-the-telephone access to interpreters who can help with constituents or customers who do not speak English. For instance, police in Lakewood, Colorado, have used the system to communicate with non-English-speakers involved in traffic accidents; Lakewood police dispatchers have also found the system useful when responding to calls for assistance. The service incorporates more than 140 different languages. Interpreters are available around the clock, 365 days per year. Government clients can gain access to the service by dialing a toll-free number and providing their account identification number.[6]

Local governments are also using recently developed technology to help locate and identify culturally diverse populations. By combining census data with its geographic information system, the city of Charlotte, North Carolina, can identify the residence location of various populations and then use that information to help direct and tailor the delivery of services. The map shown in Figure 3–2 shows the residence location of 6,693 persons of Hispanic ancestry, with each dot representing one individual. The concentration along Central Avenue, Independence Boulevard, and Providence Road, all of which carry major bus routes, can guide the city in producing route information in both Spanish and English. The city government used a similar map, indicating concentrations of residents of Chinese descent, to reorient the services of branch libraries.

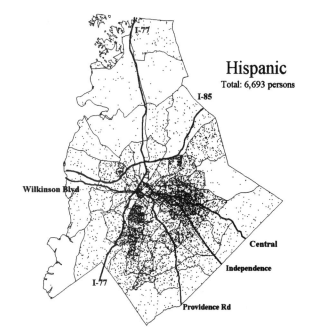

Figure 3–2.   Concentrations of Hispanic residents in Charlotte, North Carolina, 1993 (Charlotte-Mecklenburg Planning Commission).

Ways governmental agencies can use telephone interpretation services

An E-911 clerk can handle a call from someone who doesn't speak English and dispatch emergency services.

A magistrate can explain bail proceedings and other due process to a criminal defendant who speaks no English.

A paramedic can obtain blood type and allergy information from a confused accident victim who temporarily forgot his or her English.

A deputy tax collector can answer questions from an absentee property owner residing in a foreign country.

A fire or health inspector can inform the owner of an ethnic restaurant of a code violation.

A public utility representative can complete a service connection order for a new resident who speaks little or no English.

Source: Reprinted with permission from Diane Roth, "Breaking the Language Barrier," *Colorado Municipalities* (November/December 1992), pp. 13-15, published by the Colorado Municipal League.

Conclusion   By identifying the various roles citizens occupy as customers of local government and evaluating the delivery of services from their perspective, managers at all levels of local government can make sense of their own rapidly changing environment. Despite the diverse concerns of our citizen-customers, the expectation of being able to rely on government is a universal theme. Demonstrating an appreciation of the citizen as customer provides a secure foundation for the manager who wants to satisfy—and justify—that expectation.

Checklist

Just as citizens interact with local government in a variety of roles, government should perceive its many interactions with citizens as opportunities to encourage them to participate more fully in civic life.

The *service industry* provides a means of identifying citizen customers, determining what they want, and improving the local government's capacity to deliver.

Moving the point of contact for services out of city or county buildings (by such means as customer-service telephone lines and the "city hall in the mall") helps develop a sense of community and satisfaction with local government among local citizens.

The local government should foster neighborhood associations as allies in the effort to bolster both its mandate and its capacity to provide services to local citizens.

Technological advances can help the local government provide equitable, high-quality services as the population it serves becomes more and more culturally diverse.

4 Communicating With Elected Officials

Imagine a marriage in which the partners could meet face to face only once a week—and then see every word they exchanged subjected to public scrutiny the next day in the newspaper! These are precisely the conditions that elected and appointed officials have to work under in local government.

The conditions are difficult. And the personalities tend to be strong. So appointed officials need special skill and training to communicate well with elected officials. You also need to understand the elected official's job, as well as the political system in general. This chapter addresses the ways elected and appointed officials communicate with each other and gives ideas on ways to improve that communication.

Consider the following questions to help evaluate the strengths and weaknesses of your organization in its communications with elected officials:

Do your council members complain that they read stories in the newspaper before they have heard the facts from the staff?

Do your agenda packets read like unedited court proceedings?

Are agenda communications the only means the staff can use to communicate with elected officials between meetings?

Is it typical for one citizen to spend thirty minutes airing his or her views at a public hearing?

Do your elected officials pore over computer printouts to learn about the community's financial condition?

Does a typical orientation for new council members consist of several thirty-minute briefings from department heads, with only five minutes allotted for questions?

When your community faces a crisis, do you tell reporters you are too busy to talk to them?

When you have considered your organization's strengths and weaknesses in communicating with elected officials, you will be ready to take advantage of some of

the communication techniques described in this chapter.

The chapter covers the following topics:

The political environment

Roles and responsibilities

Orientation of candidates and newly elected officials

Managing the flow of information

Official and unofficial communication

Council meetings and open-meeting laws

Financial communications

Communicating under pressure

Information on ballot measures

Giving credit to policymakers

Communication in a crisis

Building the local government leadership team.

The political environment

Think back to that mythical couple who were able to communicate only once a week as television cameras rolled. Now add to those constraints the problem of a tight household budget. Maybe the family needs new clothes now, but the couple is also worried about that leak in the roof and what might happen to the house unless it is repaired in a timely way.

Communication is always easier when finances are strong and there are no difficult choices to face. Unfortunately, the trend in the 1990s is toward tighter budgets, greater demand for services, and little consensus on political solutions. While single-interest groups have become more militant, the average citizen is apathetic toward local government, often not even voting in local elections.

Council members and supervisors are increasingly being elected from districts or wards, and have strong ties to the neighborhoods that elected them. There is more diversity in local government leadership today, with a wide variety of voices seeking to be heard.

What do these trends mean for that critical communication between the manager and the governing body? For one thing, it means that you need to improve your skills in brokering and negotiating. You also need strong communication and facilitation skills to help the council focus on its strategic policy role in a more complex environment.

As the ICMA FutureVisions Report concluded, "The role of local government managers and assistants needs to be redefined. Although the traditional role of the professional manager has been to implement, it is increasingly necessary for the manager to anticipate . . . management professionals who can identify and interpret the local implications of broad demographic, economic, technological, and social trends can be valuable resources to their local governments."[1]

Roles and responsibilities

Communication between elected officials and the appointed administration works best when there is a good understanding of roles and responsibilities. Even though elected officials are primarily policymakers, they are also expected to have a good understanding of the local government's day-to-day management. Although administrators have responsibility for organizational management, they also play a significant part in shaping policy.

The local government manager's job

What are the basic responsibilities of the local government manager? Certainly they include the classic functions outlined by Luther Gulick in the 1930s: planning, organizing, staffing, directing, coordinating, reporting, and budgeting. But most practitioners agree that some of those responsibilities have gained more importance over the years and others have been added.

Coordination, for example, has become an increasingly important function, particularly in communicating with elected officials. The manager is expected to serve as the "communications center," ensuring that every part of the organization is well connected and that all important issues are brought before the council promptly.

By 1983, public managers said that they focused heavily on four key functions: managing people, managing change, building and maintaining relationships, and managing publicly. Of the many relationships that the manager must maintain, his or her relationship with the governing body is the one that absorbs the most time.[2]

One way managers can help elected officials to gain a broad perspective on important policy questions is to bring diverse groups together. When a controversial issue arises, the manager or top assistant may facilitate a process of collaboration or consensus building among all of the interested parties before the issue reaches the council. Bringing groups together *before* options are presented to the council may provide an opportunity to develop consensus on a difficult issue. Even if it is not possible to reach consensus beforehand, these discussions with community groups give the staff good background information, enabling staff members to present the policy options and their consequences more clearly to the council.

Local government management is increasingly a process of identifying a problem, directing attention to it, providing opportunities for groups to air their perspectives, seeking consensus, and developing the staff's capacity for being flexible and for handling complexity.

The local government manager can also play a key role in long-range planning processes that involve the community. For citizens participating in a long-range planning process, staff members can provide orientations, ensure that a budget and a structure are established for the process and incorporate information and ideas from the group's recommendations into relevant proposals for the council. The more effectively managers are able to educate citizens and interest groups on the variety of perspectives that need to be considered, the better prepared elected officials will be to establish policies that the community will support. The responsibility for developing good communication with all sectors of the community is one that elected and appointed officials share.

A model policy role for the city council

In Sunnyvale, California, the city manager and staff have developed several tools to enhance the city council's role in making policy. The most important tool is the city's general plan for the next 5 to 20 years, which includes more than just the state-mandated planning for housing, land use, traffic, and solid waste. It also establishes planning and management tools for all city services (e.g., support services, fiscal management, community participation, and legislative management).

Because the general plan is referenced in regular policy papers reviewed by the city council, it helps ensure that long-term goals are not forgotten. It also guides the financial planning and budgeting process for the city. Each annual budget includes service objectives and productivity measures specifically tied to the council's general plan goals and policies. This approach helps the city council focus on how quickly the city should respond to an emergency, rather than on how many fire engines should be purchased. The city council adopts the policy for service levels, allowing management to make decisions on the resources needed to achieve them.

A final tool used in this policy process is the legislative priority-setting process. Council members usually have their own personal agendas and priorities of issues that they want to see addressed. In addition, dozens of key issues arise during the year that come to the council for attention. In order to allocate staff time effectively and juggle the full list of competing priorities, the council established an agenda-setting mechanism that has them set their own agenda in an organized, thoughtful way.

Mechanically, it works like this. In early December each year, the city council conducts a workshop where they review issues that are possible study or policy topics. These may include land-use studies, potential ordinances, or policy studies suggested by council members, citizens advisory boards, staff, and the general plan itself.

In advance of the workshop, ideas for issues are solicited from council members, city boards and commissions, the general public, and staff. The general plan is reviewed to identify whether there are any action statements that specify policy studies to be undertaken. The staff prepares brief one-page issue papers that provide background on each issue and an estimate of the staff time needed to complete the study. Additional issues may be raised by council members at the workshop.

Each proposed issue is briefly reviewed. If a majority of council members think an issue should be studied, then the council ranks the relative priority of that issue against other issues that would be assigned to a city department for study. For example, the community-development department might have thirty potential issues identified by the council, whereas the finance department might have just one or two.

After the workshop is completed, staff members in each department analyze their resource capabilities to accomplish the council's priorities and recommend how many issues can be addressed, from top priority down. On the basis of the council's priorities, the staff then prepares an annual calendar, which serves as a work plan. In some cases, usually in the areas of land-use planning and development, only a limited number of policy studies can be undertaken, given resource limitations. The council decides whether to reorder the priorities or authorize additional resources to perform more of the studies.

The end result is that Sunnyvale annually adopts a "legislative calendar." It establishes the council's study priorities for the year and schedules the staff research. The calendar in effect becomes a contract between the council and the city manager that specifies which issues will be undertaken and when they will be accomplished. The calendar is flexible, however; issues and their timing can be modified during the year. Through experience, Sunnyvale's city council has gained the confidence and certainty that its priorities will be addressed and resolved, and the staff has gained a strong sense that its efforts are directed toward specific results and goals rather than mere immediate expediency.

Source: Tom Lewcock and Gene Rogers, "Strengthening the Policy Role of City Council," *Public Management* (December 1988), pp. 10-12.

It is clear that managers need to have a special kind of leadership skill. As Curtis Branscome has written, "The unending tension that managers live with is the need to be good leaders, and at the same time to be good followers . . . The key for the manager is to remember for whom the manager works. The manager works for the elected officials, not for the citizens. The manager's advocacy for public policy issues must be before the elected officials and not before the general public, unless this is at the direction of the elected officials."[3]

As James Banovetz puts it, managers are finding new and different vehicles for communicating with their councils. "Managers are participating with increasing frequency in such activities as strategic planning, goal setting sessions, and weekend retreats with council members." He defines the manager's role as that of a team builder—with the council and the staff.[4]

The governing body

The elected officials' role is defined by the priorities of the citizenry. Elected officials, expected to respond promptly to constituents, have to balance management's concerns with voters' demands. Routine requests for information or service, therefore, are high priorities for elected officials, and consequently for your staff. In particular, the governing body needs to agree on what procedures to use to handle requests or complaints. In many communities, requests for action are directed to the manager, who coordinates the staff's response.

As with the manager, the precise role of the local governing body will vary from one unit of government to another; but some duties, functions, and responsibilities apply to all of them in one manner or another and at one time or other. Generally speaking, a legislative body is performing its major duties when it

1. Sets short-, mid-, and long-range goals
2. Defines the kind and level of services to be provided
3. Approves plans and programs for achieving goals
4. Monitors effectiveness and efficiency of services
5. Exercises leadership in the community
6. Arbitrates conflicts among competing interests
7. Serves as facilitator/expediter of citizens' inquiries and complaints
8. Sends representatives to perform such ceremonial duties as ribbon-cutting, speech-making, and official greeting in their capacity as elected representatives of the community
9. Supports the "civic infrastructure" by promoting citizens' participation and sense of ownership in the community.[5]

The special role of the mayor

A key role for the governing body to understand is that of the mayor or the chairperson of the board of supervisors. James H. Svara describes this role as a policy coordinating function, "pulling together the parts of the system to improve their interaction . . . The mayor not only channels communication but may also influence and shape the messages being transmitted."[6]

An effective mayor serves as a hub for communication, particularly in the liaison role between the council and staff, and in advising on differing views of individual council members on political issues. The mayor also has significant external responsibilities, often those of acting as the community's spokesperson or representative on economic development, local disasters, intergovernmental relations, or regional issues.

Community needs and interests

Because managers and elected officials have very different backgrounds, roles, and experiences, conflicts are inevitable. The very professionalism that managers bring to the job can be a source of frustration to a council when citizens are pressing for a political solution. Elected officials win office because of their skills in connecting with the community. When they are called upon to take a position for the "long term," they risk losing the support that put them into office.

That pressure is exacerbated in places where council members are elected by district or are closely tied to a particular interest group or constituency. Many communities today have a diverse population with a wide range of nationalities, education levels, and special needs. Whether it is the frail elderly, youth at risk, or new immigrants facing a language barrier, the challenge to the council is to be aware of all of the community's interests.

Regardless of the methods, local officials need to create an understanding among the general public of the community's needs, problems, and resources. Failing to communicate a community's problems or to identify future needs creates an information vacuum. The public will then form its own impression of the community's condition and progress—often on the basis of gossip or rumor. When local officials are uncommunicative, the public tends to become suspicious and assume the worst. Taking the community's pulse will help the local government move out of its typical reactive mode of responding to a specific complaint or demand. The more adept the local government manager is at helping the governing body focus on the important policy issues, the more likely it is that sound decisions will be made.

Orientation of candidates and newly elected officials

In their relations with the governing body, seasoned managers place the primary emphasis on communication. They treat all council members equally and extend that rule to candidates for office as well. For example, if an incumbent asks for financial analysis about a controversial development, the manager will share that analysis with all the candidates and current members of the council. The manager will set up briefings for candidates to highlight current issues, finances, capital improvement plans, redevelopment projects, state ethics laws, and the local government structure. The briefings may raise the level of the political debate; they may also demonstrate the professionalism of the staff. If the council experiences turnover, the new members will be better informed and hence less inclined to make snap decisions about the competence of the staff.

Once elected, a new council member has the same difficulties as anyone else would in assuming unfamiliar responsibilities. He or she is eager to make a mark, become respected by both colleagues and the public, and exude as much confidence as a ten-year veteran. Local government managers can help newly elected officials by being aware of, and organizing, orientation programs.

Orientation by state leagues

Many state leagues offer special orientation programs for newly elected officials. The League of California Cities, for example, conducts an annual three-day program on such subjects as municipal law, conflicts of interest, financial disclosure, open meetings, press relations, budgeting, planning, employee relations, and evaluation of departmental performance. The program is offered after elections in the majority of the cities in the state. To maintain interest, the league uses a workshop format for most of its sessions, and the discussion and participation take place in small groups.

The program enjoys a good reputation. Many veteran council members have returned for refresher courses. It helps elected officials become acquainted with their peers and learn that their problems are shared by others.

Local orientation sessions   At the local level, many administrators plan orientations for new council members. Staff members who participate in orientation sessions should keep in mind that their fifteen-minute presentation may be one of many and that it is hard for anyone merely to sit and listen to others talk for four or five hours at a time. Administrators should remember, too, that newly elected officials will have specific concerns that may not be addressed in a formal presentation. For example, they may have questions about a particular project or about an issue affecting their neighborhood. If possible, administrators should answer all questions and should undertake to get back later on those needing further research.

Orientation program

Billings, Montana, uses briefing meetings as part of its overall orientation program. Conducted mostly by staff, these sessions augment information provided in a 73-page orientation manual. The manual includes details on the city organization, council meetings and agenda procedures, state open-meeting laws, home-rule authority, basic orientation to the budget process, fund accounting, types and purposes of the council's actions, conduct of meetings, and methodologies of processing citizen inquiries and requests for service. The city attorney provides information on conflicts of interest, liability, and operating procedures. Often incumbent council members take part in the sessions, offering newly elected members the benefit of their experiences.

Source: Georgene Kreinberg, "Orientation for Elected Officials," *MIS Report* (Washington, D.C.: ICMA, July 1991), p. 5.

Like any other presentation, a council orientation session should have good audiovisual aids; be lively and well rehearsed; and allow council members time to ask questions and participate in discussions. Some cities videotape topics for briefing sessions—a great service for a council member who cannot attend or who prefers to absorb new information over several days. The presentations should be as brief as possible, with the understanding that more detail is available in writing upon request. Some managers and staff members prepare council handbooks for new members, including rules of procedures, important ordinances, and background papers on local issues.

Many successful orientation sessions are made on the run, combining background information with a tour of municipal buildings, housing projects, or new developments. As the newly elected officials look over buildings, capital improvement projects, or auxiliary facilities, staff members may take the opportunity to informally brief the council on the status of a program or discuss plans for the future.

In addition to these orientation sessions, managers may meet individually with each new member of the council immediately after the election. Such meetings give newly elected council members an opportunity to discuss goals and issues in a personal way that may put them more at ease and enable them to share their concerns frankly.

Managing the flow of information   Before you can improve communication with your elected officials, you need a clear understanding of the flow of information through your organization. Most of the information communicated directly to elected officials comes either from the chief administrative officer or from citizens.

One of the most difficult tasks the manager faces is to present the concerns of the whole community to the council in a competitive environment.

The local government manager contributes to that flow of information in several ways: the staff's day-to-day contacts with citizens, employee relations, agenda communications, formal presentations at public meetings and at council briefings, and responses to individual requests from council members.

Newly elected officials are often surprised by the demands of the office and by the conflicting information they receive. Before taking office, the candidate may have been impressed by one particular special-interest group. After being elected, the official hears not only from that special-interest group but also from other interest groups, the staff, and the news media. One of the most difficult tasks the local government manager faces is to present the concerns of the whole community to the city or county council in such a competitive environment.

To make a positive contribution, you need to know what is being communicated to your elected officials. Make it a point to read all agenda communications, and to identify issues that will be of greatest concern to the council. Pay attention to the letters that you and your staff receive from citizens. Some of the complaints you receive are likely to be made to your elected officials as well. If you see some pattern to the complaints, take the initiative to alert the council to the problem and a possible solution.

Remember, many citizens see their elected officials as the court of last resort. They may have already approached the staff with the problem and not been satisfied. By the time they take it to the elected official, their feelings have grown more intense. What may have seemed like a routine problem to you may become magnified when presented to an elected official.

In this kind of environment, an elected official needs strong support from his or her staff. Prompt attention to requests from council members can help relieve the pressure on them. Likewise, your employees should defuse the ire of as many disgruntled citizens as possible. Every citizen who can be helped at the staff level is one citizen fewer who feels he or she must escalate a demand to the attention of your elected officials.

Tips for city and county managers

Give all members of the council prior knowledge of agenda items. Nothing bothers a council member more than getting questions from a reporter before having received any information on an issue. Be sure that all the agenda packets are delivered at the same time.

Discuss key issues informally before meetings. If the council has to grapple with a controversial issue for the first time in a formal meeting, individual members will not have any way of understanding each other's feelings on the matter. A word of caution, however: Be sure to follow both the letter and the spirit of the open-meeting laws in your state.

Be sure that the individual communications are well written. Give background briefings on important issues and summarize key points, to help elected officials sort through the paper blizzard. It is difficult to read a massive package of technical information in just one or two days—especially for elected officials who have other, full-time jobs.

Give the same information to all council members. If one of them asks for something special, share it with the rest of them.

Make recommendations. Elected officials expect leadership from the staff, even if they do not always take the advice. Staff members need to understand that some issues are politically sensitive, and that politics sometimes overrides long-term considerations.

Prevent surprises. Administrators who go out of their way to alert elected officials to a problem have a better chance of avoiding surprises themselves (like a sudden dismissal). Staff members should be prompt in informing the chief administrative officer or manager of any major problems.

Avoid embarrassing elected officials in public. Tell them about their mistakes in private.

Your employees are important in other ways as well. Since they are the primary link with citizens, they will be giving out the most information and answering the greatest number of questions. Be sure that you keep them up to date on decisions that the council makes on the direction of policy. You cannot assume that they will have access to all the information you have. Take the initiative to highlight important decisions or activities for them. (See Chapter 5 for more information on effective communication with front-line staff members.)

Official and unofficial communication

There are distinct classes of information, each serving a particular function. It is vital to fit the medium to the message.

Agenda communications

The weekly agenda communications prepared for the council are the most basic and important documents you and your staff prepare. Unfortunately, some of them are poorly prepared and organized. Think for a minute about what it would feel like to read such a paper. Would you want to have to make a decision affecting thousands of people on the basis of a ten-page paper pieced together from engineering specifications? Although issues for the agenda may come up suddenly, your effort in writing the communication must still be careful and thoughtful if it is to engage council members' attention.

Pay attention to the writing and the organization of each agenda communication. Although it may be necessary to include technical details in the write-up, summarize the important points in a covering memo along with a brief description of the policy options. Although many council members will not have time to read all the agenda communications completely, they still deserve the best, most concise description of the problem and the points they need to consider. (See Chapter 10 for more information on effective writing.)

Tips for elected officials

Be prepared. Study the issues before, not during, the meeting.

Avoid embarrassing the staff in public. If you have a problem with them, discuss it before or after the meeting.

Tell the staff members how well they are performing. If you are not getting the information you need, tell them that too.

Let the manager know if you want to meet with other members of the staff. It puts the manager and the staff member in an awkward position if you ask for special favors.

Recognize that the staff members have little time to prepare agendas. Last-minute changes are sometime unavoidable.

Some of the communications may be highly political. These are the ones that demand the greatest finesse. Present all the options fairly. Then, even if you are under significant political pressure, you should state your professional recommendation clearly. Keep in mind that these are the issues on which some council member may ask you for special information. It is essential that you treat all council members fairly. Be sure to give everyone the same information and to follow council policy on dealing with special requests from an individual council member.

Because of the deadlines involved, it is important for staff members to complete their write-ups on time and in the format required. There are always more mistakes and misunderstandings in agenda communications that come in late. You will want time to review the package before it goes out to council members. That important review process can prevent needless embarrassment when you are asked to explain some of your statements at a council meeting.

By understanding the importance of the weekly or biweekly agenda process, your staff can help you improve communication with the council. Be as helpful as you can in describing the various options for the council. If in your professional opinion one option is superior to the others, identify it clearly.

Informal newsletters

Besides agenda communications, there are other routine ways for elected and appointed officials to communicate with one another. Weekly progress reports are an easy way to keep the council and others up to date on important city or county news and to brief them on the status of particular projects. Progress reports may include dates of meetings, legislative news, and interesting facts about the community. A decision of the planning commission, for example, may be highlighted if it makes a recommendation that conflicts with the council's expressed policy. Or the report may focus attention on staff members' efforts that have succeeded. Even maintenance projects can be mentioned, especially if they affect the convenience of commuters.

If your community uses progress reports and newsletters, you will want to encourage staff members to contribute to them. If a department has accomplished a goal or has begun work on a high-priority project, be sure to get the news into the proper hands. Desktop publishing can add graphics and designs that help in getting important messages across.

Complaint control

Follow-up on the complaints of citizens is another important area of routine communication that merits special attention from all staff members. When an elected official makes a complaint and the staff takes care of it promptly, it is important to tell the official that the problem has been resolved. Staff members may formally respond to the council's complaints on a feedback form, on which the specific action taken should be noted.

The personal touch

Local government staff members spend hours preparing briefing papers, agenda communications, and other formal documents for the council. No matter how well prepared these papers are, though, the written word alone will not create good day-to-day interpersonal relationships with the council. It is important for administrators to maintain informal social contact with elected officials. (It is best to keep those informal contacts within a businesslike structure, however.) For some administrators, regular telephone calls to council members are effective. Others encourage weekly visits from council members to discuss whatever is on their minds. Meetings with individual council members are good times to try out new ideas.

Social gatherings after council meetings and dinners can improve the relationship between the council and staff members. As Ronald O. Loveridge observes, "In council meetings, informal working sessions, private meetings, or individual conversations the city manager is subject to the continuous face-to-face influence of the council. The success or failure of a city manager notably depends on the personal rapport he develops and sustains with the members of his council."[7]

Breakfast study sessions can also be effective in encouraging open discussion and consensus building among elected officials. They can also give the administrator an idea of the general direction in which the council is heading. No votes should be taken during those sessions, and the press should be invited. You will want to weigh considerations of informality against those of confidentiality in these sessions.

Figure 4–1 A weekly report from the city manager to the council of Scottsdale, Arizona.

March 12, 1992

TO: THE HONORABLE MAYOR & CITY COUNCIL

FROM: RICHARD A. BOWERS,
          CITY MANAGER

SUBJECT: CURRENT ISSUES REPORT

1. **WEEKLY LEGISLATIVE REPORT** (Attachment 1)
   Attached is the Weekly Legislative Report from Intergovernmental Relations. This week the City saw a major win and a close loss on two priority issues. The Annual Storage and Recovery Bill, the Scottsdale-backed water bill, was passed on a final vote in the House. The bill on open dumps that could force closure of the Tri-City Landfill, passed the House Counties and Municipalities Committee. Also attached is the League Bulletin and New Bills Introduced.

2. **ROADS OF REGIONAL SIGNIFICANCE AND SCOTTSDALE ROAD** (Attachment 2)
   This memo from Transportation explains the criteria needed to be included and identified in the Roads of Regional Significance. The roads identified were Dynamite, Frank Lloyd Wright, Shea, Indian School, Pima Freeway, and Pima Road north of the Pima Freeway. Scottsdale Road was not identified as a Road of Regional Significance.

3. **TENTATIVE AGENDA** (Attachment 3)
   Attached is the tentative agenda for the Planning Commission meeting of April 13, 1992, and the City Council Meeting for April 21, 1992.

4. **TRI-CITY LANDFILL REPORT** (Attachment 4)
   The attached report from the Chief Environmental Officer deals with the issues involved in the Tri-Cities Landfill. Recent publicity, historical correspondence, water quality data, EPA reports, and other information was compiled and analyzed. The report is meant to provide insight into the complex issues involved in the Tri-Cities landfill and offer some positive pro-active responses to the challenges.

5. **BOARDS AND COMMISSIONS ANNUAL RECOGNITION RECEPTION** (Attachment 5)
   Communications and Public Affairs Office will once again be coordinating the annual recognition reception for the members of the boards and commissions. The event is scheduled for Wednesday, April 8, at 6:30 p.m. at the Scottsdale Center for the Arts.

6. **THANK YOUS** (Attachment 6)
   Letters of appreciation are attached for the Planning and Community Development Department, Police Department, Communications and Public Affairs, the City Manager's Office, Community Services, and Economic Development.

7. **PM MAGAZINE** (Attachment 7)

   Included in this week's packet is the March 1992 issue of the Public Management Magazine. It highlights how collaboration is the key to addressing homeless issues, and diversity in the future of local governance. It also includes "Turning Government on its Head, New Perspectives on Old Problems."

RAB/cm
Attachments 7

Quick communication

Joplin, Missouri (40,000), has discovered a cost-effective way to communicate with its nine council members. Unlike other local governments, which use personal computers to communicate with their councils, Joplin chose to purchase facsimile machines for each councilor's home. The city chose the fax over the computer because it is less expensive; it is simpler to operate; it is not as intimidating as a computer; and copies of articles, complaint letters, and memoranda can be distributed without retyping. City employees no longer have to personally deliver short documents or mail out large packets of information. The council receives information literally one page at a time. The fax machines, purchased through a formal bid, cost $595 each.

Source: *The Guide to Management Improvement Projects in Local Government,* vol. 14, no. 3 (Washington, D.C.: ICMA, 1990) CCR-16.

Council meetings and open-meeting laws

The efforts made by local government staff to communicate with council members through well-prepared written documents and informal conversations will contribute to effective decision making at council meetings. The decisions made at council meetings often have a major impact on the lives of a community's citizens. So it is important that the meetings be conducted efficiently, correctly, and openly.

Living in the sunshine

Because of the public's concern that government business should be open and above board, all fifty states and the federal government have open-meeting—or "sunshine"—laws. These laws cover many types of meeting. They vary from state to state, and you should know how your state law addresses the major areas usually covered in sunshine laws. The six major areas are outlined in the sidebar on p. 58.

Local officials frequently complain that the presence of reporters interferes with the informal, candid discussions they need to have outside regular council meetings. However, elected officials may find that, in order to avoid any appearance of violating open-meeting laws, they can only meet individually with the manager.

Local officials recognize that vigilant reporters will usually learn if the open-meeting law has been violated—in fact or in spirit. For example, if managers and council members try to circumvent sunshine laws by holding informal meetings without a quorum, a determined reporter denied access to those meetings is likely to write a story saying "the public was shut out." Almost all meetings should be open to the news media.

The three topics generally exempt from open-meeting laws are discussions relating to personnel, legal matters, and collective bargaining. It is appropriate to discuss a personnel matter privately that might involve a false accusation, but it is inappropriate to use the law simply as an excuse to discuss an issue that is controversial.

It is also important to remember that even if an issue may be discussed privately, votes must be taken in open sessions.

Procedures for meetings

Council meetings themselves offer good opportunities to improve communications. Council members need to understand not only *Robert's Rules of Order* but also the informal rules that guide every meeting. New council members, for example, may not be aware of time limits. At the beginning of any public hearing, the mayor or county executive should clearly state the rules. The statement can be reinforced with brochures describing public hearings and council meetings.

Guidelines for running meetings and public hearings are essential; but it is just as important that exceptions be made. Every local government should find some way for citizens to raise their own issues or go beyond the time limits that have been set. Many local governments allow an open forum at the end of every meeting. Others require written notice in advance of the meeting describing the item to be discussed and the name of the person making the request.

Even if meetings run smoothly and administrators establish a good rapport with elected officials, all can be lost if certain kinds of information are not communicated. Among those crucial types of information are finances, long-range goals, labor negotiations, ballot measures, and updates on emergency conditions.

Financial communications

Council members expect a complete, timely budget from the staff, with regular updates on the financial condition of the community. The council expects not only information on finances but also recommendations for action as financial conditions change.

Administrators should pay attention to the quality of the financial information they provide to elected officials. Summaries of key information, charts, and graphs, are more effective than detailed financial reports. Many local government staffs now provide their elected officials with concise monthly reports summarizing information on revenues and expenditures. The reports generally show year-to-date estimates and appropriations and compare those data with comparable-period data from the preceding year. Quarterly fiscal reports typically supplement the monthly reports with more intensive analysis of the community's fiscal condition. They can be used to forecast the year-end fund balance.

Open-meeting laws

You may have questions as to what constitutes an "open" meeting. The questions answered below pertain to the six areas common to sunshine laws in all fifty states of the United States.

Who's covered by the law? Actions by elected officials are almost automatically covered. In some cases, advisory groups, citizens committees, and staff members are covered as well.

What's a meeting? This may seem like a simple question, but it has caused more controversy and confusion than any other area covered by sunshine laws. Depending on the size of the council or commission, even two people getting together for dinner and talking over some business may be considered a meeting—and may require a public record.

What are the requirements for advance notice of meetings? Almost all state sunshine laws require public advance notice for at least some types of meeting. Commonly the minimum time required is 72 hours. Some laws describe the kind of announcement required (e.g., newspaper, community bulletin board, etc.).

What are the requirements for recording sessions? Some sunshine laws require that you keep a taped record. Others require a transcribed record. The requirements may vary depending on the type of meeting; requirements may be different for executive sessions than for other types of meetings.

May any meetings be closed? Some states offer few if any exceptions to the rule that meetings must be accessible to the public. You need to be sure that you can legally hold a closed meeting or executive session before you try to do so. And you need to follow the procedure prescribed by the law.

What happens to officials who violate the law? In many states, public officials who violate sunshine laws are subject to criminal or civil penalties. Many sunshine laws also provide that actions taken in violation of sunshine laws are automatically void or voidable. This section of the law also explains who can initiate action against violators.

Beyond the budget

The key to communicating financial information is that it is a continuous process, not just a once-a-year budget requirement or a crisis memo. Many managers find it helpful to weave financial information into routine communications. A weekly newsletter or memo to council members, for example, can highlight important financial information. Some of the best newsletters are personal, brief (never more than a single page, two sides), and topical. They may include short articles on finance, such as the amount of money collected from a particular revenue source during the previous month, or a longer analysis showing trends or summarizing a longer report. Some financial directors and managers keep bar graphs and charts on display in their offices to encourage questions

Figure 4–2. Page from the 1992-93 budget of Phoenix, Arizona.

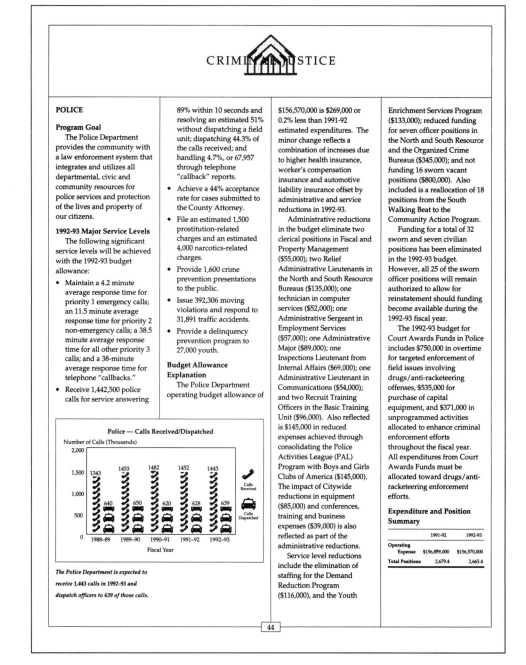

CRIMINAL JUSTICE

POLICE

Program Goal

The Police Department provides the community with a law enforcement system that integrates and utilizes all departmental, civic and community resources for police services and protection of the lives and property of our citizens.

1992-93 Major Service Levels

The following significant service levels will be achieved with the 1992-93 budget allowance:

- Maintain a 4.2 minute average response time for priority 1 emergency calls; an 11.5 minute average response time for priority 2 non-emergency calls; a 38.5 minute average response time for all other priority 3 calls; and a 38-minute average response time for telephone "callbacks."
- Receive 1,442,500 police calls for service answering

89% within 10 seconds and resolving an estimated 51% without dispatching a field unit; dispatching 44.3% of the calls received; and handling 4.7%, or 67,957 through telephone "callback" reports.

- Achieve a 44% acceptance rate for cases submitted to the County Attorney.
- File an estimated 1,500 prostitution-related charges and an estimated 4,000 narcotics-related charges.
- Provide 1,600 crime prevention presentations to the public.
- Issue 392,306 moving violations and respond to 31,891 traffic accidents.
- Provide a delinquency prevention program to 27,000 youth.

Budget Allowance Explanation

The Police Department operating budget allowance of

$156,570,000 is $269,000 or 0.2% less than 1991-92 estimated expenditures. The minor change reflects a combination of increases due to higher health insurance, worker's compensation insurance and automotive liability insurance offset by administrative and service reductions in 1992-93.

Administrative reductions in the budget eliminate two clerical positions in Fiscal and Property Management ($55,000); two Relief Administrative Lieutenants in the North and South Resource Bureaus ($135,000); one technician in computer services ($52,000); one Administrative Sergeant in Employment Services ($57,000); one Administrative Major ($89,000); one Inspections Lieutenant from Internal Affairs ($69,000); one Administrative Lieutenant in Communications ($54,000); and two Recruit Training Officers in the Basic Training Unit ($96,000). Also reflected is $145,000 in reduced expenses achieved through consolidating the Police Activities League (PAL) Program with Boys and Girls Clubs of America ($145,000). The impact of Citywide reductions in equipment ($85,000) and conferences, training and business expenses ($39,000) is also reflected as part of the administrative reductions.

Service level reductions include the elimination of staffing for the Demand Reduction Program ($116,000), and the Youth

Enrichment Services Program ($133,000); reduced funding for seven officer positions in the North and South Resource and the Organized Crime Bureaus ($345,000); and not funding 16 sworn vacant positions ($800,000). Also included is a reallocation of 18 positions from the South Walking Beat to the Community Action Program.

Funding for a total of 32 sworn and seven civilian positions has been eliminated in the 1992-93 budget. However, all 25 of the sworn officer positions will remain authorized to allow for reinstatement should funding become available during the 1992-93 fiscal year.

The 1992-93 budget for Court Awards Funds in Police includes $750,000 in overtime for targeted enforcement of field issues involving drugs/anti-racketeering offenses, $535,000 for purchase of capital equipment, and $371,000 in unprogrammed activities allocated to enhance criminal enforcement efforts throughout the fiscal year. All expenditures from Court Awards Funds must be allocated toward drugs/anti-racketeering enforcement efforts.

Expenditure and Position Summary

	1991-92	1992-93
Operating Expense	$156,889,000	$156,570,000
Total Positions	2,679.4	2,665.4

Police — Calls Received/Dispatched

Number of Calls (Thousands)

Fiscal Year	Calls Received	Calls Dispatched
1988–89	1343	640
1989–90	1453	650
1990–91	1482	620
1991–92	1452	628
1992–93	1443	639

The Police Department is expected to receive 1,443 calls in 1992-93 and dispatch officers to 639 of those calls.

44

from elected officials. The charts should be changed or removed frequently, to sustain interest. Similarly, visual aids work well in newsletters to highlight important trends.

Long-range goals

Although elected officials recognize the need to focus on broad policy questions, they may need help in working together to set goals. Some administrators use the budget as a way of drawing attention to the community's long-range goals. Since voters seldom reward officials for long-term planning, managers need to be creative in making points about structural financial issues and their relationship to quality of life (and bond ratings). An orientation session for the new board of supervisors, for example, might be combined with a briefing on the budget and a retreat. As discussed earlier, it might include a bus tour of all the buildings operated by the government, recently completed capital projects, and areas of the community that need attention. Staff members could follow the tour with presentations and reports on levels of service, results of surveys, and budgetary needs. This kind of activity is especially effective in a relaxed setting, which allows ample time for an exchange of ideas and questions.

Nothing is more important to the public than to know that their tax dollars are being managed wisely. It's best not to wait until a crisis looms. Keep your elected officials fully informed of all financial trends and changes in the budget.

Communicating financial information with indicators

To help appointed and elected officials put financial information into an intelligible format, the International City/County Management Association developed the Financial Trend Monitoring System (FTMS), a system of thirty-six indicators that translates difficult financial data into the kind of decision-making information that managers and elected officials can conveniently use for policymaking. (The FTMS is described in ICMA's *Evaluating Financial Condition: A Handbook for Local Government.*)

Some of the indicators are revenues per capita, cost of fringe benefits per employee, shortfalls in revenue, debt service to operating revenues, and maintenance of the capital plant. The system also includes indicators that are signs of the health of the underlying economic base, such as the employment rate, property values, and personal income of residents. Those indicators are trended throughout a five- to seven-year period so that decision makers can also see how their community's financial condition has been changing and what problems have been developing.

Managers have used the indicators in presentations they have given to the council before budget sessions, to provide a perspective from which elected officials can view political demands. Several managers have used the indicators to help the council focus on important issues when decisions to cut back have to be made. Other managers have used them as a tool for setting and monitoring long-range financial policies. Several local governments have used the indicators in presentations before credit rating firms such as Standard & Poor's and Moody's. Often the indicator charts are included in the budget or the annual report to explain the meaning of the tables of data.

Communicating under pressure

Another sensitive subject that requires special attention is labor negotiations. In some localities negotiations between management and labor take place in a business-like way. In other places, the news media—and by extension, the public—get to be players.

Administrators who hand their council members a 150-page computer printout can easily improve their financial reporting.

There is considerable opinion that elected officials should stay away from the bargaining table. Still, they need reliable information about the negotiating process. Elected officials need to be informed about both the financial constraints of the government and the procedures the negotiator will follow.

In some communities it seems best for the council to stay removed from the day-to-day discussions. In others, the chief negotiator briefs the council regularly. Negotiators say that such briefings can be helpful in determining how much political support there might be for a particular package.

Some council members want to be actively involved in the process. In some localities it might be desirable for a well-informed council member to serve as an observer at the bargaining table. Without actually taking part in the discussions, he or she could listen to the issues and give progress reports to the rest of the council.

There is no consensus among elected officials or administrators, however, as to how much information should be shared with the council. Many administrators argue that the council needs some psychological distance from the process in order to make sound policy. Administrators who argue that way also say that keeping the council away from the day-to-day flow of information makes it easier to stay objective at the bargaining table: the negotiator is then able to honestly say that the union has a point, but he or she is not sure whether the idea can be "sold" to the council. It may be harder to talk about the possible pressure on the council from tax-shy citizens when council members are present.

The question is moot in states such as Florida and cities such as Dayton, Ohio, where bargaining is done in the sunshine. In these places, the news media exert tremendous influence on the negotiating process. Although the news media show only sporadic interest in the day-to-day activities, the way they report specific wage proposals affects the substance and the style of negotiations. Although it may be more difficult to determine each party's bottom-line position in open meetings, some observers believe that unions tend to screen their proposals better before bringing them to the bargaining table if the proceedings are open to the public.

Information on ballot measures

Ballot measures also require sensitivity in communication between elected and appointed officials, particularly if the council is divided in its opinion. This is true whether the issue is a ceiling on property taxes, a new bond obligation, or a city/county consolidation. A good way to prevent problems is to be certain that each council member receives the same information.

There is a fine line between disseminating information and promoting an issue, so use great care. For example, some states prohibit the use of public funds for preparing promotional materials. If you are able to publicize a ballot issue, it's a good idea to ask the council to review any printed matter you plan to distribute. Taking this step will help to ensure that you have the support of the council for both the content of an election brochure and the desirability of publishing one.

You should be wary of engaging in discussions with individual elected officials on the merits of any ballot measure. You might find comments made by any staff member misunderstood or used in the crossfire of political debate. All elections create a great deal of pressure for elected officials. When council seats are up for a vote, be particularly careful to treat all individuals, both incumbents and candidates, equally.

The manager is often operating on a tightrope.

Giving credit to policymakers

Elected officials are in the public eye, but more often than not, the publicity they get is either sensational or negative. Many elected officials find it annoying that the more positive stories about local government often give credit to the local government staff. Without becoming political, administrators who want the public to recognize the community's excellent programs and accomplishments can often do that best by giving credit to the elected officials. So, for example, when the police department unveils its new communications system or announces a new crime-prevention program, the city council or board of supervisors should get credit for financing the program or for setting the policy. Too often, in the excitement of launching a new program or in reporting its success, the elected officials who authorized it are forgotten. In planning publicity for new programs, make sure that the elected official's personal expertise and interests are tied into the story.

There are, of course, times when publicity is best left to individual council members. If a city publishes a regular newsletter addressed to citizens and discusses council activities routinely, there should be no complaints. On the other hand, if a city or county distributes an election-eve newsletter in which individual council members are praised, challengers will naturally accuse the staff of engaging in political activity. Any city or county manager who wants to work on an official's reelection campaign—or on a challenger's campaign—should resign first. Elected officials, too, should be sensitive to the potential for the appearance of favoritism and refrain from asking anyone on the staff for assistance in writing campaign literature or in organizing "Meet the

Candidate" breakfasts and other events. Administrators must always weigh the need for publicity against the equally important need to maintain the organization's impartiality in serving citizens.

Tenets 5–7, *ICMA Code of Ethics with Guidelines*

Every member of ICMA . . . shall:

5. Submit policy proposals to elected officials; provide them with facts and advice on matters of policy as a basis for making decisions and setting community goals; and uphold and implement municipal policies adopted by elected officials.

6. Recognize that elected representatives of the people are entitled to the credit for the establishment of municipal policies; responsibility for policy execution rests with the members.

7. Refrain from participation in the election of the members of the employing legislative body, and from all partisan political activities which would impair performance as a professional administrator.

Guidelines

Elections of the Governing Body. Members should maintain a reputation for serving equally and impartially all members of the governing body of the municipality they serve, regardless of party. To this end, they should not engage in active participation in the election campaign on behalf of or in opposition to candidates for the governing body.

Elections of Elected Executives. Members should not engage in the election campaign of any candidate for mayor or elected county executive.

Communication in a crisis

When disaster strikes, local officials will need all their energy to resolve the crisis. Organizations that are well prepared and have involved top management and elected officials in disaster planning are the ones that cope well in a disaster. The first step is to develop a disaster plan that lays out responsibilities for key officials and resources that are available. For example, the disaster plan should outline how the emergency operations center will be organized and who will coordinate emergency services. Emergency operations require changes in reporting relationships and decision-making processes, and they test an organization's capabilities in unprecedented ways.

Shared responsibilities

"Organizations that extend decision-making prerogatives and responsibilities throughout their ranks will perform well. For there is no time in emergency circumstances to run everything through the usual chain of command. Judgment and responsibility must have been cultivated far in advance of the emergency."[8]

The mayor or chairperson of the board of supervisors takes on a critical role in a disaster, speaking for the community and setting the stage for recovery. That leader's words and deeds will be the focus of media attention and can be critical in giving hope to a community under siege. In many communities, authority is vested in the elected leader to request a declaration of emergency from the governor of the state (who in turn may request a presidential declaration). Because the elected leader is often speaking for the community, it is critical for that person

Pressures on the council

or the board increase

during disaster recovery.

to work closely with the director of emergency services so as to have up-to-the-minute information and to understand recovery strategies.

The mayor or chairperson of the board of supervisors can also be helpful in guiding many of the state and federal officials through a disaster site. The elected leader can give officials a perspective on the community's needs and help pave the way for financial or other assistance. Keep in mind that the visitors will want access to the emergency operations center, so be sure there is a good space where they can observe, but not hinder, operations.

Pressures on the city council or the board of supervisors increase during disaster recovery. Often they must hold daily meetings, some of which will deal with the adoption of ordinances or the threat of litigation. Other meetings will serve as a forum for citizens to discuss the hardships or to learn more about the community's recovery plans. Some

Figure 4–3. The *City Manager's Report* from Arlington, Texas, gives credit to elected as well as appointed officials.

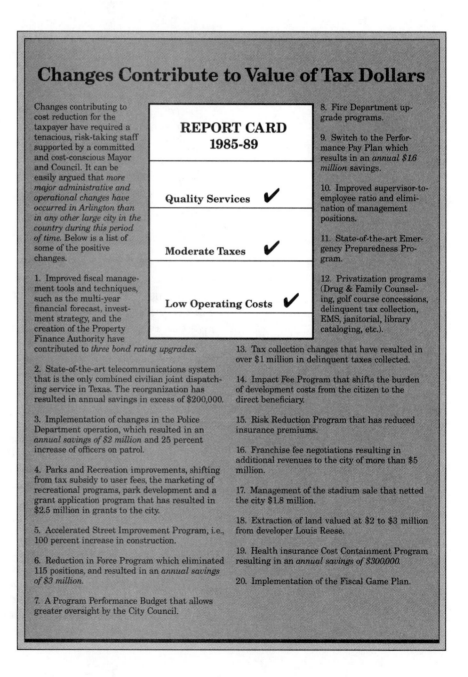

Changes Contribute to Value of Tax Dollars

Changes contributing to cost reduction for the taxpayer have required a tenacious, risk-taking staff supported by a committed and cost-conscious Mayor and Council. It can be easily argued that *more major administrative and operational changes have occurred in Arlington than in any other large city in the country during this period of time.* Below is a list of some of the positive changes.

1. Improved fiscal management tools and techniques, such as the multi-year financial forecast, investment strategy, and the creation of the Property Finance Authority have contributed to *three bond rating upgrades.*

2. State-of-the-art telecommunications system that is the only combined civilian joint dispatching service in Texas. The reorganization has resulted in annual savings in excess of $200,000.

3. Implementation of changes in the Police Department operation, which resulted in an *annual savings of $2 million* and 25 percent increase of officers on patrol.

4. Parks and Recreation improvements, shifting from tax subsidy to user fees, the marketing of recreational programs, park development and a grant application program that has resulted in $2.5 million in grants to the city.

5. Accelerated Street Improvement Program, i.e., 100 percent increase in construction.

6. Reduction in Force Program which eliminated 115 positions, and resulted in an *annual savings of $3 million.*

7. A Program Performance Budget that allows greater oversight by the City Council.

REPORT CARD 1985-89

Quality Services ✔

Moderate Taxes ✔

Low Operating Costs ✔

8. Fire Department upgrade programs.

9. Switch to the Performance Pay Plan which results in an *annual $1.6 million* savings.

10. Improved supervisor-to-employee ratio and elimination of management positions.

11. State-of-the-art Emergency Preparedness Program.

12. Privatization programs (Drug & Family Counseling, golf course concessions, delinquent tax collection, EMS, janitorial, library cataloging, etc.).

13. Tax collection changes that have resulted in over $1 million in delinquent taxes collected.

14. Impact Fee Program that shifts the burden of development costs from the citizen to the direct beneficiary.

15. Risk Reduction Program that has reduced insurance premiums.

16. Franchise fee negotiations resulting in additional revenues to the city of more than $5 million.

17. Management of the stadium sale that netted the city $1.8 million.

18. Extraction of land valued at $2 to $3 million from developer Louis Reese.

19. Health insurance Cost Containment Program resulting in an *annual savings of $300,000.*

20. Implementation of the Fiscal Game Plan.

council members may want to become more deeply involved in the emergency, perhaps donating their time or expertise. Because a new organizational structure goes into operation during an emergency, the mayor or chairperson has a higher profile than usual—and the nature of the government's policy process changes. In reviewing emergency plans with elected officials, it is helpful to discuss what they can expect and how they might contribute in a disaster situation.

Surviving Hurricane Hugo

On Friday, September 22, 1989, Hurricane Hugo unexpectedly hit Charlotte, N.C. (404,500), with winds in excess of 87 miles per hour. Charlotte suffered extensive damage from the high winds, losing 10 to 15 percent of its trees. Homes throughout the city and region lost roofs; trees damaged houses and blocked roads; and nearly 90 percent of the city went without electrical power. An emergency operations center was immediately activated. One of its priorities was providing information to the community.

The Hugo information plan had two parts: (1) the emergency phase, in which information on services and compliance with guidelines were the primary messages; and (2) the cleanup/recovery phase, in which the primary message was how to prepare for debris collection. The need for emergency information was evident once the storm had cleared. With 90 percent of the city without power, more than 50 percent without telephones, trees blocking streets, and all traffic signals damaged, information on basic services (fire, police, traffic control, sanitation, water/sewer safety) became critical.

During this phase, the city followed a predetermined communications plan for emergency operations that, while specific in its structure, was flexible enough to accommodate the disaster situation . . . The plan's objectives were as follows:

To provide citizens with accurate and timely information

To keep the news media informed

To provide information on and recognition of city employees

To keep the city council informed of the status, procedures, and costs of the emergency and cleanup/recovery phases

To solicit support from the opinion leaders of the community.

The emergency communications plan contained four major strategic components, namely: media relations, the Hugo Hotline, employee relations, and city council updates. An estimated 302 staff hours were spent in the emergency phase.

Source: Jeannine Clark, Public Service and Information Department, Charlotte, North Carolina.

Informing the public

Planning also pays off in coordinating public information. The public information function needs to be centralized—ideally, in a place removed from the Emergency Operations Center, but with complete access to it. This round-the-clock operation needs to provide accurate and consistent information for the public. Since the media will focus on the worst situations, the public information officer will be challenged to provide perspective on the magnitude of a disaster. For example, the public information officer is likely to be pressed for data on casualties or financial estimates of damage. It is better to acknowledge that good information is not yet available than to release inaccurate or misleading information. Likewise, if mistakes are made during a disaster, they should be addressed openly and with candor.

Integrating disaster planning

Planning for disasters needs to be an ongoing activity.

While dealing with intense media pressure, escorting government dignitaries through the disaster site, and responding to one emergency after another, local government staff must still carry on daily operations. Many local governments assign the assistant city or county manager to take charge of ongoing operations. Whoever has this assignment must be well connected to the emergency operations to ensure coordination. Like other citizens, employees too have fears and concerns that need to be addressed. Making sure that someone contacts their family and friends can give emergency workers peace of mind as they carry out their duties.

Because people and resources frequently change, planning for disasters needs to be an ongoing activity. New technological developments may improve a community's emergency response or save precious staff time. Cellular phones, though commonly used in emergencies, have not replaced radios. Commerce, California, is testing an automated telephone system that can contact 3,200 residences and 1,700 businesses with a recorded emergency message in just one hour and 40 minutes. The system can call 50 numbers simultaneously, and will even return calls two times if a line is busy.[9] Many local governments periodically "walk through" a simulated disaster to check the effectiveness of their disaster plan and to update the information in it.

As Richard C. Wilson observes, disaster planning requires a commitment from elected officials, the chief executive, and department heads. "It will take time away from other things. And it may take resources away from other priorities. But if you are called upon to face the real thing, every disaster planning effort you have made will pay enormous dividends."[10]

Building the local government leadership team

Communicating with elected officials involves much more than meetings, agendas, and newsletters. It is also involves interpersonal relations, particularly among elected officials and between elected officials and the city or county manager. Several techniques have been credited with improving the effectiveness of a group. Most of these techniques have to do with interpersonal skills, a subject that many administrators and elected officials find uncomfortable.

Consider, for example, the difference between managers and elected officials in skills and styles. Managers are usually skilled in analyzing information and in making sure staff members are organized to carry out their responsibilities. Elected officials need skill in persuading citizens that they deserve their votes, and tend to enjoy talking about their goals for the community.

A survey of the work styles of elected and appointed officials would probably show that managers have a tendency to be introverted and highly analytical, while elected officials are more extroverted and oriented to people's feelings. Those differences can be valuable to the community, but they can also lead to misunderstandings and frustration.

If most of the council members would rather talk about issues or listen to ideas, they will be frustrated with the manager who gives them a mountain of reading. The manager, in turn, may feel frustrated that the council members are not "doing their homework." If you grasp the differences between styles of learning, you can achieve much more. Executive summaries will be more widely read than long papers. Informal discussions may be critical to some council members' understanding of important issues. Be sensitive to different people's styles of learning.

Some groups of elected officials may be willing to explore communication styles with facilitators, using assessment tools such as the Myers-

Briggs Type Indicator. (See Chapter 8 for a description of the Myers-Briggs Type Indicator.) Others may see it as a waste of time or a lower priority than other activities. Without proper attention to both potential and existing interpersonal conflicts, however, the broader needs of the community may become lost.

Plan against pitfalls

Your local officials can benefit from training activities if they recognize they have communication difficulties and want to deal with them. The following are some examples of typical energy drainers that can impair the effectiveness of a governing body.

Council meetings that should never take more than two hours always take more than four. One or two elected officials habitually disagree with others on matters the staff presumed to be noncontroversial. Stories of disagreements among elected officials and staff members fill the newspapers.

One faction of the board of supervisors assumes that the staff members favor another faction.

Staff members contradict the manager at public meetings.

At public meetings, elected officials frequently ask whether the manager has filled a particular pothole.

The administrator waits until an elected official has gone out on a limb before giving the facts that make the point absurd.

Once these conflicts have been acknowledged, they can be tackled in a variety of ways. Among the most effective approaches are goal-setting retreats, team-building sessions, orientation sessions (discussed earlier in this chapter), and other special group activities.

The usefulness of retreats

Weekly meetings of the city council or board of supervisors are generally taken up with immediate decisions and routine business. To deal with long-range issues, many local officials leave the county or city offices to go on a retreat.

Retreats last one or two days and are generally held in relaxed settings. They might be held in the lodge in a state park, a ski lodge during the off season, or any comfortable hotel meeting room. It is important that retreats be held away from telephones, offices, and other reminders of day-to-day work.

All elected officials should be present, along with the city or county manager, and any staff members needed for the discussions. An outside facilitator can be hired to lead the discussion, giving all others freedom to participate. Hiring the right facilitator is one of the most difficult aspects of setting up a retreat. He or she should be someone who has had experience in leading organizations in goal-setting discussions. One of the best ways to find a good facilitator is to talk with officials of other communities that have held successful retreats or with executives from private firms in your community that may have conducted similar sessions. Thoroughly interview anyone being considered as facilitator to make sure that his or her approach will be acceptable to your organization.

Before the retreat begins, all participants should have a clear idea of the agenda. Because each participant brings a set of concerns to such a session, it is wise to interview all participants ahead of time so that as many of those concerns as possible can be dealt with. Participants can also be asked to fill out questionnaires to help set priorities among the issues to be discussed. Results of the questionnaires and interviews can provide the basis for the agenda, which can be narrowed further when the retreat begins.

Staff members can prepare any necessary background information or issue papers needed for the discussion. One way to organize written information for retreats is in the form of an outline. In a single page, describe the issue, list any technical barriers (such as outdated equipment or lack of staff), and outline any opportunities (such as a new source of funds or "executive loans" from interested private businesses). The concerns of management and questions of policy should also be noted.

You should invite representatives of the news media to attend the retreat. Although reporters may be skeptical about the worth of such an event, they generally become more enthusiastic after they observe the work that takes place. In planning a retreat, be sure to keep costs to a minimum. If the bill for lodging and food is unusually high, you can expect critical stories in the press.

If you are involved in planning a retreat, hold it away from the office and at a time and place planned so that all council members can attend. Survey the council members ahead of time. Work with an outside facilitator in running the meeting if possible. Encourage the news media to send representatives to the retreat. Follow up with a written report of council decisions and actions planned.

Team building

One of the most difficult jobs for elected officials is to learn to work together as a team. In the process of getting elected, few candidates consider the importance of working well as part of a group on the city council or board of supervisors. They are elected because of their powerful individual personalities. Once on a council or board, however, they may become aware that they lack other skills they need to be effective in the new daily environment.

Some local governments have used team building as a long-term approach to improving the policymaking skills of the elected body. Team building is much like organization development, designed to help a group help itself. An important element of team building is discovering the perceptions that elected officials have of their community's policymaking process. The individuals involved then design their own solutions, put them to work, and periodically evaluate their progress.

Outside consultants may assist in team building by gathering data and sharing them with elected officials and selected staff members. Consultants can also conduct workshops and identify resources that elected officials can use in making improvements.

The city or county manager can share significantly in the team-building process.

The city or county manager can share significantly in the team-building process. Managers can help identify problems and help make the changes in the local government administration that elected officials say are needed. Managers can also help gather support for a training program as they counsel individually with elected officials about conflicts. Once a training program has started, managers and staff can reinforce the process with meetings, reports, and updates on results.

Though more and more elected officials recognize the need for better training in group processes, there are clearly some risks involved. Some elected officials resist the idea. Others report only temporary improvements in relations and fall back into bad habits. Administrators who have worked with a number of different councils say that the success of team-building exercises depends largely on the particular group of individuals involved. Some councils are so tense that administrators introduce only so-called "safe" subjects, such as capital improvement projects. With that type of council, administrators take fewer risks and avoid most team-building exercises. The one constant in local politics, however, is change; sometimes the arrival of one or two new personalities is enough to change a council's attitude toward training.

City and county officials who want to improve their effectiveness as a team need to understand the processes that they use in making policy. You can help them by introducing the idea of team building to them, suggesting consultants that they might want to use, collecting data, and drawing attention to the progress they are making.

Special group activities

Elected and appointed officials have many occasions to work together as a group outside the weekly council or board meetings. The occasion may be a one-day working meeting on the budget, the manager's evaluation, an emergency meeting to deal with the implications of new federal or state legislation, or a briefing on labor relations.

These meetings are good times to reemphasize improved communications. For example, the manager's evaluation requires the manager to listen carefully to learn what he or she needs to do to meet the council's expectations. A good discussion can help clarify the elected body's goals and clear up misunderstandings about the respective functions of the manager and the elected body.

The manager should be sure that the agenda for any special meeting is well understood before any discussion begins. It should be clear what is expected of elected officials, and how the follow-up will be handled. Once the discussion begins, the manager can help by periodically bringing up key issues so as not to lose sight of the questions that need to be resolved. Managers can encourage the elected officials to be as specific as possible in describing their objectives and the actions they think are needed to meet them. Once the meeting is over, you should write a summary and distribute it to all the participants.

Taking an activist approach to communications

Communicating with elected officials involves style as well as substance. It makes a difference how we present information to busy people in an era of too much information. It needs to be visually interesting, well organized, and timely. You can use fax machines to get information to elected officials more quickly, but the information may be confusing or useless without being put into context.

Perhaps more than anything else, managers need to hone their listening skills. What are the concerns of the neighborhood groups? Make sure their voices will be heard among the special-interest groups that frequent council meetings. Successful managers are devoting more of their time to that kind of external communications activity, while still fostering good communication with each member of the elected body. Managers must also pay attention to the voice of the mayor or the chairperson of the board of supervisors, recognizing the growing importance of the community's key political leader.

The manager has a responsibility to help the elected officials sort through the competing priorities and focus on long-range issues. When the elected officials make a decision that seems short-sighted, you will need to remember that citizens sometimes expect a "purely political" decision.

Good communication with elected officials involves much more than clear presentations, a good orientation program, and easy-to-read progress reports. Sometimes it takes flexibility, a perspective on the other person's job, tolerance of ambiguity, and a good sense of humor. Most of all, it requires a passion for public service that shows respect for the men and women who have been elected to make the difficult political decisions today's citizens demand.

Checklist

Recognize that the manager often walks a tightrope, balancing the needs of elected officials, citizens, and employees.

Encourage citizens to get involved in setting goals for the community. Be sure to follow through.

Pay attention to what is communicated to elected officials. Keep employees well informed of important issues.

Write concisely and summarize the main points in agenda communications. Identify your recommendation clearly.

Give prompt attention to citizens' complaints. If a complaint comes through an elected official, let that official know when the problem has been resolved.

Keep informal meetings with council members open to the news media. Invite representatives of the media to retreats.

Use the budget as a way of expressing long-range goals. Provide continuous financial information to the council throughout the year, and use good graphics to underscore key points.

Give credit to elected officials when a program is launched or a project has been successful.

Encourage retreats, team training, orientation programs, and evaluations of the local government manager, to improve communication with (and among) elected officials.

Listen to your elected officials.

5 Employees: The Local Government Team

Whether they are motivated by the search for excellence, a commitment to "total quality," a desire to "reinvent" government, or the simple need to answer the wake-up call of fiscal austerity and accountability, a growing number of local government managers are gaining a fresh appreciation of the crucial role that front-line employees play in achieving the increasingly daunting objectives mandated by local citizens and their elected representatives. Indeed, many local government administrators now consider their employees the single most important audience for their communication efforts—even ahead of legislators and the news media.

Effective communication with your front-line team doesn't happen all by itself. In many instances it takes the form of a planned process requiring the concerted effort of a number of people in various managerial positions. But concurrent with this process, or even in its absence, effective communication ultimately must start with *you,* regardless of your job title or the organizational level at which you manage.

You can begin your efforts to enhance communication at the most basic level— by taking steps to make yourself a more effective speaker, listener, reader, and writer. Among the ways you can enrich your dialogue with your staff, and in turn provide them with the best possible tools to work as an effective team, are video materials; electronic mail; timely and low-cost computer-generated publications; and formal and informal surveys ranging from scientific polls to conversational inquiries.

The following pages offer practical tips on effective (and cost-effective) ways to share information upward, downward, and laterally with the people who are entrusted with serving the public in your community. The subjects covered are

Making your staff the "first team"

Some managers aren't listening

Orientation for new employees

Local government is different

Sharpening your communication skills

Studying your audience

Preparing a communication plan

Choosing the right channels

Communicating in tough times

Communicating quality

Staffing the internal communication function

Making your staff the "first team"

As a manager in city or county government, you're usually battling for the approval of one group or another: neighborhood associations, the municipal council, the news media, the business community. Although you have a long list of target audiences, you may feel that *you're* the one in the gun sights!

But before you resign yourself to seeing your furrowed face on the six o'clock news with picket signs in the background, remember that you've got an army of talented people on your side who can help you sparkle in front of all those groups. That "army" is made up of your *employees,* perhaps the most misunderstood, underutilized, and under-appreciated "public" you deal with.

Too many managers never get acquainted with their employees. They're too busy dealing with other executives, poring over paperwork, or putting out fires to realize what a potent asset their staff members can be. But it's well worth reminding yourself that it's your employees, not you, who actually deliver the services on which *your* performance is judged.

Jerry Dalton, former national president of the Public Relations Society of America, says that for too long, employee communications has been viewed as the least important, least glamorous of all the functions of public relations. But, he observes, the truth is that a "case can be proved—almost without exception—that the internal audience is our *most* important public. More so, in many instances, than taxpayers, legislators, customers, neighbors, contributors, suppliers, investors, or even news media."[1]

Over the years, administrators have come up with a litany of questions to ask themselves for reassurance whenever they feel the need to rationalize their us-versus-them mentality toward employees: Can we really trust them with vital information about the organization?—Wouldn't some of them run straight to the news media with some half-baked version of the truth?—They're never going to understand the reasons behind management decisions anyway, right?—If information is power, why give it away?—And who has the time?[2]

Recognizing these questions for what they are—nothing more than rationalizations for an increasingly ineffective status quo—communications specialist Alvie L. Smith says a new bible is being written on management/employee relations, one that articulates the need for managers to respect employees' opinions and ideas and commit themselves to a partnership that fosters sharing and trust. One means of reaching these goals is the *employee communication program,* a structured effort to facilitate the movement of information through the organization upward, downward, and laterally. Smith cites the contributions that a disciplined employee communication program can make:

> *A new bible is being written that articulates the need for managers to respect employees' opinions and ideas.*

Create a climate for open dialogue that stimulates new and different ideas and encourages candid criticism without fear of retribution

Inform employees about the enterprise so that they might better understand its mission and its leaders

Motivate employees to come to work every day, to provide high-quality service, and to give top performance on the job

Make it easier for people to accept unpopular decisions, because the reasons have been given to them

Instill feelings of pride, confidence, and commitment in employees because they are trusted with key information and authorized to make decisions affecting their jobs

Engage the brainpower of all employees by listening to their ideas and encouraging them to reach out more and more.[3]

That last point about brainpower is especially worth remembering. Generally well-educated and eager to contribute, your employees *want* to help meet the challenges facing your organization. Your job is to harness and focus their enthusiasm while providing a clear, honest voice, an ear that is willing to listen, and a mind that is willing to learn.

Informed employees are capable of better performance because they understand how their efforts contribute to the overall success or failure of the organization. The manager who fosters such an awareness can expect the results to include greater job satisfaction, less absenteeism, better quality, and higher productivity. Putting forth sincere efforts to nurture communication with staff members is particularly important for the manager whose opportunities to provide incentives in the form of increased compensation are limited.

Some managers aren't listening

In "Employee Communication in the '90s," Julie Foehrenbach and Steve Goldfarb describe a "trust gap" between employees and senior management. Their research into nearly 300 organizations showed that no more than 45 percent of employees think management is aware of the problems they face in their jobs. Although top executives are the preferred source of information for 62 percent of employees, *only 15 percent* report receiving information from their organizations' leaders. (See Table 5-1, "Current vs. Preferred Sources of Information.")

It seems that although front-line supervisors continue to be employees' overwhelming preference for their primary source of work-related information, those supervisors are being given low grades by the people who work for them. Research turned up this scenario: "In survey after survey we conduct, employees say loudly and strongly that they want to contribute. They want to be involved in the company, they need to feel their work is important. They believe they have viable ideas for improving productivity, for increasing quality, for streamlining operations. But they remain frustrated in their attempts. Management isn't listening."[4]

Table 5–1 Current vs. preferred sources of information.

	Current source	Preferred source
Top executives	15%	62%
Small group meetings	37	70
Immediate supervisor	59	90
Orientation program	22	45
Local employee publication	18	41
Large group meetings	28	49
Annual business report to employees	17	37
Audiovisuals	13	29
Upward communication programs	14	29
Employee handbook	33	46
Company-wide employee publication	29	36
Bulletin boards	38	38
Mass media	15	12
The grapevine	42	9

Source: *Communication World,* May-June 1990, pp. 101-6. Reprinted with permission from International Association of Business Communicators and from Towers Perrin, Management Consultants, New York.

It's hardly surprising that many employees know little about their own organization. Managers who have toiled in the local government for decades have amassed a wealth of practical knowledge that they sometimes assume everybody else has, too. Ever try to get clear, concise information about your own local government's policies on benefits, discipline, long-term disability, or pensions? How about accessible material on your goals and objectives, along with strategies to attain them?

Even if you could lay your hands on these policy materials, though, how relevant would they be? The Illinois Commission on the Future of Public Service asked government professionals to list the greatest barriers to recruiting and retaining top-notch professionals. Almost all of the respondents cited outmoded personnel rules, established decades ago, that weren't flexible enough to advance talented people, reward creativity, or increase efficiency.[5]

Ways to encourage teamwork

In the city of Commerce [California], employees are informed about and involved in the city's mission, projects, and programs in a variety of ways, including attending quarterly meetings hosted by the human resources department, receiving the monthly city and Chamber of Commerce newsletters in addition to the employee newsletter, receiving a copy of the city history book, being trained to use city video and editing equipment, and helping produce programs for the city cable channel. Informed and involved employees create a team spirit that translates into top-quality service to residents of Commerce and to the industrial community.

Source: Karen A. George, Scott Summerfield, and Sheri Erlewine, "Establishing a Public Information Program," *Western City,* September 1991, pp. 26-28, 55.

Similar problems pervade governments and private companies alike. Not long ago, Pratt and Whitney, a leading manufacturer of aircraft engines, realized that communications between management and the company's forty thousand employees had broken down. As part of a complete overhaul, a communication task force attacked *138 volumes* of outdated policies and procedures. Thirty-five percent were eliminated for redundancy or irrelevance, and the remaining volumes were rewritten in clearer language. The new, seven-part employee communications strategy began: "1. Employees are to be the company's most important audience." With this guiding philosophy, sales skyrocketed and employee morale improved measurably.[6]

Orientation for new employees

An effective orientation program can instill a sense of mission in workers from day one. Though many localities have invested in sound-on-tape slide presentations or videos in order to tell the story of their local government in a memorable fashion, the city of Hampton, Virginia, has gone further, by taking every new employee on a van tour of all major city facilities.

In larger jurisdictions, orientation is often the responsibility of the public information office. If your city or county does not have such an office, you can develop your own relatively inexpensive orientation program by writing a script and shooting some appropriate slides or video. (See Chapter 9 for guidance on script writing.) If there is a corporate headquarters, military installation, or other large employer in your area, its public information office likely can probably provide you with an example and some advice. If you would like to develop an orientation program or presentation but lack the time or doubt your ability to put one together, consider pitching the project to the nearest university as an internship for qualified students in mass communications, photography, journalism, public administration, or some other relevant major.

During the orientation, an up-to-date employee handbook should be distributed. Employees should sign for it to ensure that everyone gets a copy.

An engaging, informative orientation can provide the basis for a team-building communication program. In *Employee Communications in the Public Sector,* Geoffrey Perkins recommends dividing the information you intend to communicate into five categories—*progress, profitability, plans, policies,* and *people.*

Progress Information on improvements taking place can be used to measure not only individual advancement, but how effectively the organization is moving toward its goals. There is little point in setting a budgetary target, Perkins says, if the employees most responsible for meeting it are unaware of its existence. Even if they are aware of it, they must be given continuous feedback so that their performance can be charted, redirected if necessary, and improved.

Profitability How profitably, in terms of value returned, is your city or county spending the revenues it receives from your citizens? How much do your employees understand about the financial side of your organization? Public-sector employees should know more than other people about the general economic conditions of your community, including employment levels, production and sales, investments, and financial trends. In many instances, your people are already competing against other jurisdictions for the opportunity to provide local government services.

Plans If your employees hear about the plans of your organization through the grapevine, or read about them in the newspapers, you're likely to have

---

Narrowing the communication gap

If you'd like to narrow the communication gap in your own city or county, consider some of these communication policies suggested by the editors of *communication briefings.*

1. All managers and supervisors shall promote, by both attitudes and actions, an open communication climate both vertically and horizontally.

2. All managers and supervisors shall be readily available to employees.

3. Operational, communication, and action-plan goals shall be developed annually for individuals, the work unit, and the organization. These goals shall be shared with all appropriate parties. Goal achievement will be evaluated annually and the results publicized.

4. All employees shall develop joint annual goals with their immediate superior and have him or her approve their action plan.

5. All managers and supervisors shall have their communication attitudes and competencies evaluated annually as an integral part of their annual performance evaluation.

6. The ratings for achieving communication goals and for related competencies shall be directly tied to the employee's compensation for the upcoming year.

7. All managers and supervisors shall receive appropriate communication training related to their job goals and responsibilities.

8. One person shall plan, coordinate, and administer the organizationwide communication program and information dissemination.

9. No more than three levels shall exist in the organization's communication network.

10. An organization-wide crisis communication plan shall be developed and updated annually.

11. An organization-wide communication council shall be established. It should be composed of representatives of a cross section of the organization to provide input and feedback as well as to share ideas on how to improve communication. This council shall meet regularly in accordance with approved guidelines.

12. All employee ideas, suggestions, and complaints shall be acknowledged within three working days and followed up by the time stated in the acknowledgement message. No employee shall be penalized for sharing ideas, suggestions, or complaints.

13. All important information shall be distributed internally before being released to the news media.

14. The management information system shall be driven by the needs of the users. The system shall balance the need for ready access by users with the data-processing staff's need to protect confidential and proprietary information.

Source: *The Guide to Employee Communication* (Pitman, N.J.: Communication Publications and Resources, 1990), p. 3.

morale problems. Wise employers make sure that their managers and front-line employees are briefed, particularly on plans that affect them directly, such as reorganizations, closures, expansions, and relocations.

Policies Any change in your policies should be communicated quickly, especially if it affects employment conditions. It's not uncommon for the grapevine, or for union representatives, to convey information to employees about new policies and procedures even before your line managers know about them. Everyone deserves to hear it straight from the source, with an explanation of what the changes mean and how they will be implemented.

People If an organization can foster strong social ties among its people, it is likely to provide better service to its community. Employees need to see each other more frequently, share both professional and personal information and news, and develop a sense of camaraderie. Where your employees are situated on the organization chart should not present a barrier to a team-building type of social interaction.[7]

Local government is different

It's difficult to apply a textbook communication plan to cities and counties, because they're so different from private companies or even other governmental units. For one thing, cities and counties are conglomerates, offering a mixture of seemingly unrelated services, such as law enforcement, fire protection, libraries, mass transit, and education. Any communicator, no matter how skilled, may have trouble convincing such diverse departments that they have common interests, needs, and objectives.

Even the smallest incorporated localities encompass physically large areas. In many cases, employees at locations miles from city hall or the county seat rarely come into any contact with even their supervisors, let alone a city or county manager. Many local departments have twenty-four-hour work shifts, which make getting everyone together at the same time impossible. Cities and counties also employ part-time staff or unpaid volunteers, workers who present unique communication challenges to supervisors. Staffs are likely to represent a diversity of cultures, backgrounds, ages, and education levels.

Another major difference between the public and private sectors is that cities and counties carry out the *public's* business. This means they are nearly always being scrutinized by news reporters racing to beat a daily deadline. Getting basic information to your own employees before or at the same time it is reported in the media often becomes a contest. Nonetheless, your work as a manager—and as a principal communicator of your organization—must be done. Smith says that managers should communicate instinctually and from the soul, encouraging good ideas and radiating them in all directions in order to build understanding, resolve conflicts, and motivate positive actions. He has devised the following six commandments on communications with employees:

1. Employee communication is a fundamental component of the organizational management system.
2. A clear statement of commitment by top management, as well as its participation and support, is essential.
3. Communication must be a planned process—there must be a strategy—involving both professional communicators and key managers.
4. Managers are the key conduits and catalysts for effective communication.

5. The highest-priority business issues should be the core content of the employee communication program and should be discussed in an understandable and open manner through various channels of communication.

6. The communication system should undergo regular evaluation to prove its worth.[8]

Although there are differences between the public and private sectors, many principles of employee communication apply to both. Most of the items in the accompanying sidebar describing the employee communication policy of a fictional corporation are also relevant to local government organizations.

Sharpening your communication skills

Anyone who wants to communicate well must master a few basic skills first. Even if the next few paragraphs don't apply to you, other managers or supervisors in your organization may be able to benefit from them.

First, learn to *listen.* For most managers this is not an easy task. It takes discipline. Next time you're in a meeting, concentrate on your listening skills. Repeat the major points that are made by others and invite them to comment on your summary. Instructional audiotapes available at your local library or bookstore can help you become a better listener. Or you could take a class on developing listening skills. Identify role models in your organization and watch how they listen and learn

---

Employee communication policy, R. Ehrenberg, Inc.

PREFACE

To achieve its goals, R. Ehrenberg, Inc., depends on the skills and commitment of each employee. Knowledge, truth, understanding and positive motivation are critical for each to participate effectively in the company's future. Internal communication, effective at all levels and all forms, is necessary to achieve this participation.

POLICY

1. Internal communication in R. Ehrenberg, Inc., will be designed to
   a. Be carried out at the lowest level of authority practical.
   b. Provide open, accurate and timely communication in a climate of mutual respect.
   c. Exchange information about company goals, plans, policies and activities, including all lines of business.
   d. Share information about the progress of and challenges faced by our company.

   e. Advise employees of company decisions prior to informing the public, whenever possible and practical.

2. The management of R. Ehrenberg, Inc., at all levels will encourage two-way communication by
   a. Soliciting, promoting, and facilitating feedback from employees through formal and informal systems.
   b. Responding to feedback so that employees know that they have been heard.
   c. Listening with minds open to the best interests of the company and its employees.

3. Communication in R. Ehrenberg, Inc., will be practiced
   a. Honestly and with care and sensitivity
   b. Openly and in a timely fashion
   c. Consistently and with no bias for only the good news
   d. Ethically and in a way that does not jeopardize the legal, civil or moral rights of any employee or the company

RESPONSIBILITIES

1. Each R. Ehrenberg, Inc., management person is responsible for assuring conformance to this policy.

2. Each R. Ehrenberg, Inc., employee is responsible for promoting effective and responsible communication within the company and for doing his/her part to stay informed.

3. Company responsibility for this policy is with the Director of Public Affairs, who
   a. Participates in company planning and decision making to assure that internal communication is part of the process.
   b. Advises functional areas at all levels on how best to achieve effective communication.
   c. Participates in communication training programs as part of an ongoing commitment.

from those around them. At Federal Express, the express-mail service consistently identified as one of America's best employers, managers attend workshops where they learn not to talk, but to listen and to probe their employees for more input.[9] (See Chapter 8 for more information on listening skills.)

Second, develop your *writing* skills. Start by asking for a critique of your writing from someone generally acknowledged within your organization as a good writer. If your letters and memos don't ring with clarity, consider enrolling in a writing class at your local college or learning center. One of the many self-help books for writers available at your local library or bookstore might also be useful. One widely available text is *Write to the Point!*, by Rosemary T. Fruehling. (For a complete citation, see the list of suggested readings for this chapter at the end of the book.) It's a good idea to write the way you talk; most people speak in short, simple sentences. Read your next written report aloud to see whether it sounds like you. Ask your associates for continual feedback on your writing. It will also increase your power as a communicator. (See Chapter 10 for further guidance on writing.)

Third, sharpen your *speaking* skills. Have you ever listened to yourself speaking? Get someone to videotape your next public address and watch it later on a VCR. If you put yourself to sleep, it may be time to join a Toastmasters Club or invest in some professional help from speech experts. As with your writing, don't hesitate to ask for feedback from colleagues and friends. (For detailed guidance on speaking, see Chapter 9.)

Fourth, improve your skills in *reading*. Every good communicator needs to know what's going on, and a great deal of what we know comes from reading. You can improve your speed and comprehension by taking a refresher course at a community college or learning center, or by following the exercises in one of the many reading manuals you can find in bookstores or the public library. A classic of the genre is *The Evelyn Wood 7-Day Speed Reading and Learning Program*. (See the list of suggested readings for this chapter at the end of the book for complete citations.)

Fifth, if you're serious about becoming a better communicator, don't always play the role of the boss; reveal your human side. Admit your mistakes and add "I don't know" to your vocabulary. Maybe it's time you loosened your tie or scarf, rolled up your sleeves, and got to know your employees by their first names. Broaden your conversation so that you're not always talking about jobs and work assignments. Show your employees that they count as *individuals,* not just as members of a group. A thoughtful memo of commendation, a bedside visit to an employee with a prolonged illness, or a telephone call to express birthday greetings are small gestures that will have a big effect on loyalty and team spirit. And—always—remember your sense of humor.

Reveal your human side. Admit your mistakes and add "I don't know" to your vocabulary.

Studying your audience

Knowing your audience (in this case, your staff) is the heart of effective communication. You can begin the process by doing some on-the-job research. It can be done informally at little or no cost, or it can entail a complete communication audit performed by an outside consultant.

The least expensive—though least scientific—research method is simply to ask your employees informally how they feel about communication in the organization. As you walk around the department or office you manage, ask people how they get their information and how credible they consider that information—and its sources. What changes would they like to see made? It shouldn't take you long to get the pulse of your organization.

Some localities are increasingly using employee *focus groups* on a range of subjects such as safety, compensation, and customer services. Focus groups usually involve a cross section of eight to ten employees chosen at random who are invited to discuss their opinions on a particular topic. In a typical session, a focus group gathers around a table for an hour to ninety minutes, guided by a meeting facilitator who introduces the subject and directs the conversation. To stimulate a free-flowing discussion, it's a good idea to choose the facilitator from outside your department (or perhaps even outside your city or county government) and to conduct the session away from the workplace. Occasionally a focus group will go off on a tangent or become dominated by a bias that is not representative of the total group. That's why two focus-group sessions on the same topic are often scheduled sequentially, to improve the opportunities for meaningful discussion.

Your internal publications can be improved by *readership surveys*. You may find that your employees would rather read about a change in their health benefits than see yet another "manager of the month" feature story.

You may want to use a professional research firm to design a brief *telephone survey*. Done randomly, surveys by phone can give you a statistically sound analysis of employees' opinions. Because the people you reach through this method are probably not the ones you see on a daily basis, the results may surprise you. If you decide on having a *comprehensive audit* done, it should be performed by an independent consultant. The package should include a spectrum of approaches: one-to-one interviews with top executives, focus-group discussions, a written questionnaire administered in sit-down meetings, and a critical analysis of your communication program.[10]

If your budget precludes hiring a professional research firm, check with your local college or university—you might find a faculty member who could use your institution for a research project. The expertise you need may be available in any of several academic departments—business, communications, marketing, political science, or public administration, among others.

Another way of learning from your employees is to devise an *employee attitude survey*, making sure it includes a section dealing with communication. It is sometimes helpful to have a private research firm conduct the opinion survey, to limit bias in the questions and to insulate your employees from feeling obligated to tell management just what it wants to hear. And be sure to include a couple of open-ended questions so that employees can offer suggestions for improvements.

These surveys can reveal how informed your employees are on matters that are key to the success of their departments. Surveys can tell you where your employees get their information, which sources are considered most believable and which ones are ignored, and how well your supervisors rate as communicators. (See Figure 5–1 for a composite questionnaire based on several actual employee surveys.)

It is invaluable to have an active *upward* communication program. More than thirty years ago, IBM became a communications pioneer by starting its Speak Up program, a confidential way for employees to ask questions or comment on company policies, actions, and procedures. More than 300,000 inquiries later, IBM employees continue to enjoy a unique communication channel that has produced improvements in their work environment. Speak Up also gives the management some insight into employees' attitudes and concerns. Similar programs are now found in

It is sometimes helpful to have a private research firm conduct the opinion survey, to limit bias in the questions.

numerous organizations worldwide. (See Chapter 8 for more on upward communication.)

Starting—and supporting—an *employee suggestion program* is often productive. For many years, suggestion awards were widely used by the federal government to encourage employees to come forth with money-saving ideas. If your office or your local government is in a position to do so, consider applying this practice to employees whose ideas save your city or county money by giving them a percentage of the savings. Acknowledge all suggestions quickly, and don't penalize anyone for offering their opinions or complaints.

You can also learn a great deal by doing *exit interviews* with employees who are retiring or moving into another job. It is a time when some

Figure 5–1   A composite employee communication survey.

How good a job does Anytown do in keeping employees informed about what is happening in the Anytown government? *Circle one.*
Very good   Good   Fair   Poor

From which of the sources listed below do you obtain your most useful information about Anytown and its activities?
Check as many as apply.

☐ City/county management ☐ Employee newsletter ☐ Radio
☐ My supervisor ☐ Departmental memos ☐ Newspapers
☐ Other employees ☐ Television ☐ Bulletin boards

Can you suggest ways that Anytown could do a better job of keeping employees informed? _____
_____
_____

How *visible,* do you think, is Anytown top management (department heads and above) with. . . *Circle one number for each item.*

	Very	Somewhat	Not very	Not at all
Me	1	2	3	4
My fellow employees	1	2	3	4
Middle management	1	2	3	4
Customers	1	2	3	4
The news media	1	2	3	4

How *credible,* do you think, is Anytown top management with. . . *Circle one number for each item.*

	Very	Somewhat	Not very	Not at all
Me	1	2	3	4
My fellow employees	1	2	3	4
Middle management	1	2	3	4
Customers	1	2	3	4
The news media	1	2	3	4

How informed does Anytown keep its employees? *Check one.*

☐ Completely informed ☐ Gives us only a limited amount of information
☐ Fairly well informed ☐ Doesn't tell us much at all about what's going on

When Anytown gives out information to employees, how do you feel about it? *Check one.*

☐ I can always believe it ☐ I can believe it about half the time
☐ I can usually believe it ☐ I can seldom believe it ☐ I can never believe it

people will share criticism or ideas they might previously have felt uncomfortable about expressing.

The fact is that news will travel through your organization whether you've officially communicated anything or not. The grapevine is marvelously efficient at distributing information rapidly—and usually with a twist—throughout the rank and file. Smart managers will realize that the grapevine is an invaluable source of feedback on almost any management action. Fort Collins, Colorado, for example, has established a rumor-control hot line that gives employees an opportunity to share, by phone or electronic mail, the latest topics of hallway conversation. All rumors are either verified or debunked by management and are published electronically.

From which of these sources do you prefer to get your information? *Check as many as apply.*

- ☐ City/county management
- ☐ My supervisor
- ☐ Other employees
- ☐ Employee newsletter
- ☐ Departmental memos
- ☐ Television
- ☐ Radio
- ☐ Newspapers
- ☐ Bulletin boards

When you talk about Anytown with friends and neighbors, what are the three most-talked-about subjects?

(1) _____

(2) _____

(3) _____

How important is it for you to get information on the following subjects? *Circle one number for each item*

	Very important	Somewhat important	Not very important
Pay policies and procedures	1	2	3
Anytown's plans for the future	1	2	3
Employee benefit programs	1	2	3
Training courses available	1	2	3
News about activity within Anytown	1	2	3
What employees can do to improve their work performance	1	2	3
Reasons behind important decisions within Anytown	1	2	3
News about activities in other departments	1	2	3
How your work fits into the total picture	1	2	3
News about promotions, transfers, and retirements	1	2	3
News about changes in management	1	2	3
Work rules and how they are applied	1	2	3

Other (please specify):_____

Please use the space below for any additional comments you may wish to make on any topic, regardless of whether it was covered in the questionnaire. For example, you may wish to discuss the city/county's major strengths or major problems, or make suggestions for improvement. Your comments will be typed, edited to protect your confidentiality, and presented to top management.

_____

_____

_____

Suggestions and awards

A well-administered city- or countywide employee suggestion and awards system provides departmental managers with a supplementary means of encouraging employee initiative. Such a system calls for

1. Clearly defined procedures
2. Prompt review of and reporting on all proposals
3. A process that is viewed to be both competent and without favoritism as, for example, use of an independent review panel composed of business and academic persons
4. Financial awards ranging from a substantial percentage of small savings to a small percentage of higher savings
5. In-house and public recognition of significant achievers.

The capstone to such a system is a public recognition ceremony, in which you and your chief elected official have prominent roles.

Source: Adapted from Coalition to Improve Management in State and Local Government, *Cities and Counties: Implementing an Executive Management Improvement Program*, Management Guide 5 (Pittsburgh, Pa: n.d.), p. 36.

Preparing a communication plan

Your research should help you put together a communication plan tailored to meet the overall goals of your department. A plan that gives specific assignments to each manager and pushes many of the key responsibilities down to the line supervisors is good because employees prefer to get their information firsthand from their supervisors. Develop a system that gets vital information to supervisors *quickly* so that it can be disseminated accurately and with confidence to the entire work force.

Your communication plan should stress honesty and integrity above all. It should protect the interests of individual employees. And it should accommodate the dissemination of both good and bad news, essential to your credibility during tough times. In *Communications in Practice,* the Institute of Personnel Management lists five benefits that result from instituting an employee communications policy:

A more aware and efficient work force

Fewer misunderstandings among all levels of employees

Less alienation of employees

Increasing interest in the organization's aims and objectives and in meeting them

Increasing identification with the organization.[11]

Employees prefer to get their information firsthand from their supervisors.

The flow of communication needs to go two ways. Employees have a right to hear basic information from their managers and also should have the opportunity to express their ideas and opinions regularly. A well-organized communication plan opens the channels—not just for words and data, but for respectability and empowerment of front-line employees. In their *Guide to Employee Communication,* the editors of *communication briefings* emphasize agreed-upon job responsibilities, goals, and priorities in the workplace as being essential to mutual understanding. If you want to increase productivity and promote high morale and job satisfaction, they say, you must grant employees these seven basic entitlements:

1. An up-to-date, comprehensive, relevant job description for each position that the employee had a voice in developing
2. Clear, understandable, worthwhile, challenging, but attainable goals adopted jointly with the supervisor
3. Clearly defined priorities for each goal
4. Specific target dates, along with an approved plan for attaining each goal
5. The necessary authority and freedom to do the job
6. Sufficient time, resources, training, and assistance to do a good job
7. Standards that allow the effectiveness of performance to be measured fairly and objectively.[12]

Chances are, your organization needs to improve the flow of information—upward, downward, laterally, and diagonally. Executives, middle managers, and front-line supervisors should develop communication plans within their own departments and share them widely. Results should be evaluated and publicized. If possible, the ratings should go into managers' annual performance evaluations and compensation plans.

Choosing the right channels

Creative managers have devised myriad channels to carry messages to and from employees. In the following paragraphs, several are described that have been used in cities and counties across North America.

One to one

The most fundamental form of communication takes place when the sender and the receiver share information face to face. So your first assignment is to get your face out of the office! See how many other faces you can look into. Set up a regular circulation schedule and mark it on your calendar. Visit staff lounges and lunchrooms. Vary your walking patterns so you'll run into different people every day.

When you visit the field, don't breeze through as if you were on a presidential tour. Take time to listen and share a little personal warmth.

Figure 5–2 It is important to visit and listen to employees in the field. Here, the city manager (right) and assistant city manager for operations (center) of Raleigh, North Carolina, visit Raleigh's yard waste center.

Teach this routine to your other managers. Peter Dallow, director of administrative services for Fort Collins, has invented a "Me and My Shadow" program that takes him into the field with a different employee every month. It's been an eye-opener and a money saver, he reports.

Group meetings

Group meetings can involve a handful of people or everyone in the organization. Either way, a few ground rules and preparatory steps will make your meeting more successful:

Settle on your messages and objectives in advance. Prepare and distribute an agenda so your employees will know the purpose of the meeting.

Send out question cards before the meeting so attendees can submit comments or inquiries anonymously if they choose. This approach also gives your management people time to prepare responses.

Include speakers from several levels of your organization for two reasons. First, employees identify with peers; second, it will keep the same faces from appearing before every meeting.

Use visual aids to make comparisons, simplify new concepts, and explain relationships. Make use of blackboards and easels. If you use projection equipment, make sure you've pretested the sound system and lighting in the room, focused the slides, and kept the extension cords out of the way. Bring a spare bulb. Keep text on your slides and overheads to a minimum. Build your oral presentation on bulleted lists. Too many presentations are ruined when entire sentences are printed in illegible microtype.

After the meeting is over, distribute evaluation forms to help you determine whether you covered the right topics in the right way. Compile the results and send them back to the participants.

Formats for meetings can vary greatly. Some cities report success with breakfast roundtables of a panel of managers rotating from department to department. Others have scheduled peer-group meetings without managers. Some conduct "diagonal-slice" meetings of groups of employees mixed by rank and department. In situations where innovative thinking may be transferable, department-level meetings can benefit by inviting guest speakers from other city or county departments. When you have monumental news—good or bad—a mass meeting with *everyone* may be appropriate, although the logistical aspects may be difficult because of varying work shifts and field locations. Central service departments, such as finance or personnel, can benefit from open houses that allow them to can explain the workings of their departments in an informal atmosphere.

Printed publications

Most local governments rely heavily on printed publications to get the word out to their employees on a variety of topics. Your staff is undoubtedly inundated with fliers, posters, newsletters, and pamphlets. But how many of those publications get read, understood, and remembered? And how good a job are you doing in coordinating all this literature?

Researchers at the University of Wisconsin-Green Bay found that the typical newsletter is published monthly, with an average circulation of 3,000 copies, at a cost of 40 cents each.[13] Virginia Beach, Virginia, trimmed the cost of producing its employee newsletter, the *Beam,* by accepting paid advertising from local merchants.

Many organizations continue to struggle with the content of their newsletters. Studies show employees would rather read about changes in corporate policy than see scores from the bowling league. In other words, information that affects their jobs is more important than such personal tidbits as who has the most unused sick leave.

Publishing both organization-wide and departmental newsletters is justifiable, but make sure to integrate your local government's strategic goals into all news sheets. Some organizations set aside a page or two in their site publications for news affecting all employees.

Here are some tips to editors who seek a responsive employee readership:

Give priority to news about the organization. This includes changes in services, budgets, job assignments, or employee benefits.

Strike an editorial balance. Don't let your newsletter become a management mouthpiece, presenting only one side of the issues. Nor should your newsletter become too chatty and omit management messages altogether. If you must run a column by a member of management, save it for truly important announcements.

Devote space to an idea exchange. Ask your employees to suggest improvements. Let them speak about the major problems facing their sections and ways they're solving them.

Keep it fresh. Consider such features as rumors run side by side with the facts, comments from recipients of your services, or insights from employees into what creates a sense of pride in the performance of their jobs.

Employees don't read all the "clutter" they get with their pay envelopes.

Every payday, employees are likely to be bombarded with a flurry of fliers urging them to attend a workshop, donate blood, ride the bus, or recycle their aluminum cans. Employees don't read all the "clutter" they get with their pay envelopes. In fact, during tough economic times, many of them resent what they perceive as a waste of money on printing. Here's how one county manager dealt with a division head's request to send an "important" flier to every employee: "If it's *really* important," the manager said, "let's put it in the employee newsletter." (See Chapter 10 for more information on employee newsletters.)

A well-organized employee handbook is essential to effective communication. It should contain guidelines on salary and benefits, rights and responsibilities of employees, information on health and day care, and key administrative regulations. In some jurisdictions, the handbook is bound in a loose-leaf binder so that it can be updated easily. No matter what its format, though, your handbook should *communicate* in simple, nonbureaucratic language and serve the team-building objectives of your organization as effectively as possible. If, as is often the case, the production of your employee handbook is the responsibility of the personnel department, the time you spend helping personnel ensure that the employee handbook is forthright and informative will be time well spent.

Managers who regard the handbook as a formality, or who feel threatened by the prospect of employees acquiring a full understanding of personnel policies, can rest assured that staff will spend hours of work time trying to figure out just what city or county policy toward them entails.

Teletips

Employees in Hampton, Virginia (125,000), can call a 24-hour phone number to have basic employee benefit questions answered. *Teletips* allows employees to use a touch-tone phone to access prerecorded messages about benefits. The personnel department purchased the system because it felt that employees were not receiving accurate information from a centralized source. Although a benefits manual was available, employees were apprehensive about searching through it for answers. The director of human resources wrote easily understood scripts for each personnel policy. A professional narrator was paid $6 per script to record the tapes. Requests by type, total number of calls, and number of messages accessed can be tracked by the personnel department. The system has received as many as 135 calls in a month. Personnel department employees now spend less time answering routine questions, and the information being given is now consistent.

Source: *The Guide to Management Improvement Projects in Local Government*, vol. 14, no. 3 (Washington, D.C.: ICMA, 1990) PRM-15.

Another publication gaining popularity is the employee annual report. The best of these not only recognize the work of employees but also give them a greater awareness of where they fit into the organization's activities. These reports should include relevant financial information, presented without accounting jargon.

Other publications are tailored for managers or supervisors. Still other publications reach out to retirees, a growing and influential group that—if kept well informed—may help you win that next bond election or ballot proposition. Large organizations can economize by printing these types of publications on newsprint in tabloid format.

Video Communication by videotape is becoming an increasingly common practice in cities and counties large and small. Many of the larger jurisdictions are home to government-access cable television channels. That means they probably have an array of professional video equipment and people who know how to use it. Smaller towns and counties can make use of camcorders to carry messages in words and moving pictures whenever people are unable to congregate personally.

Video cameras can record departmental meetings to be replayed later for wider groups of employees. Training and development programs can now bring the wisdom of motivational speakers to many more of your staff (as long as you get written permission in advance from the speakers). Alex Briseño, the city manager of San Antonio, uses video to highlight the work of employees in a two-minute feature he shows every month at city council meetings. Nominated by their departments, the spotlighted employees attend the meeting, where they are saluted in person by the elected officials. Afterward, copies of the tape are played in the department so that colleagues can share in the recognition.

Video can be used to explain complex situations, such as a budget crisis, so that all employees, including those who have difficulty reading, can better understand the fiscal challenges facing the city or county. Tapes should be distributed throughout the organization, but only after you have taken an inventory of your VCRs and monitors and established a network of communication personnel or training officers to show the tapes in the field. If employees do not consider it an infringement on their break periods, television monitors may also be placed in lunch-rooms or lounges.

As part of their franchise agreements, many cities and counties require cable companies to wire their facilities for closed-circuit television. Other methods of projecting images involve microwave or fiber-optics systems that transmit video messages to remote work sites. Some cities now use two-way interactive teleconferencing to provide employee training and to set up a video dialogue between managers and field employees.

City connection

The institutional network (I-Net) in Newport News, Virginia (154,560), is a 57-mile system of cable that connects city hall with other public facilities throughout the city. The two-way interactive system is a sophisticated method for providing training and education; conducting business between opposite ends of the city; and transferring data to various offices including fire stations, school, and libraries.

Source: *ICMA Newsletter,* May 20, 1991, p. 8.

In the private sector, some major companies with their own production facilities put together regular video newsmagazine programs for their employees. Every morning, for example, employees at twelve hundred Federal Express work sites watch a video newscast with highlights of the previous day's performance and tips on improving service. If your organization has no video equipment, there may be someone on staff with a camcorder and a desire to demonstrate his or her directorial talents. One caution: the quality of your videos may not receive rave reviews. Like most Americans, your employees are used to seeing high-quality television productions at home, so be prepared for your productions to suffer a bit by comparison. (For more information on video production, see Chapter 11.)

Bulletin boards

Surprisingly, as was shown in Table 5-1, employee surveys rank bulletin boards as one of the top sources of information in the workplace. But unless someone is assigned to keep bulletin boards tidy and current, your notices won't be read. Organize the board space into categories so that people know where to look for particular kinds of messages. Use headlines and eye-catching colors. And be sure to include an expiration date on all notices. Most important, put your bulletin boards in well-traveled corridors so they can't be missed.

If your employees receive thank-you notes from satisfied customers, show them off on the bulletin boards. This not only helps build pride among employees but builds respect for your office from visitors who read your rave reviews.

Some cities and counties turned their employee bulletin boards into "information centers" with pockets for leaflets or newsletters.

Electronic mail

Electronic mail, popularly known as *e-mail,* allows a computer user to send a message to other employees' "mailboxes" instantly. Not only is e-mail quick and relatively inexpensive, it vastly reduces time lost playing "telephone tag" by allowing recipients to read messages at their convenience. The effectiveness of e-mail, though, depends largely on the number of users who have access to the system.

Some organizations use e-mail to disseminate daily news summaries of interest to employees. Pratt and Whitney issues a daily on-line news summary programmed into the company's ten thousand computer terminals. E-mail users can become part of an even wider communication network, copying messages onto preprinted news sheets that can be distributed to employees who are not connected to the computer system.[14]

Administrators of one Fortune 500 company reported that 60 percent of the messages they received via e-mail would not have been sent over other channels, illustrating how electronic messaging is opening a new channel for increased employee communication.[15]

Telephone systems

Telephone hot lines are commonly used to provide both recorded and "live" messages on special programs, emergencies, and other matters of interest. *Voice mail* goes a step further by giving callers an opportunity to leave a confidential message at any time or send voice messages to larger work-force audiences. One city auditor has given all thirty-one of his employees access to a voice-mail system. Every Monday morning they hear his weekly announcements, and they're also encouraged to record their own concerns and comments.

In the private sector, the Travelers Insurance Company reported a 30-percent increase in staff productivity after voice mail was installed. Its study showed that 60 percent of the phone calls placed before voice mail required no response and that 70 percent of those calls never reached the intended person anyway.[16]

Another way to speed your messages to employees is through *electronic sign boards*. Generally located in high-traffic areas such as shop floors or cafeterias, sign boards can provide a continuous flow of breaking news or information about your local government.

Communicating in tough times

Every city and county has critical moments, when a trusted communication link to your employees becomes indispensable. It is in times of crisis that good managers—who have been forthright with their employees through good times and bad—will find themselves surrounded by allies. Candor is powerful. If employees feel that management has leveled with them on the shape of the budget and has sincerely sought their participation in the search for solutions, they will be far more willing to accept reductions in force and the loss of promotions, pay increases, and training opportunities.

Shortly after slicing 450 positions out of its fiscal 1991-93 budgets, Phoenix conducted an opinion survey in which it was found that 97 percent of the employees still considered the city a good place to work. One of the communication tools used during the budget crisis was a video that included interviews with employees whose positions had been eliminated. They spoke of the retraining they were getting in order to assume vacant positions in other departments, and of the warm receptions they had received from their new colleagues. Circulated to all employees, the video showed in a convincing and personal way how much the city cared about the welfare of its workers.

One of the ways Phoenix has raised employees' morale is by pitting some of its own work crews against private companies, in a sealed-bidding process, for the opportunity to perform government services. After some initial losses, the city crews won back a good share of the contracts, with two positive side effects—the competition drove costs down and job satisfaction up.

Likewise, San Diego improved service to customers by instituting a service enhancement program and asking employees to act as if they were competing against an imaginary "City Hall A." The city used the slogan: "If our customers had a choice, they'd choose us." The program was credited with prompting more than 350 procedural changes and realizing $2 million in savings.

In some organizations, representatives of labor unions and management are extending the lines of communication so that when trouble arrives, the two sides won't automatically revert to their traditional roles as combatants. Regular meetings during non-negotiating periods can help build rapport. Some public agencies are sharing bulletin boards and offering space for union news in the house organ.[17]

You're likely to have employee-performance problems at any time, and a policy of open communication can help solve them. It's normal to shy away from confronting difficult employees, but the experience doesn't have to be negative or punitive. Evelyn Massengill, a program manager at the Department of Social Services in Raleigh, North Carolina, asks herself, "Am I doing anything to contribute to the problem? If I am, how can I avoid it?" Dennis Sheehy, Montana's deputy state auditor, says simply listening to employees helps. "You need to communicate with these people," Sheehy says. "Part of the problem may be that they just want someone to hear them out. You might discover that their work isn't challenging them enough, or that personal problems are spilling over into the job. Whatever's happening, by just letting it go, you end up with a more difficult situation than you do by confronting it."[18] Bankers Insurance Group in St. Petersburg, Florida, has systematized the process by holding regular one-to-one meetings every month between supervisors and employees. The purpose is to improve overall communication and provide mutual feedback to sharpen performance.[19]

Communicating quality

Good staff-management communication lies at the core of the Total Quality Management (TQM) movement, which began taking root in many cities and counties in the late 1980s and early 1990s. Cooperation is the key to quality management, says Jonathan Walters in *Governing* magazine. He cites the Milwaukee County (Wisconsin) vehicle maintenance shop, where TQM's emphasis on training, consultation, and "coaching" rather than "bossing" saved hundreds of thousands of dollars and kept the shop from being privatized, outcomes that helped convince the local union council and management that working together could be a win-win proposition. When asked why changes had not been implemented years earlier, shop steward Bill Hicks replied: "We had no one to talk to before." Walters reported that the people-oriented, consultative approach embodied in TQM had been implemented in "jurisdictions as disparate as New York City; Fort Collins, Colorado; Dallas and Austin, Texas; Palm Beach County, Florida; and the states of Arkansas and North Dakota."[20]

Staffing the internal communication function

How you organize your internal communication function depends largely on the type of city or county you serve. Most large local governments employ public-information officers who are communication professionals with strong writing and media-relations skills. Smaller jurisdictions may wish to place this function in the human-resource department, an area traditionally responsible for handling salary, benefits, and labor/management issues affecting all staff members. But the job of employee communication is larger than any single function. It requires maximum cooperation among all departments—and a network of communicators strategically located throughout your organization.

The person(s) you choose to take on this responsibility should be intimately involved in the key issues facing your organization. "They should be asking not what to communicate, but 'What are the organization's issues? How can I help it address them?'" advises Dean Landeche, manager of internal communication for PMI Food Equipment Group. Landeche believes communicators should stop communicating and instead offer counsel on communication. "If I'm doing the communicating, then I'm alleviating someone of their responsibility. That's not the way to get work done."[21] (See Chapter 7 for more information on staffing of the communication function.)

Conclusion

In governments throughout the world, the value of communication as a means of fostering teamwork is gaining increased recognition. By unleashing the flow of information throughout your area of managerial responsibility, you'll be giving every member of your staff a heightened sense of purpose and a broader understanding of his or her value to your organization.

Checklist

Always remember that as a communicator, you have no more important audience than your own employees.

Front-line managers are employees' overwhelming preference as the primary source of work-related information, so don't let the news media become your staff's first source of information about important developments in your organization. Widen employees' participation in the decision-making process so that they won't be caught off guard by newspaper or television reports.

An effective orientation program can instill a sense of mission in employees from day one.

The careful manager plans for effective communication with employees while recognizing that no two communication plans can be alike, any more than two local governments can be.

Improve your own communication skills and thereby set an example for others on your staff. Remember that listening can be just as important as speaking.

Surveys—both formal and informal—can help you learn what's on the minds of your staff, and make devising a communication plan easier.

A good communication plan will help you empower your front-line employees.

Don't let the way your organization is structured impede the flow of information that your employees need in order to work effectively.

Candor is a powerful tool for communicating in tough times.

Good communication between management and staff is the key to quality management.

How you organize the communication function depends largely on what type of local government you serve.

Use every device at your disposal—electronic and print technology as well as personal contacts—to keep people informed.

If your employees know how their work fits into the overall goals of the city or county, you'll find their enthusiasm and their productivity on the rise.

Keep in mind that the best ideas are likely to come from the people who actually do the job, not from the person who oversees the operation.

6 Working with the News Media

The three preceding chapters of this book cover communication with three groups: *local citizens, elected officials,* and *local government employees.* A fourth group must also be included in any discussion of local government and communication: the *news media.*

To be or not to be involved with the news media is not a choice that is open to local government officials. The role the media play in the democratic process necessitates a relationship between media representatives and representatives of local government. The quality of the relationship is often determined by the level of local government officials' respect for the role of the media in a democracy and their willingness to be active partners in the relationship.

The relationship between local government and the media is not one-dimensional, with both parties playing well-defined, unchanging roles. On the contrary, the relationship is complex and ever-changing. One day, the media are the aggressors, seeking information that government officials may not possess or may prefer not to release at that moment. Another day, the government approaches the media to air an issue of interest to the community.

As governments adopt marketing techniques of the private sector and seek to promote "products" such as fee-supported

and revenue-producing services and facilities, the relationship becomes more complex.

The most important goal of a media-relations program is to develop a two-way relationship between the government and the media in which government plays an active role instead of simply responding to inquiries. Taking an active stance is important if local government is to function effectively in encouraging communication and the sharing of information on all sides of important community issues.

An active stance is even more crucial to local government's efforts to disseminate factual, objective information about public services, special events, public hearings, voter registration, and the many other matters that governments would like citizens to be informed about.

As many local officials can painfully attest, it is all too easy to obtain media coverage of controversy. It is not so simple, however, to obtain column inches in the papers and air time on TV and radio when the offering is an item of less appeal, such as a successful recycling program that depends on continued public participation for its existence or the details of a hold-the-line budget.

The challenge becomes even stiffer when local government has to compete with other newsmakers in business, finance, and real

estate for the reporting of economic-development efforts, or when it has to work hard to attract the attention of sports reporters to cover fee-supported golf courses, or when it seeks coverage of performing-arts programs or other services that depend on ticket sales or memberships for success. Editors in those subject areas are wary of private sector efforts—and increasingly, of public sector efforts—to seek news and feature coverage for "non-news" items as substitutes for or supplements to paid advertising.

The purpose of this chapter is to help local officials in their efforts to develop and maintain an effective media-relations program. This chapter covers the following subjects:

Developing a media-relations program

Building a working relationship with media contacts

Basic tools in media relations

Meeting the media's varied needs

Keeping the news new

Effective news releases

News conferences and briefings

Photography

Legal issues in media relations.

Developing a media-relations program

The successful practice of media relations by local government is based on several basic principles:

Knowing the news media in general and the characteristics and needs of the local media in particular

Being willing and able to understand the journalist's viewpoint

Building credibility through honesty, consistency, and availability

Respecting the agenda of the media, even though it is often at variance with that of local government

Dedicating sufficient staff time to plan and implement campaigns, develop and distribute information, and make media contacts.

The planning and organization of a media-relations program should follow essentially the same process used in developing other local government programs. The first task is to set realistic goals and objectives, considering the particular needs of the local government and the community as a whole, and establishing priorities within the constraints of staff time and funds.

An important initial consideration, particularly for small local governments, is deciding who will be responsible for developing and implementing the media-relations program. The city or county manager must either assume that responsibility or—more likely—assign it to an assistant in the manager's office, the director of communications, or the public information officer, if there is such a person on staff. (A 1990 survey showed that 73 percent of responding communities had a public information officer on staff.)[1]

The important thing is to assign someone primary responsibility for media relations.

The important thing is to assign someone primary responsibility for media relations. Doing that will give reporters, editors, and news directors a source to call on when they want authoritative information from the local government. It will also give the local government a measure of control over its image in the community.

The long-term goals of the public information program, which includes media relations, should include the following:

Developing and maintaining an informed citizenry that participates in the local government's decision-making process and uses city or county services effectively

Ensuring that local government services meet the needs of the various components of the community

Ensuring that citizens are aware of the depth and breadth of services of local government and the qualifications and dedication of the people providing those services

Fostering a sense of community among local citizens.

An effective relationship with the news media can contribute to the fulfillment of the above long-term goals. In the short term, you need to develop media plans that deal with specific issues or promote individual services or facilities. The goals are usually written in behavioral terms (i.e., in terms of how people act), for example:

To build support in a particular neighborhood for construction of a stormwater-management project

To help citizens understand the necessity of new taxes or user fees for various city or county services

To sell enough tickets to support a performing-arts series.

Stating goals in behavioral terms helps define the target audiences for various kinds of information and gives you a yardstick to measure results by. Note that the goal statements do not include such objectives as obtaining coverage in the daily newspaper, getting television coverage of the mayor's speech on a certain issue, or increasing the visibility of a government spokesperson. Though those accomplishments (with the possible exception of the last one) may be effective means of getting the desired results, media coverage is a *means,* not an end in itself.

When you have determined the desired behavioral results, the next step is to formulate specific plans laying out how best to proceed to obtain these results. The kinds of media strategies you use and the tone and content of informational materials will vary, depending on whether the aim is to inform, persuade, or promote. Designating the objectives also will help determine which media outlets would best serve the local government's purposes.

The type of coverage you need will vary with the issue. In the case of a controversial issue, editorial support for the local government's position might be appropriate. For an upcoming public hearing on a proposed new swim center, though, a short, informative news story might suffice. To solicit proposed solutions to a problem in a particular neighborhood, it might be more effective to publicize a forum in a municipal or civic association newsletter than to obtain daily newspaper or broadcast coverage and thus give the issue wider coverage than it warrants. And for some issues, media coverage may not be desirable at all.

Building a working relationship with media contacts

To function effectively in the dual roles of (1) news source and (2) aggressive promoter of the local government's services and activities, staff members who work with the media must develop and maintain credibility. The basis of credibility is honesty. Reporters and editors value consistency and reliability above all other qualities. They respect the news source who admits it when he or she doesn't have the answer to a question and then comes back as soon as possible with the requested information, or puts the reporter in contact with someone who can help. Once stung by a source who "wings it" or, even worse, intentionally misleads them, reporters are wary of future contact. "We just want people to tell us what they know or to say they can't release the information—to be honest," explains one city editor.

Professionalism is also important in developing credibility. Reporters expect their sources to be familiar with format requirements, deadlines, and the organization of various media, and to share the information with others in the local government who work with the media. One newspaper reporter, for example, says she often receives criticism for a headline or for the placement of her articles from government officials, who apparently do not realize that she has no control over those factors.

Special aspects of local media outlets

Besides understanding the general requirements of the various news media, you must also become familiar with the local media. What are the deadlines for the various editions of newspapers, for radio and television broadcasts, for regional magazines? What are the requirements of different radio and television stations for public service announcements? What is the least hectic time to call a television news assignment editor to ask for some discussion of a local issue or to talk about an event?

To be successful in media relations, staff members must read local daily and weekly newspapers, noting bylines and issues currently being covered; must watch the news and become familiar with interview, talk, and public affairs programs on local TV; must keep up to date on the format, public service policies, and interview and talk programming of local radio stations. This kind of close observation of the local media yields several types of information:

Reporters' current beat assignments

Issues and trends already being covered

The ages and interests of the audiences of certain media outlets

The frequency with which specific radio stations use public service announcements, the time of day they are aired, and their typical format and wording

The existence of local interview, talk, and public affairs programs on radio and television that offer opportunities for coverage.

The human factor in the equation

Local government officials need to get to know key people in the print and broadcast media—reporters, managing editors, editorial writers, news managers, wire-service staff, and even camera crews. Keeping information on contacts current is a time-consuming and continuous process because of the news media's tendency to make frequent changes in format and personnel. It will bring rewards, however. By cultivating relationships with journalists, you are likelier to be rewarded with fair, substantive coverage of issues important to your local government.

Local government staff members who work with the news media should also be sensitive to the constant space-constraint problem facing newspaper editors and the time limits of the broadcast media. Failure to use a news release or to cover an event should not be regarded as a personal put-down. Sharing information about media constraints with other local government employees—such as the fact that a local television station has only one crew on weekends and is thus limited in the number of events that it can cover—helps prevent misunderstandings and enhance cooperation.

It has been said that "good media relationships can be best achieved by the practice of a few basic principles: (1) shoot squarely, (2) give service, (3) don't beg or carp, (4) don't ask for kills, (5) don't flood the media, and (6) keep updated lists."[2]

Improving media relations

To assist the city in developing a successful working relationship with the media and to encourage accurate media coverage of programs, events, and decisions, Claremont, California (34,650), developed a *Media Relations Manual* for city employees. The manual provides concise information on the functions of the community information office, appropriate responses to media inquiries, public disclosure, and press conferences. It also includes a handy list of publications offered by organizations involved with local government administrative services, cable television, community development, human services, public safety, and public works.

Source: *The Guide to Management Improvement Projects in Local Government*, vol. 14, no. 4 (Washington, D.C.: ICMA, 1990) PRM-26.

Here are several other helpful suggestions that elaborate on these basic principles:

Always be honest. Mark Twain said we should always tell the truth, because it will please half the people and astonish the other half. This doesn't mean that you have to tell media representatives everything you know—only that everything you tell them should be true. Deliberate attempts to mislead the news media will almost always backfire.

Don't play favorites. It is always tempting to give preferential treatment to one reporter or editor over another, especially if that person seems more sympathetic. Over time, this approach generates resentment among others in the media.

Be consistent, no matter whether the news is good or bad. One city department head loved to see his face on television and in the papers. When his department was developing a new facility, he took advantage of the opportunity to give interviews almost every day. Later in the year, however, problems developed in his department, and the city's prosecuting attorney began an investigation. The department head dropped out of sight, even having his secretary lie to the media about his whereabouts. Local journalists, perceiving that they had been used by him, turned on him in the bad times, thus making his life more miserable than it might otherwise have been under the circumstances. It's a bad idea to court the media when times are good and then hide when things go wrong. Remember your public role. You are representing the local government and not yourself. Don't use media relations as a means of self-promotion.

> *It's a bad idea to court the media when times are good and then hide when things go wrong.*

Be available. The media contact for the local government (whether it is the city or county manager, an assistant manager, the director of communication, or the public information officer) should be available around the clock. The media should know who this person is and have phone numbers for his or her office, home, car, and beeper. The contact should take all calls from the media or return calls as soon as possible. In cases of emergency, the contact—or someone else temporarily designated as the media contact—should be available at the scene of the emergency or in an easily accessible center.

Develop two-way relationships. Getting to know the people in the media during times when there are no deadlines or crises builds rapport. Go to lunch with an editor, or set aside some time to talk with reporters in a relaxed setting to explain a complicated issue that soon will be in the news. Get to know them and their interests, and let them get to know you.

Be sincere in your approach. Make sure the relationships are genuine. Trying to develop phony friendships is just a way of trying to manipulate the media, and it will sooner or later backfire. It's a good idea to give media representatives candid feedback about their news and feature reports, being as specific as possible about the good points and the weak points of their reports.

Be positive in your attitude. Don't complain about every story in the newspaper and on television. Tell the media representatives when they do things right as well as when they do things wrong.

Local government officials who work in media relations sometimes face delicate situations. For example, the more aggressive local governments market their services by seeking different types of coverage. As they work with the media to promote a city or county "product," public officials must avoid the pitfall of trying to place "puff pieces" if they wish to keep the respect of media representatives and obtain coverage of local government endeavors in these less traditional areas.

Policies on payment

Governments also should not risk losing the goodwill of public service directors of local radio and TV stations by trying to get free air time for information that is more appropriate for paid advertising. Even if the media cooperate, local business people may find it difficult to understand why a revenue-producing public facility, which may be regarded as competition for a particular business, should receive free air time that is unavailable to private sector services and facilities.

Local government needs to be especially careful about how it places paid advertising in a campaign in which advertisements and news releases are combined. Do not penalize the broadcast media for providing free public service time by spending all your advertising dollars on print media. Broadcasters can read—and you are likely to get a bill instead of a complimentary credit slip.

Designating government contacts

An important role of the local government's key media contact is to facilitate smooth relations between other city or county staff and elected officials on the one hand, and media representatives on the other.

Develop and disseminate a clear policy about who on the staff handles media inquiries (and who does not). In some local governments, only elected officials, the city or county manager, and the director of communications or a public information officer will talk with reporters. Some cities use a more decentralized approach, in which department directors and other designated staff deal with the media.

Anyone designated to provide information directly to the media should receive professional training. A casual approach invites disaster—for

---

For guidance to training

The following organizations can direct local government staff members to training in the field of public information:

City-County Communications and
  Marketing Association (3CMA)
409 Third Street, SW
Washington, DC 20002-4414

Continuing Education for Professionals
  and Organizations (CEPO)
6990 Soquel Drive
Abtos, CA 95003

International Association of Business
  Communicators (IABC)
One Hallidie Plaza, Suite 600
San Francisco, CA 94102

International City/County Management
  Association (ICMA)
777 North Capitol Street, NE
Suite 500
Washington, DC 20002-4201

Public Relations Society of America
  (PRSA)
33 Irving Place
Third Floor
New York, NY 10003

Local colleges and universities are also increasingly likely to offer courses—and even degree programs—in areas such as corporate communications and public affairs.

example, allowing anyone who answers a telephone to handle media inquiries. A more effective approach is to authorize several people to handle factual questions but only a few to comment on policy questions or controversial issues. One town has a written policy stipulating that only elected officials discuss policy questions, whereas appointed officials limit themselves to questions of implementation or programs. It is wise to limit the number of sources on controversial or tough issues, to make sure that the local government presents a clear and consistent message.

Clarifying the rules of engagement

Make sure that elected officials and everyone else who makes contact with the media understand the rules concerning and distinctions among the following: information for background, attribution, direct quotations, and "off-the-record" comments. (These terms are defined and discussed later in this chapter.) It is a good idea for staff to share information about particular reporters—those who play by the rules, those who don't, and those who appear not to have been introduced to the game.

Enlist the help of your city or county's legal department in presenting a workshop for appropriate staff members on legal issues relevant to media relations. These include questions such as: What is considered public information under state law? What are the time and cost issues involved in answering public inquiries? What should be done when the right to know appears to conflict with the right to privacy? What is privileged information under the law? Who is available in the attorney's office to assist with emergency or on-the-spot legal questions? (See the "Primer in communications law," later in this chapter.)

Modesto, California's media-relations workshop

The city of Modesto's public information office coordinates a half-day media relations workshop annually for city management personnel frequently contacted by news outlets for information. The session includes:

A presentation by the city attorney, "To Be or Not to Be Public," a refresher course on the Public Records Act.

A presentation by the public information officer, "The Interview Process: Advantage City of Modesto." The PIO uses news clips, radio interviews, and print articles featuring comments and interviews of city employees to discuss interview techniques and the most effective ways of getting the city's message out.

A question-and-answer session with representatives of local news media concerning coverage of the city and how and why they report what they do.

The workshop has resulted in better relationships between the staff and the local news media; different departments using the public information office as a resource when preparing comments for the news media; and more human-interest stories about the city because the media have been introduced to more staff contacts through this process.

Source: Karen A. George, Scott Summerfield, and Sheri Erlewine, "Establishing a Public Information Program," *Western City* (September 1991), p. 28.

Easing the way for everyone

Develop clear rules about referrals. A person who receives a media inquiry and needs to refer the caller to another source should tell the caller that the call will be returned. That will give the recipient of the

Solicit feedback from the reporter to be sure his or her interpretation is correct.

call time to alert the appropriate staff member, relay any impressions he or she may have of the type of story the reporter has in mind, and suggest how the inquiry might be handled. This procedure will give the other staff member time to make a quick review of the facts before returning the call. The person making the referral should ensure that calls from the media are returned promptly and may want to check back with the other staff member—or, better, call the reporter back to ask whether he or she received a sufficient amount of the type of information needed for the story. The show of concern will be appreciated.

Assist others in getting their messages across. Recommend that when discussing a complex subject, people try to "begin at the beginning." Some reporters may be reluctant to confess their ignorance or confusion and may go ahead and write a story the way they interpret it. To avoid this pitfall, never deliver a monologue. Solicit feedback from the reporter to be sure his or her interpretation is correct.

Protecting local government's legal interests

Suggest that when staff members give a reporter an impromptu statement over the telephone about a controversial issue, they jot down what

---

Effective interviews with the media

Most reporters get news stories by covering city-council meetings. Often during a meeting, a topic will pique a reporter's interest and the reporter will want an interview for a more in-depth story on the topic.

When a reporter calls for an interview, ask what the topic is, the deadline for the story, and the other people the reporter is planning to interview. Many times, reporters don't have a focus on the story until after the interview, but they do know the general topic of the article.

City officials do have the right to set ground rules before the interview. Limit the length of the interview; in order to prepare, limit the number of topics you will discuss during the interview.

City officials should look at media interviews as a marketing opportunity to sell your point of view. The following are guidelines to remember when a reporter is interviewing you:

Prepare. When you are preparing for an interview, ask yourself these questions.

1. Who is the audience? The reporter is not your audience. The reporter is the messenger to your audience.

2. What is your objective or message? By thinking through your objective before the interview, you will be more in control of the message you are sending to your audience. Always come back to your message.

3. What are the benefits? How will people benefit from the program, issue, or change the city is proposing? Speak in terms of benefits, not features.

Edit before you speak. Most people talk through the process to get to the conclusion. With reporters, start with the conclusion and then give supporting information and examples. This requires you to know your message and say it concisely.

Jargon and technical terms complicate your message. Use terms the public will understand. Using technical terms does not make you look more of an expert— in fact, the opposite happens. The interviewee looks as if they are hiding the truth by using technical jargon. If the reporter asks a technical question, begin your response by explaining that the question is technical and requires a more complicated answer.

Use examples. This is a powerful way to communicate and helps the audience understand your objective.

Develop a style. Most people underestimate the power of how you present information. If the interview is about a new and exciting program, act and sound excited. If it is bad news, show your concern. Your style should be consistent with your message.

Repetition. The more you repeat your message, the better your chances of getting that message into the story and to your audience.

Listen to the question the reporter asks. If you do not understand the question, rephrase it back to the reporter so that you get clarification before you answer.

Be comfortable with silence. Answer the question the reporter asks, then be quiet. Most people are uncomfortable with silence when speaking with someone. Reporters know this, and use it to get more information from a person.

Practice. Preparing and practicing will mean a more successful interview.

Source: Debra Nyberg, "Dealing with the Media for City Officials," *Minnesota Cities* (March 1992), p. 5.

was said to the reporter. The notation will come in handy if a second reporter calls about the same issue, or in case someone is misunderstood or misquoted.

From the standpoint of both the local government official and the reporter, most conversations and interviews between the media and city officials should be *on the record*. That means that everything said by the person being interviewed can be directly attributed to that person in a news or feature story. Local government officials should always assume that they are talking to reporters on the record—even if interviewed in a phone call at home at night or on a weekend. Consistently speaking on the record adds to the credibility of the local government official as a news source, and provides reporters with the information they need to complete an assignment.

If a city or county official decides to provide information to a reporter under other than on-the-record conditions, those conditions must be made clear at the beginning of the conversation. Stating the conditions at the beginning of the interview also gives the reporter the opportunity to refuse the interview under those conditions and look elsewhere for information.

Dealing with "problem" journalists

Most local government officials and most journalists work hard at developing relationships built on trust and respect. Sometimes, despite the best efforts of everyone, journalists seem to distort the news and (perhaps intentionally) make local government look bad. Here are some useful steps to deal with problem journalists:

1. Talk with the journalist first. Explain exactly why you are concerned. Point out specific passages in news stories, features, or editorials. Do it on the phone or in person, as soon as possible after the item in question is printed or aired. Don't mention threats or penalties. Listen to the journalist's response. Describe how you feel about the situation (angry, embarrassed, disappointed) and ask the journalist how he or she feels. Give him or her the benefit of the doubt (at least the first time). Give the journalist feedback the next time he or she writes or airs something about you—especially if it seems to indicate that the situation, from your perspective, has been corrected.

2. Discuss the situation with a friend or colleague. If the situation persists, have a confidential talk about it with someone you trust—preferably a third party who is not affected by the subject of the news item. Seek that person's advice as to whether you are being too critical or thin-skinned, and ask for his or her evaluation of the seriousness of the situation. Ask the third party if he or she thinks you're justified in taking corrective action.

3. Talk with the journalist's editor or boss, either in person or on the phone. Be calm and analytical. Explain exactly what the problem is, as well as the results of your discussions with the journalist. Ask if others have complained about the journalist's reporting. Expect the editor to defend the journalist to a point, and don't press for corrective action on the spot. Give the editor a chance to look into the situation, talk with the journalist, and get back to you. Listen carefully to the editor's feedback.

4. Continue trying to work the situation out. Don't panic or feel paranoid, especially if the situation gets worse in the short term (as it may well do).

Continue to speak specifically with the journalist to make it clear what you expect him or her to do. Continue to test your feelings and instincts with third-party friends. Keep in touch with the journalist's editor.

5. If nothing seems to work after a few months, take action within your organization to rectify the situation. Make efforts with other journalists to get your story to the public, or (even better) develop direct communication links with the target publics to get your message across. Treat the problem journalist with special care—consider telling your staff to refer all inquiries from that journalist to you. Tape conversations with the journalist or have a third party present when you talk with him or her. (You may want to check with your city or county attorney to make sure you are not violating any of the journalist's rights—such as access to public information.) Tell the journalist what you are doing and why, and make it clear that you are not seeking preferential treatment, that you only want the journalist to treat you professionally and impartially.

Reporters need direct quotes.

In stating any conditions for the interview, be sure that both parties agree on terms. Generally, *off the record* or *for your information only* mean that the reporter will not use information from a source in a news or feature story but will use it solely to put things into better perspective before writing. *Not for attribution* means that the reporter can use information however he or she deems appropriate but will not quote a direct source. Local government officials should be cautious about giving interviews that are not on the record, particularly with a reporter they do not know well. There are plenty of stories of officials who were "burned" by a reporter—or thought they were—at the cost of great embarrassment, or worse.

The worst possible response to a reporter's question is "no comment." To a reporter, "no comment" means that the government official is hiding something, shielding someone, or otherwise avoiding a truthful answer for devious reasons. A public official who consistently uses "no comment" soon gets branded as uncooperative and untruthful. Reporters also feel that it is fair to report that a source said "no comment," which can destroy the official's credibility with the public. A better answer is "I don't have that information," or "I can't release that information right now," or "Let me get back to you," or any of a number of other similar answers, provided they are truthful.

The public official should assume responsibility for setting the ground rules for any dialogue with a media representative. The best rule is: Take nothing for granted. When telephoned by a reporter, especially one you don't know, you may have to assume that your conversation is being recorded until you are able to ascertain otherwise.

Be especially careful with new or inexperienced reporters, or with reporters with a reputation for being troublesome. Make it clear to all journalists that they must let you know when they are recording your conversation—especially radio and television reporters. One former government information officer tells of the time he picked up his phone during a local emergency and quickly realized he was live on the air in the middle of a nearby town's morning newscast. He gave cordial, informative, but very brief answers to the reporter's questions. As soon as the interview was over, he put in a call to the station's general manager.

Basic tools in media relations

Staff limitations may prevent some local governments from assigning even one person to handle media relations full time. This limitation does not, however, prevent such governments from being accessible to the media. Local governments can use several methods—with little impact on either resources or staff time—to assist the news media in covering the city or county beat.

Media representatives point to a calendar of city events as the most basic piece of information they need. A calendar is useful because it alerts editors and reporters to the times, places, and dates of public hearings, board and commission meetings, voter-registration deadlines, and other public activities.

Although calendars are less informative than news releases or public service announcements on individual events, they do have several advantages. They can be assembled quickly and easily, and they provide a lot of information. Also, the news media can be directed to the appropriate point of contact for each event in case they need further information.

Another service that the media regard as basic is being mailed an agenda several days in advance of each council or board meeting. Editors and reporters review agendas to decide whether they should cover a meeting. Often the agendas alert them to issues and legislation likely to merit future coverage.

Sending out background material on agenda items several days before meetings is helpful to reporters who cover local government. This service gives reporters time to review materials in advance so that they can follow discussions of the issues more easily and gather supporting information they need for their stories, which are often written to meet tight deadlines. Generally it is to the advantage of local government to provide as much information as possible to reporters. The direct result is that local residents will receive more accurate and substantive news accounts.

To add depth to their stories, the media need access to the local government's elected officials and to top-level staff from whom they can obtain more information and statements. Reporters also need direct quotations from key officials—a feature as important to the vitality of a news story as dialogue is to a novel.

Elected officials and staff should make every effort to speak to reporters when they call or else to return their telephone calls *promptly*. A return call after the deadline for a newspaper or a news broadcast has passed is worthless. Failure to return calls promptly is the most frequent complaint among reporters about local government officials. Could these officials be the same ones who continually complain that the media never tell the government's side of the story?

Meeting the media's varied needs

Good media relations require that local government officials understand the general requirements of the various media as well as the specific deadlines, staff assignments, formats, and other characteristics of the individual newspapers and radio and television stations in the community. News releases and public service announcements should be written in a style appropriate to the medium and should be directed to the appropriate staff member.

The needs of newspapers

Although the style and format of daily and weekly newspapers may be similar, their differences in staff organization and frequency of publication affect the way local government staff members work with editors and reporters.

Because the staff of a daily paper is usually large and specialized, government staff members will have contacts with numerous editors and reporters.

The most frequent contacts will be with reporters and editors for the local news section. The editor in charge of this section is usually called the *metropolitan editor* or *city editor*. On larger newspapers, editorial responsibilities may be further broken down, with editors for specific jurisdictions reporting to the metropolitan editors. Depending on the size of a community, contacts with reporters for a daily newspaper will range from frequent interactions with several reporters assigned to cover different aspects of local government to infrequent contacts with a single reporter assigned to a larger geographic area.

Many dailies publish zoned sections to allow for more local news. In some instances, these sections will have their own editors and reporters, whose requirements will be more like those of weekly newspapers than those of their colleagues on other sections of the daily.

Staff members responsible for publicizing or marketing sports activities and events, recreation classes, special events, performing-arts programs, and the like will need additional, separate contacts with editors and writers assigned to the lifestyle, sports, and calendar sections and

Regardless of the size of the weeklies serving the community, their needs should not be neglected.

to the Sunday magazine. If the city or county has an aggressive economic development program, contacts with the staff of the business and finance and real-estate sections will be essential. Probably less frequently, contacts on the editorial staff may also be needed.

The staff organization of large weekly newspapers such as the ones serving populous suburbs or middle-sized towns is similar to that of dailies: editors for news, lifestyle, sports, and business sections reporting to a managing editor. In smaller towns, a single editor may be responsible for editorial copy and production and be assisted by no more than a couple of writers. But regardless of the size of the weeklies serving the community, their needs should not be neglected.

Weekly newspapers offer an effective, direct, and intimate means of reaching the people of the suburbs, small towns, and farms, who are often sources of grassroots opinion. Weekly newspaper readers are loyal and read their paper from the front page to the classifieds. The weekly newspaper may exert a far greater impact on opinions in ratio to its circulation than the average daily does.

To facilitate coverage, news-release mailing lists should reflect the organization of the area's newspapers. Mailing to the specialized staffs of dailies and large weeklies will direct releases to the appropriate section editor, critic, or calendar editor. Releases to small newspapers may be sent to a single editor.

Reaching the right audience through radio

Although radio is one of the major media, the audience for an individual radio station is seldom as general as that for a daily newspaper or a commercial television station. A radio station's format—whether rock, classical, country, urban contemporary, all-news, all-talk, or Spanish language—affects the way staff members will work with the station and provides the opportunity to direct the local government's message to a particular age cohort or interest group within a community.

The diversity of radio provides opportunities for targeting specific audiences.

Contacts with all-news stations or stations that devote considerable air time to local news and public affairs will be more extensive than contacts with stations devoted entirely to popular music, for example. Staff organizations of the former usually include—among others—a news director, reporters assigned to local beats if the station is relatively large, a public affairs director who handles interviews and talk shows, and a public service director.

The news director and appropriate reporters should be on news-release mailing lists for hard-news coverage and should be called with breaking news. The public affairs director or the producer of specific shows should be approached if the local government seeks discussion of an issue in an interview or on a talk show. For public service announcements, the public service director is the person to contact.

Considering the differences among radio stations

Staff organization varies greatly on smaller stations or stations that give little air time to news and public affairs. Stations with various music formats, for example, may limit news coverage to wire-service copy read by the announcer. This is known as the "rip-and-read" type of news programming. A few music stations may air no news at all. Still other stations may use news provided through well-written releases but will not have any reporters who actually cover events or originate stories.

To obtain the greatest possible news coverage, vary your methods of contact according to the format and staffing of the individual stations. An all-news station or one with a news department should be on the mailing list for news releases, should be notified of news conferences and other events it might wish to cover, should be reached through the wire services, and should be called promptly with up-to-date information about breaking news. At the other end of the scale will be the stations that have no news coverage, for which such contacts are both unnecessary and inappropriate.

Vary your method of contact according to the format of the individual stations.

In between fall stations using the rip-and-read approach. Local government can reach them only through the wire services for news coverage. Some stations want to be on news-release mailing lists and receive calls about breaking news. Still other stations are able to develop their own stories through telephone interviews but are seldom if ever able to send a reporter out to cover a story.

The diversity of radio-station formats provides opportunities to aim at specific audiences. Keep that in mind when planning information programs and attempting to place public service announcements to reach the community's Spanish-speaking or African-American residents, young people, potential concert-goers, senior citizens, and other discrete segments of the population.

Timeliness—crucial to the medium of radio

Radio is an "immediate" medium with frequent deadlines. The urgency is magnified at stations that have all-news formats or that broadcast news on the hour or half-hour. Dated stories will not be aired.

News releases on topics with a short "shelf life" are usually worthless to radio stations unless they are delivered immediately. The delivery can be either by fax or by hand. Or you have the alternatives of calling major stations about important stories and having the story placed on the audio services of the Associated Press and other news agencies. There are several avenues for placing a story on a newswire. Staff members can (1) call the local bureau directly, (2) talk with the local stringer for the wire service, or (3) suggest that a reporter for the local station place a story on the wire. The immediacy of radio news requires that the local government representative return telephone calls from radio reporters as soon as possible.

Formats for releases to radio stations
Although in some instances working with radio means preparing two releases—one appropriate for print, the other for broadcast—two releases are not always necessary. At a news conference, for example, one release will suffice. Radio reporters who cover the conference will use the release as background information. It will help them flesh out their stories, which will consist of taped remarks made by the principals at the conference and the reporters' commentary.

The local government contact should work with radio stations to help them obtain *actualities* (recorded comments by principals in a story for use on air), by arranging for elected officials, the city or county manager, and other local government staff members to be available for phone or taped interviews. The contact should also encourage local officials to make themselves available for interviews, either over the phone or in person. Another method of providing actualities on important issues is to tape a statement by the mayor or another official that can be recorded by radio news operations over the phone.

> *One means of providing easily accessible information to the radio stations and other media is a hot line that is kept up to date as news develops.*

Tips for local government broadcast writers
Use short, simple sentences. Avoid clauses and parenthetical material as much as possible, and use well-known acronyms only. As a touchstone, you should be able to read your copy without tripping over your tongue or getting short of breath. It's acceptable to use contractions; they save time and make your copy sound more natural.

Your opening sentence should hook the reader with some interesting but simple bit of news—for example, the announcement that the city will be spraying the east side for gypsy moths next week. Then add the essential details such as the exact time and place, if you are writing about an upcoming occurrence.

Avoid using unfamiliar names. If you mention individuals whose title will interest local listeners more than their name, use just the person's title—especially if you are making only one reference to the person. Also, unlike in print journalism, in short broadcast pieces it's acceptable to use a locally prominent person's title and last name only. Thus: "Mayor Smith will call on the mayor of Victoria, British Columbia, next week as part of Anytown's effort to encourage tourism."

Do broadcasters—and yourself—a favor and include pronunciation guides in parentheses for technical, foreign, or otherwise uncommon words. For example: RIBONUCLEIC (RYE-BO-NYU-KLEE-IK). If for some reason your script has a lot of difficult words in it, put a note to that effect at the top.

Before sending off your radio spot, read it one more time—preferably to another person. If you can't shake a feeling that it's hard to follow (or glib)—go with your instinct and simplify.

One means of providing easily accessible information to the radio stations and other media is a hot line that is kept up to date as news develops. If resources are available to do so, copy for the newscast may be prepared by a staff person, then recorded on tape. Reporters are given an unlisted number for access to this recording of breaking news. The hot line may include information on forthcoming council and commission meetings and recent council actions as well as taped statements on important issues. The hot-line approach to information and news becomes particularly valuable in an emergency, when ready access to the latest facts is important.

Although radio stations are not required to dedicate a specific amount of air time to public service programs, many do aim for a certain percentage of public service time, which includes news and public affairs programs as well as public service announcements. Such programming is doubly useful to the station—it is (1) an asset to the station when applying for a renewal of its license from the Federal Communications Commission and (2) an aid in developing a loyal listening audience.

Although radio stations are not required to dedicate a specific amount of air time to public service programs, many do so.

The particulars on public service announcements

Public service announcements (PSAs) are the type of material most likely to be broadcast verbatim. Prepared by not-for-profit agencies, including all levels of government, public service announcements are short spots, rarely exceeding thirty seconds, that may be aired numerous times. Observing guidelines for good broadcast writing should increase the chance that the public service announcement will be aired. They can be distributed as written scripts only, or on audiocassettes. Local government contacts should ask local radio stations about their preferences.

The simplest version of the PSA is the written script. The heading for public service announcements should include contact information like that of news releases. "Start" and "stop" dates (indicating when to begin and end use of the PSA) are important to include, along with the length of the announcement. Allow about seventy-five words for a half-minute spot. Taped announcements should be of broadcast quality, and a written script should accompany any tape sent out. The standard format is a script typed in capital letters or in large and small caps, triple spaced. A simple phonetic spelling should be provided in parentheses after any difficult names or unusual words.

Figure 6–1 A sample script for a public service announcement.

PUBLIC SERVICE ANNOUNCEMENT

From: Anytown City Government
1 Municipal Plaza
Anytown, USA 00000

Good until: 9/30/94
Contact: Mike Smith
ph. 555-0000, ext. 000
Duration: 0:30

ANYTOWN'S CIVIC AUDITORIUM WILL CELEBRATE ITS FIRST ANNIVERSARY FRIDAY WITH A FREE PERFORMANCE OF MEXICAN FOLK DANCING. AN EVENING OF SPIRITED MUSIC, COLORFUL COSTUMES, AND INSPIRED DANCING WILL BE PRESENTED BY BALLET DE LA CIUDAD (DAY LAH SEE-EW-DAHD). THE TWO-HOUR PROGRAM WILL BEGIN AT 8 P.M. ON FRIDAY, SEPTEMBER 30TH. THE ANYTOWN CIVIC AUDITORIUM IS LOCATED ON RANCHLAND (RANCH-LIN) HIGHWAY, DIRECTLY ACROSS FROM COUNTY CONSOLIDATED HIGH SCHOOL. PARKING IS FREE. FOR MORE INFORMATION, CALL THE CITY MANAGER'S OFFICE AT 555-0000.

####

Proposals for public affairs programs

Some homework is required before approaching local radio stations with ideas for public affairs programs. First, listen to and assess the interview, panel discussion, talk, and call-in programs of each station that interests you. In a community with few radio stations, that is a simple task. In a large metropolitan area, the city staff can turn to local media directories, often produced as fund-raisers by nonprofit organizations, or to the national media directories, found in most libraries.

Make program proposals specific and show why the subject would interest the station's audience. Broach the subject with the producer of a show by telephone and then follow up with more details in a written proposal, or write first and follow up with a telephone call.

Make program proposals specific and show why the subject would interest the station's audience.

Unless you have already established a relationship with the producer, a letter followed by a phone call will probably be the more appropriate approach when dealing with a major station in a large market. Make absolutely sure you have the name of the producer—with correct spelling—and his or her full formal title. Even if you've consulted a media directory, it's worth the effort to have someone on the staff call the station to double-check that information is current before a letter goes out, because there's a high rate of turnover in the radio business.

If a government serves a small community in a large metropolitan area, radio stations with large broadcast areas may consider the community's issues too parochial for their large audiences. Such objections can be overcome by developing proposals on topics that are highly relevant to the community but also have appeal throughout the metropolitan area. For example, a proposal for a panel program on how changes in the federal budget are affecting communities could call for a forum of several mayors or local government managers.

Producing radio programming in house

Local government can also reach the radio audience through programs it develops on its own. Depending on the willingness of local stations to air them, these shows can be produced in a variety of formats. The simplest is a short spot (thirty seconds to a couple of minutes) taped by telephone for a single station on a regular basis, most likely weekly or daily. If your local government has no recording facilities, consider approaching the station itself (if its management is willing) or the nearest community college or university radio station.

The short spot can be used to provide timely information on public hearings, local services, special events, or council actions.

The job experience (and willingness to go on the air) of employees of various agencies of local government may be used to develop series of public information spots. Some ideas for programs:

Health tips for elderly people from the commission on aging

Advice on gardening and lawn care from the city or county extension service

Series on local museums and cultural centers operated by the city or county

Crime prevention tips from the police department.

Some local governments produce longer shows, in an interview format, on current community issues. The programs are taped and then distributed to radio stations that have agreed to broadcast them as public affairs programs. This type of program requires a substantial commitment of time and resources because it entails doing a number of shows, as well as developing ideas for programs, reserving studio time, and scheduling—and working with—guests, many of them prominent members of the community who have little time to spare.

Taking on the challenges of television coverage

The organization of the staff of a television station is similar to that of a radio station that emphasizes news and public service programming. Nearly all television stations have a news director, public affairs director, and public service director. The news staff also includes assignment editors responsible for reporters and video crews.

Local government's most frequent contacts will be with the assignment editors, or with reporters assigned to regular beats. Many stations have different people handle assignments on weekends, often rotating the responsibility. The contacts are all important.

Angles to consider for effective TV publicity

Although many of the suggestions for working with the press and radio also apply to television, TV's emphasis on the visual makes special demands. If an event or program has no appealing visual element, it is unlikely that TV stations will be interested. For instance, the opening of a new exhibit at the city zoo is more likely to get TV coverage than the reorganization of the municipal port authority, regardless of the relative importance of the two events.

News conferences and other events scheduled between mid-morning and 2 p.m. have a better chance of being covered than those that take place later in the day (and thus closer to the evening news). Council and board meetings, usually scheduled in the evening for the convenience of citizens, are not so convenient for television news operations. Not only is there less time to prepare the story for the late evening news, but many stations have fewer camera crews available during the evening. This is more of a problem in the suburbs, if the television stations are all in the central city. In such instances, travel time has to be incorporated into an already tight schedule.

Television news operations consider the central city their primary beat, because it has a larger population, its leaders are usually more active politically, and it is geographically more convenient to cover. Suburban government officials may find television coverage of their area limited to controversy and novelties.

Making it easier for TV to cover local news

Local government communicators can provide certain services to television news staff, however, that may make coverage possible even if reporters and camera crews are not assigned to a story. For example, it is possible to call television newsrooms with information on major actions of the council or board in time to make newscasts. The story may be run without visuals, or the visuals could be filmed earlier in the day.

Television news staffers should be alerted to the visual possibilities of the story. If the event to be covered is a news conference, the availability of graphs, charts, demonstrations, or models of future development projects should be mentioned.

Local television stations also provide opportunities for public service announcements and public affairs programming. Public service announcements prepared for television can be as simple and inexpensive as the written script prepared for radio or as elaborate as a professionally produced spot with music, actors, and an "on-location" setting. The introduction of computer-generated art and animation since the late 1980s has transformed the possibilities for video products produced in house by a local government.

Some TV public service directors or their staffs will work with the local government on its public service announcements, perhaps even making copies that can be sent to other stations. Often this can be done at little expense to the government other than that of staff time. Local governments that have television-production facilities, or have access to such facilities through public-access cable or other sources such as local universities or colleges, can produce their own public service announcements. In such cases, it is still a good idea to contact the public service directors at local television stations before producing PSAs, to ensure that an announcement meets specifications.

As is the case on radio, local public affairs programs and talk shows on television offer further opportunities for coverage. Get acquainted with formats, types of issues and activities covered, producers, and on-the-air personalities before making specific proposals.

Many local stations have morning news and talk shows. Some have "magazine" shows in various formats and at various times. Producers of these programs are looking for human-interest stories, unusual entertainment opportunities, a new book about some aspect of the local community, or interviews with local celebrities, as well as lively, visual treatments of more serious subjects such as health, education, crime, and fire prevention. Assess the community's resources imaginatively. The people who operate the city or county's zoo, port facilities, sports stadium, concert arena, or firehouses all have interesting stories that can get them on the air. Once on the air, they can inform viewers of the diverse services available from their local government.

Keeping the news new

News-media coverage of local government information, events, and activities varies from community to community, depending on a number of factors. On one hand, the suburbs have to compete for coverage with large cities and counties. On the other hand, large cities and counties will sometimes receive more attention than they want.

Regardless of size, nearly all local governments face some hard work persuading editors and reporters to cover softer issues, to do stories on routine government programs and services, or to be interested in the noncontroversial items or "product publicity."

Besides becoming familiar with the general demands of the various media, learning particular requirements of the local media, and developing personal contacts, there are specific techniques that are helpful in working with editors and reporters in the various news media. Although local methods may vary, the following suggestions will be generally helpful:

Learn what news is, from the media's point of view. Many local government officials give in to the temptation to define news as what *they* would like to see printed or aired—a sure way to invite conflicts with editors and reporters. Many definitions of news have been offered, but most incorporate the ideas proposed by pioneer journalism educator William Bleyer: "anything timely that interests a number of persons, and the best news is that which has the greatest interest for the greatest number."

Remember to consider the "qualities of news," including such characteristics as proximity, prominence, novelty, and human interest. And before becoming cynical about the media's propensity to focus on the negative, controversial, or sensational, consider your own preferences in reading, listening, and viewing.

Tie news stories to today's interests. To do this well, you must stay informed on current issues, social trends, and social change on both the local and the national levels.

Show that a local government program is a new way of dealing with an old problem. If the problem is widely shared, the new program will be of interest to readers and listeners who do not directly benefit from the program. Some examples: programs dealing with crimes committed by youths, drunken driving, housing problems for the elderly, and local efforts to counteract effects of cuts in federal programs.

Look for a human interest or an unusual angle. Such material is interesting to people simply for its own sake, regardless of its effect on them. Stories appealing to the emotions or exhibiting irony or coincidence have human interest. The cliché that children, old people, and animals are winners for coverage still holds true.

Place news of important decisions made at evening council meetings on the local wire service or fax it to appropriate media that night, when it may be difficult to reach reporters. This diligence can bring coverage on late-evening radio and television news broadcasts, on high-listenership drive-time radio news programs, and in morning newspapers. Follow up the next morning with individual calls to the principal broadcast and print media to provide additional information.

Give reporters copies of complex documents such as budgets, with accompanying news releases, as far in advance as possible. That will allow time for reporters to digest the materials and for visuals to be filmed for television. It is possible to give reporters information with a release date in the future, as long as they agree to the release date in advance. Make sure they clear this arrangement with their editors.

Follow up on major releases. Reporters and editors urge local government communicators to make follow-up telephone calls after mailing news releases, because of the vast amount of mail received by the media. Follow-up differs from nagging in duration, frequency, and level of insistence.

Keep media lists up to date; if at all possible, address releases by name to reporters, critics, editors, or news directors. For a local government with a small staff in a large metropolitan area where there are thirty or forty radio stations, numerous newspapers, and several television channels, however, close and frequent monitoring of staff changes for all the outlets may be impossible. In this type of case, it is preferable to address public service announcements to titles like "Public Service Director," and send calendar notices to "Calendar Editor," etc., rather than persist in sending information to staff members long gone to other jobs.

Send releases only to appropriate media. In addition to categorizing media mailing lists by editorial position, organize lists around such topics as performing arts, sports, business, and real estate, so that the appropriate media receive only releases of interest to them. Sending releases about the symphony to art critics or information about recreation programs to real-estate editors projects an unprofessional image. Worse, recipients of irrelevant releases soon will toss away all unopened relevant mailings from that source.

Don't take the first no as the final answer. Rejection of a story suggestion by a reporter does not preclude contacting the lifestyle editor of the same newspaper; nor should a turndown by a broadcast reporter mean that the news director cannot be called.

Schedule requests for coverage to correspond to slow news periods. It is usually easier to get coverage in Saturday, Sunday, and Monday issues of daily newspapers.

Schedule special events for "fifth weekdays"—the occasionally occurring fifth Monday, Tuesday, etc., of a month. Editors looking for news generally find less of it on the days following a fifth weekday.

Compile and periodically update a list of feature-story possibilities to have ready when reporters complain that they have nothing to write about.

Develop new angles for old stories. The media annually note such occasions as the coming of spring, the beginning of hot weather, Independence Day celebrations, the first day of school, Halloween, and other holidays. Suggestions for a fresh approach for photographs, articles, or broadcast coverage incorporating city programs, events, or facilities are often welcomed by the media.

Create variations on shopworn events. For example, a groundbreaking ceremony for a new building often features a row of smiling elected officials posed with shovels. For a variation, give each official a turn on the backhoe. Instead of a ribbon-cutting ceremony—a row of smiling elected officials armed with scissors—hold an open house for the new facility with appropriate opportunities for photos and video visuals. If the facility is a swimming pool, officials can take the first dip. They can tee off to inaugurate a city or county golf course or answer a call at a new dispatching center.

Look in the membership directories of local writers' or publishers' associations to determine the special interests of freelancers who write for local newspapers or magazines, then approach them with ideas for articles. Their suggestions may be more persuasive to an editor than ideas that come from local government staff.

Along the same line, wire services may be more amenable to taking stories from the newspapers or broadcast media that subscribe to their services or from stringers than from local government sources.

Effective news releases and information packages

News releases will vary in form, depending on their intended purpose and subject. But in most situations the traditional inverted-pyramid style will be the most appropriate form for releases to newspapers. The term *inverted pyramid* is a graphic description of the form of organization of the standard news story. The most important information is placed in the first few paragraphs (at the apex of the pyramid), with following information in descending order of importance. The *who, what, when, where, why,* and *how* (the "five Ws and the H") of the story are explained in the first few sentences.

The advantages of this format have long been known to reporters, who use the formula for organizing facts into a story; by headline writers, who need only to look to the first paragraphs for the point of the article; by makeup editors, who can cut the article from the bottom in the confidence that they are eliminating the least important information; and by readers, who can decide early in a story whether they are interested in the subject or have read enough at any point.

News releases that follow the formula provide some related advantages for local government officials. Reporters and editors need only a few paragraphs to obtain the gist of the release and to determine whether they will print it, cover the event described, or take any other action that the release elicits. If the release is used but must be cut, the makeup editor will probably cut information that the writer considered the least important.

A good news writer determines the "news peg" of the subject at hand. What makes it news? Why is it timely? How is it significant? The most important and interesting aspect of the story should be used to capture the reader's attention. Seldom are the five Ws and the H of equal importance; rare is the story that should begin "At 4 p.m. Saturday . . ."

Releasing the appropriate news to an audience

Length, depth of detail, the inclusion of background material, and other characteristics must depend on the subject and purpose of the release. Is this release intended to give the media insight into the city's annual budget, to highlight the most important portions of a legal document creating a public/private partnership, to announce registration for recreation classes, or simply to provide information appropriate for calendar listings?

In the case of a release about the budget, reporters who cover the local government will probably use the handout as the skeleton of their story, supplementing the release with direct quotes from key officials, comments from business or political leaders, and their own understanding of local government. The same release may be used verbatim by other publications and should be written accordingly, with appropriate direct and indirect quotations and adequate background information.

Although some public relations textbooks recommend limiting news releases to a single page, for important stories more detailed information is both appropriate and appreciated. In some instances you should distribute a detailed release on a subject such as the budget, but soon afterward follow it with a brief version that provides only the highlights and some new information, such as dates for public hearings. Some newspapers may use both; others that will not devote space to a long budget story may use the shorter version.

Many of the news releases written for newspapers are similar in nature to public service announcements for broadcast media. Such releases concern local services or special events rather than hard news. To facilitate publication of such releases, the writer should keep them brief and to the point, avoiding adjectives and gimmicks.

Using calendar publicity

Calendar editors should also receive announcements about events. Such information should not necessitate a treasure hunt for the who, what, when, and where. A short paragraph or two, with a telephone number for additional information, is adequate.

The closer any release is in length, degree of detail, style, and format to that of the finished newspaper product, the better the chance that it will be used. The relatively detailed budget release saves time for the reporter by providing a base to build a story on; the brief release about a forthcoming trip provides the lifestyle editor with a short, ready-to-use article, not a complete rewrite job that entails eliminating gimmicks and ferreting out buried leads. The calendar notice is just that—a notice.

To provide a sense of identity, the local government can develop a standard heading for preprinted news-release stationery, probably a variation on government letterhead. The news-release stationery should provide space for the date of writing and the release date, which specifies when the release may be printed or aired; at least one, but preferably two contacts, with telephone numbers; and the address. Although many news-release headings also include headlines, they are almost never used.

Developing useful fact sheets
A handy complement to the news release, for journalists, is the fact sheet. Fact sheets can be used to summarize important information, giving

Figure 6–2 A sample news release from the city of Claremont, California.

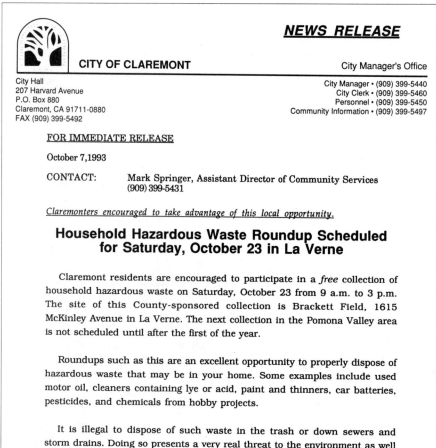

NEWS RELEASE

CITY OF CLAREMONT

City Manager's Office

City Hall
207 Harvard Avenue
P.O. Box 880
Claremont, CA 91711-0880
FAX (909) 399-5492

City Manager • (909) 399-5440
City Clerk • (909) 399-5460
Personnel • (909) 399-5450
Community Information • (909) 399-5497

FOR IMMEDIATE RELEASE

October 7, 1993

CONTACT: Mark Springer, Assistant Director of Community Services
(909) 399-5431

Claremonters encouraged to take advantage of this local opportunity.

Household Hazardous Waste Roundup Scheduled for Saturday, October 23 in La Verne

Claremont residents are encouraged to participate in a *free* collection of household hazardous waste on Saturday, October 23 from 9 a.m. to 3 p.m. The site of this County-sponsored collection is Brackett Field, 1615 McKinley Avenue in La Verne. The next collection in the Pomona Valley area is not scheduled until after the first of the year.

Roundups such as this are an excellent opportunity to properly dispose of hazardous waste that may be in your home. Some examples include used motor oil, cleaners containing lye or acid, paint and thinners, car batteries, pesticides, and chemicals from hobby projects.

It is illegal to dispose of such waste in the trash or down sewers and storm drains. Doing so presents a very real threat to the environment as well as to workers that may come in contact with the material while collecting your trash.

Claremont residents pay for the County's collection program through a surcharge placed on all refuse dumped at County-operated landfills. Instead of duplicating these costs by holding a similar collection day, the City decided to evaluate, on a trial basis, the effectiveness of having residents

– MORE –

the who-what-when-where-how in a simple format. A relative of the fact sheet is the question-and-answer (Q & A) format, in which key questions are anticipated and succinct answers provided. That information can be supplemented by other background information such as biographical data, brief histories, examples, and case histories.

All of the components—news release, fact sheets, Q & A sheets, background information—can be packaged in a news kit. Some local governments have preprinted news-kit folders that can be used for many occasions. Others simply buy blank folders from stationery suppliers and then put a label on the outside when appropriate. News-kit folders are especially useful when several sheets of information are to be given to each representative of the news media. They are also useful to the local government in packaging information to be retained by reporters and editors for background.

The advent of video news releases

With the growing accessibility of video technology, video news releases (VNRs) have also become common. The problem is that some television stations have a policy of *not* using video news releases, and others use them only rarely. However, many will use *B-roll,* videotape without an audio narrative (or *voice-over*). (Information on more technical aspects of the relationship between local government and television is given in Chapter 11.)

News conferences and briefings

Anyone who has been responsible for a news conference on a subject that the media did not find worth covering can attest to the embarrassment for everyone involved. In general, the fewer the news conferences the better. The general rule is that when you need to give the same information at the same time to everyone in the media, and when it is information that they want and need quickly, then a news conference is in order. When in doubt about calling a news conference, don't.

Local government officials may find it appropriate to call news conferences to announce important economic development proposals, to discuss labor/management disputes, to bring the media up to date during natural disasters or other crises, and to provide briefings on other timely and complex subjects.

The types of news conferences

A *news briefing* is a low-key alternative that can provide the advantage of offering additional information to the media without the fanfare of a news conference. Reporters can be given a news release and background material in advance and told that if they wish further information, a briefing may be held, depending on the response.

A similar approach is to distribute materials and tell the media that the mayor, city manager, or other spokesperson has cleared his or her calendar for a specific period and will be available to handle inquiries from the media concerning the topic. This sometimes is referred to in the journalists' trade as a *media availability.*

Localities that reserve the full-fledged news conference for topics appropriate for such a buildup can be more confident that reporters will attend when conferences are scheduled.

Having determined that a topic warrants a news conference, local government staff members should plan carefully to ensure its success.

An agenda should be set, speakers selected, and time set aside to brief staff who will be involved in the conference. Likely questions should be determined, information gathered, and the local government's stance defined, if appropriate. In many instances it is wise to have a practice conference, with staff asking questions of the planned speakers. This type of exercise can be helpful when the city faces any controversial issue, whether or not a news conference is called. It helps clarify the government's position and can reveal any inconsistencies or gaps in the available information before policy statements and news releases are developed, reporters are faced in interviews, or inquiries from the public are fielded at hearings or forums.

Practical preparation for news conferences

When scheduling a news conference, consider deadlines for print and broadcast media. The specific restrictions on weekly newspapers should also be a consideration, if their reporters are the ones who cover local government most regularly.

Before making the final decision on the day and time for the conference, check into the possibility that other events already scheduled will compete with the conference for media coverage.

Phone representatives of appropriate media to inform them of the news conference. Even if written announcements are distributed by mail or fax, follow-up calls are a good idea, both to remind the media and to give local government an idea of who plans to attend.

Select a room for the conference that is appropriate for the number of reporters, photographers, and video crew members expected to attend. When in doubt, go small. It is much better to pull in some extra chairs if the turnout exceeds expectations than to provide a cavernous room for two or three reporters and a lone photographer.

Depending on the subject of the news conference, a news release may be supplemented with background material, photocopied documents, photographs, artists' renderings, and color slides or even videocassettes for television. The media packets should be given in advance to the speakers to allow time for review. The packets can also be sent to reporters unable to attend the conference.

If possible, provide something of greater visual interest at the conference than a row of people behind a table. Models, maps, charts, graphs, diagrams, and other props are important for both television coverage and newspaper photographs. In selecting props, remember that any copy should be easily readable, that small details will most likely be undiscernible, and that the fabrication should be of high quality. If television coverage is expected, provision should be made for cameras, lights, and microphones.

Allow some time after the conference when speakers will be available for taped interviews with radio reporters, videotaping for television, or mini-interviews with newspaper reporters who want to develop special angles that were not presented during the news conference. (For more information on public speaking occasions such as news conferences, see Chapter 9.)

Photography

Some cities and counties have substantial on-staff photographic capabilities, including darkrooms. Many others find the cost of on-staff photography prohibitive. From time to time it is useful to obtain photographs to supply to the media and for other uses, such as slide shows. Several low-cost alternatives are available to the full-time staff photographer:

Student photographers. The faculty of the photography, journalism, or mass-communication departments of local colleges and universities may be glad to locate capable students. Often students will work at intern rates or for college credit in exchange for professional experience and a portfolio of published photographs.

Job-market re-entrants. Local residents returning to the job market may be interested in updating their experience and portfolios and might—at least in the short term—be interested in arrangements similar to those offered to students.

Local government staff members. In some cities and counties, various departments have skilled amateur photographers on staff. Those employees have access to government-owned cameras and lenses and take shots of their departments' various events and services. Developing and printing is handled by the city or county graphics shop or by an outside vendor.

Interns. Cities and counties that have intern programs can benefit if interns assigned to the public information office have skills in photography.

Special arrangements with professionals. Although professional photographers usually have set rates and policies about ownership of negatives and other matters, special arrangements are worth checking into. One city maintains its own files of negatives. The staff has agreements with photographers who take the shots, develop the film, and provide contact sheets. The city then prints the photographs and keeps the negatives available for future use. Maintaining good relations with these photographers and meeting the government's part of the agreement is important, both to maintain goodwill in the local business community and to keep the photographers willing to continue the arrangement.

Share the costs. Although purists might shudder at this "perversion" of the traditional adversarial relationship between media and government, it may be possible to share with a newspaper the cost of hiring a freelance photographer. Different shots can be selected by the paper and the local government so that the photographs the city or county distributes are not the same as those published by the newspaper.

In implementing cost-cutting measures, make sure in advance that both parties fully understand the nature of the arrangement and that you are not inadvertently violating local government regulations or agreements with labor unions.

The following further guidelines can help prevent unnecessary expense and waste:

Research the need. Whether photography is handled by an employee or by an outside vendor, both materials and labor are expensive. So it pays to know whether local newspapers have policies or agreements with their photographers that preclude using all photographs supplied or that prevent using them in certain sections of the newspaper. Policies concerning use of supplied photographs vary widely. Some weeklies and small-town papers are overjoyed if the government can provide timely, good-quality photographs. Some dailies will use only photographs taken by their staff photographers for news sections but will accept shots to accompany news releases used in listings of coming events. Check your local situation.

Consider the format. Don't waste money by distributing shots that would be difficult to use. A photo in horizontal format will generally have the best chance of being used. Vertical shots requiring a deep, narrow space will make page layout difficult.

Limit the number of people to appear in the photograph. Photographs of more than six or eight people are unlikely to be used because of the space required for identification in the accompanying story or cutline (caption). Also, each face will be so small that the identities will be difficult to discern.

Primer in communications law

As a public manager, you have found that your words and actions are constantly spotlighted, publicized, and scrutinized. As a manager of information, it is essential that you understand the laws affecting communications.

Here is a brief summary of significant communications law areas. Have your legal staff or outside experts periodically brief you and your staff on the latest developments in the following areas of law:

Defamation

Defamation—also referred to as "libel" if printed or broadcast, and "slander" if spoken—includes communication that exposes an individual to hatred, ridicule, or contempt; lowers him or her in the esteem of others; causes him or her to be shunned; or injures his or her business or calling.

Libel per se indicates the specific words of the defamatory message. *Libel per quo* occurs when facts extrinsic to the exact words add additional meaning that results in defamation.

The U.S. Supreme Court decision in *New York Times Co. v. Sullivan* held that public officials may successfully sue for defamatory communication that focuses on their official conduct only if they can prove either:

1. Known falsehood—the communicator knew the statement or comment was false

2. Reckless disregard for the truth—the communicator acted recklessly when considering the truth of the message.

Sloppy reporting is not the same thing. Look for fabricated quotes, headlines that defame by distorting the meaning of a story, and other actions that show blatant disregard or ill will.

Tip: Tape all communication with the press. And tape all your public statements.

Public officials, in turn, should be particularly cautious when they communicate. In most states, private citizens, including non-policy-making subordinates, only have to show negligence to win a defamation action.

Tip: Avoid unproven accusations and name calling.

Intentional emotional distress

In many states, an alleged victim who can prove an act or a pattern of communication behavior intentionally designed to cause emotional distress may sue for damages. Tip: This has particular significance in management and leadership scenarios. A temperamental management style may be a quick ticket to the courthouse.

Privacy

Privacy is best defined as the right to be let alone. "Invasion of privacy," as the tort is known, generally involves one of four types of actions:

1. Making public private matters in violation of state or federal privacy laws or community norms.

2. Intruding on a person's physical solitude, as in trespass.

3. Portraying an individual falsely. Examples include placing a person's name on a petition, or falsely alleging their support for a view or program.

4. Using an individual's identity without his or her consent for commercial gain.

Tip: Review your state privacy and confidentiality laws. Make certain your policies and staff actions comply with them.

Copyright

Proprietary communication is protected by copyright. This may include written and spoken communication, video and audio recordings, software, art, and other works.

Tip: Be certain to obtain written permission before duplicating and distributing copyrighted work to your staff or the public.

Freedom of information

James Madison wrote: "A popular government without popular information or the means of acquiring it is but a prologue to a farce or a tragedy, or both." Freedom-of-information (FOI) laws are written to provide public access to government information.

While often considered a press tool, FOI laws should be given a broader view: they are written to serve everyone. A wise public manager recognizes that cooperation with FOI laws can generate public support, whereas a secretive approach may raise doubts and distrust.

Also recognize the research opportunities that state and federal FOI laws offer you and your staff. Use the opportunity to gather timely information.

Tip: Be helpful. Develop a "Glad you asked" attitude when dealing with freedom-of-information requests. Such as attitude can generate public interest and awareness and stimulate public support.

Regulations of the Federal Communications Commission

The increased use of public broadcasting and government cable-television channels by localities calls for awareness of the rules of the Federal Communications Commission. Have a staff attorney include broadcast regulations as one of his or her specialty areas.

Source: Frederick Talbott (President, Talbott Communications, Franklin, Tennessee).

Order extra prints. Unit cost decreases with the number of prints ordered, so have file copies made for future use.

See Chapter 10 for more information on photography.

Legal issues in media relations

Staff members who have media contact should be aware of the legal implications of their actions. It is not necessary to know all the laws that affect public communications, but be familiar with some of the principal issues and possible problems:

Freedom-of-information laws and the right to privacy

Statutes concerning libel and slander

Copyright laws, which protect publications, artwork, photographs, audiovisual materials, literature, and music.

Generally, the members of the staff who have the most frequent contact with the media will be required to seek legal advice from the city or county attorney in reviewing news releases, draft statements, contracts, or other materials that concern

Negotiations between management and unions or other employee groups, striking employees, or other labor/management issues

Charges of violation of civil rights made by an employee

The termination or acrimonious resignation of an employee

Any suits in which the local government is involved, either as a defendant or as a complainant

Other civil or criminal cases that are pending

Negotiations concerning distribution or acquisition of property

The use of photographs of individuals in advertising or promotional materials

Relations with freelance photographers, graphic artists, and other design professionals.

Checklist

The most important goal of a media-relations program is to develop a two-way relationship between local government and the media in which the local government takes an active role.

A media-relations program will be significantly more effective if it is carefully planned and organized and one person is made responsible for coordination with the media.

Be sure to consider carefully the range of choice beyond straight news stories—public service announcements, reader-exchange columns, and talk shows, for example—as you seek the most effective way to get your message across in each instance.

Effective media relations depend on knowledge, professionalism, and, above all, honesty in dealings with reporters and editors.

Keep in mind that the various media—newspapers, radio, and television stations—have differing patterns of organization, different formats, different deadlines, and different news policies. It is important to be aware of these differences and work within them consistently.

Learn to think and write like a reporter to increase the likelihood that your news releases will get used by the various media.

News conferences and media briefings provide opportunities for exchange and discussion of issues and should be used only for topics that warrant the discussion format.

All local government staff members who have contact with the media should be aware of the legal implications of certain of their actions.

III

Communication Techniques and Tools

7 Communication Planning and Staffing

The first part of this book (Chapters 1 and 2) addresses themes that underlie communication in the context of local government: the need for effective communication and the significance of identity and image. The second part (Chapters 3 through 6) covers communication between local government and its four most important "publics": citizens, elected officials, city employees, and the news media.

The third and final section of the book (Chapters 7 through 11) covers specific techniques and tools of communication that are used in offices of local government. As the introductory chapter of this section, this chapter deals with two major areas of importance to the local government: (1) how to organize the communication function to achieve organizational goals in the most cost-effective way and (2) how to develop a general communication plan, as well as specific plans for various communication needs.

The size of a local government will largely determine the size and capabilities of its communication staff. Other factors that come into play include (1) the way a local government has traditionally handled communication matters and (2) the communication philosophy of the current administration. Considerations such as the strengths and weaknesses of the incumbent communication staff also affect the effectiveness of the organization in its communication duties.

Many cities and counties have master plans for land use and zoning. Many also have strategic plans for economic development, revitalization of the central business district, and dealing with natural disasters such as floods and earthquakes. There are more and more communication plans for specific undertakings such as an impending bond referendum or development of a new park or community center. However, few localities have developed comprehensive communication plans. Communities that develop comprehensive communication plans are more likely to see their communication efforts bring the results they want.

This chapter covers the following topics:

Organizing the communication function

Changing the way communication is organized

The communication plan

What results do you want from your communication program?

REPACE: Six steps to success

Research: An information base

Evaluating research

The planning process

Selecting target audiences

Setting goals and objectives

Developing communication strategies

Time lines, budgets, and assignments for specific tactics

Implementing the communication plan

Internal communication during implementation of the plan

Evaluating the program.

Organizing the communication function

Colorado Springs, Colorado, has a director of public relations. College Station, Texas, has a public relations and marketing manager. Oklahoma City, Oklahoma, has a public information officer. Charlotte, North Carolina, has a director of the department of public service and information. Scottsdale, Arizona, has a director of communications and public affairs. San Jose, California, has a director of marketing and public relations. James City County, Virginia, has a communications coordinator. Dallas has a manager of marketing and media relations. Clearly there is diversification in their job titles.

The people with these different titles, though, have one major thing in common: Although their duties are as varied as their titles, they are professional communicators who are responsible at least in part for the communication activities of the local government that employs them. Given the plethora of communication titles and the variety of functions across the United States, it is understandable that a local government official might ask: How should I organize the communication function?

In a memorable scene at the beginning of the movie *Butch Cassidy and the Sundance Kid,* an upstart member of the Hole in the Wall Gang challenges the Sundance Kid for leadership of the gang. They decide to settle the matter by fighting. Sundance asks what the rules of the fight are. His scruffy challenger responds, "The rules are that there ain't no rules."

So it might seem to a local government official talking to counterparts around the country about the best way to organize the communication function. With only minor variations, localities are similarly structured. Planning is handled by the planning director, legal matters by the city or county attorney, and personnel matters by the personnel or human-resources director. But when it comes to the communication function within local government, the rule seems to be that "there ain't no rules."

Community size

The size of a locality is one consideration in determining how to organize government communications. Charlotte, North Carolina (approx. pop. 400,000), has a departmental director and a staff of communication specialists. That city even has television production personnel assigned to a sophisticated telecommunications center. Charlotte has established a national reputation in telecommunication productions, serving as a model for many other communities. Such an extensive program, however, is unnecessary for much smaller communities such as Urbandale, Iowa (approx. pop. 25,000), where the city manager serves as a one-person communication staff and the city's telecommunications program operates within the context of the greater metropolitan area of Des Moines, Iowa.

Functional responsibilities

Function is another consideration. As noted throughout this book, most local government officials must concern themselves with communication with four major target audiences:

Citizens

Elected officials

Local government employees

The news media.

The ideal situation is to have a director of communication with responsibility for overseeing communication activities that affect all four of those target groups. Such consolidation of functional responsibility would allow a coordination of all of the local government's communication activities, greatly enhancing the chances of success of all of them.

Taking that route, however, is not so simple and straightforward as it seems. Some city and county managers believe that communication with elected officials, for example, is the exclusive domain of the manager and should not be delegated to anyone else—for many reasons, one of them being the perils of exposing a staff member to possible political cross fire between local elected officials. Even in such a case, however, the communication director can assist the manager, especially with communication strategy and tactics involving elected officials.

Another organizational "turf" is communication with local government employees. In the past, responsibility for that activity often rested with the director of personnel or human resources. The city or county manager generally is either pleased with the communication job that the personnel director is doing or else is reluctant to transfer such an important function of the organization without a pressing need to do so.

The result is that some cities and counties have a communication director who produces regular newsletters and annual reports for citizens, while the employee newsletter is produced by the personnel department. That type of division of functions within the organization not only hampers (and in some cases prevents) a coordinated organizational communication program, it can also lead to counterproductive competition between local government offices.

PIO—or director of communication? Not many years ago, local governments that had a communication professional on staff typically called that person the "public information officer" (PIO) and assigned him or her the primary (and sometimes sole) function of dealing with the local news media. Usually someone either from the news media or with a media background was recruited to do the job. Many factors have caused that model to change over the years, including the following:

The growing importance of communication as a function of local government management (discussed in detail in Chapter 1)

The growing number of communication professionals—both generalists and specialists—in the private sector

The emergence of professional communication as a career choice for which an increasing number of universities offer courses and degree programs.

Many cities and counties still have a PIO whose primary responsibility is to deal with the news media. Nevertheless, the trend is toward having a director of communication or of public relations who is an experienced professional communicator. That person will be entrusted with a number of functional responsibilities—almost always still including media relations.

Outlining job expectations
When a local government establishes or reorganizes a public information program, the program will get off to a surer start if there is a clear understanding between top management and the public information officer of what the PIO's job will entail. A sample memo outlining job expectations and means of meeting those expectations is available from the California Association of Public Information Officials (CAPIO), 1400 K Street, Sacramento, California 95814.

As more and more local governments take on "marketing" functions, the communication director frequently is given or assumes the responsibility for marketing municipal services. Sometimes that person is given a new title (such as director of communication and marketing) to reflect the additional duties. Then the director of communication or public communication officer sometimes is given other assignments not closely related to either communication or marketing, such as employee training, handling grievances, or running the print shop. In those cases, a manager should study the functions to determine whether they are an essential part of the mission of the communication office or department, or whether they might more logically belong in some other more suitable office.

Departmental communicators

Some cities and counties are large enough to have communication professionals in some or all of their operating departments. For example, one large East Coast city does not employ only the usual spokespersons for the mayor, the fire and police departments, and the school system. That city also employs information specialists of various types in the following departments, among others:

Municipal art museum

Housing and community development

Public library system

Public works

Recreation and parks

City zoo.

Organizations and facilities that operate on separate or "enterprise" budgets, such as a utility department or a county arena, are also likely to have their own public information officer.

Local government managers should try to ensure that the efforts of department-level communicators are consistent with the communication policies of the organization as a whole. It is not in the organization's best interests to have communication "fiefdoms" throughout the structure. One city solved this problem by forming an organization of professional communicators within the city government and having a meeting

---

Government communicators form regional association

Hampton Roads is the second-largest region in the state of Virginia and ranks just behind the Northern Virginia area as the fastest growing. Almost 1.5 million people make up this region, which is the nation's 27th largest metropolis.

A representative group of public information directors from Hampton Roads local governments met in August 1988, to discuss common problems associated with communicating with citizens. These included competition for media attention and the duplication of efforts to get the same message out.

The communication professionals formed an innovative regional organization, the Hampton Roads Municipal Communicators (HRMC). The group represents the cities of Chesapeake, Hampton, Newport News, Norfolk, Portsmouth, Suffolk, and Virginia Beach, as well as the counties of James City and York.

After designing a logo and a video public service announcement promoting a regional focus, the group established the following goals:

To consolidate efforts to increase public awareness about issues common to all Hampton Roads localities

To serve as a regional resource for the Hampton Roads media

To share information that would enable all members to serve their municipalities most effectively.

The group discussed and resolved common problems, shared and compiled resources, and met with representatives from the print and broadcast media. To minimize travel between localities, the HRMC rotated meeting locations and relied heavily on fax machines to transmit paperwork.

Source: Michele Frisby, "Public Information: Educating and Communicating," *MIS Report* (March 1991), pp. 12-13.

once a month to touch base on current communication issues in local government. They would bring one another up to date on work in progress, discuss new faces and trends in the local news media, and coordinate their efforts in graphics and other areas of common interest and responsibility. The organization was chaired by the city's director of communication and became an effective means of making sure the communicators communicated among themselves.

The local government might also want to work on communication issues with other governmental and quasi-governmental agencies in the region. A regional association of public sector communicators is often an effective way to do it. Membership in such groups can offer a wider perspective.

Responsibility for communication

Regardless of the number, location, titles, and functions of full-time professional communicators within a local government, the point made at the opening of Chapter 2 merits reiteration here: Everyone within the organization has a responsibility to be an effective communicator for the organization, and the manager, assistant managers, department heads, and division heads are the chief communicators. Specific communication responsibilities, projects, and tasks can be—and in many cases should be—delegated to others within the organization. However, there is no question that the ultimate responsibility for communication rests at the top.

Changing the way communication is organized

Several possible current political scenarios can cause a city or county to take a fresh look at its communication organization. Some typical situations are described below.

Under new management

A new city or county manager comes on board, with new and different ideas about how the communication function should be organized. For clues to how the new manager will assess communication needs, staff members can take a look at the communication organization where their new boss last worked, if he or she comes from outside the community. If the new manager's former staff included a director of communication or a public information officer, the odds are good that he or she will feel more comfortable with a position of that kind in the new office also.

Departure of a key communicator

A longtime director of communication or public information officer leaves the city or county. Often a city or county communication office is built around one or more individuals who staff that office. A director of communication or PIO functions as an internal "status quo" mechanism, tending to keep the communication organization pretty much as it is.

When a communication director leaves the organization after a long tenure, there is often a reassessment of the communication organization. Management wants to determine whether any changes need to be made. This juncture may well be the time when the title of "public information officer" is changed to the more current "director of communication" or even "director of public relations."

In such instances, some cities and counties hire consultants to survey the internal communication needs of the local government. Consultants will research what other cities and counties are doing with their communication organizations and help to resolve issues that may have been the subject of debate or even conflict in the past. (One such issue might be that of responsibility for production of the employee newsletter.) The usefulness of such consultants will depend on how carefully they are chosen. As with the selection of any consultant, the local government must take care to chose a company or person with considerable expertise, relevant experience, and evident enthusiasm for the task. Sometimes an internal committee or task force can serve the same purpose, if staff can be found who meet the criteria of expertise, experience, and enthusiasm.

Learning from a crisis

A crisis or emergency hits the community or the local government, with the consensus being that poor communication was to blame. Some examples: A bond issues fails. A local newspaper goes on an editorial campaign against government waste. The community rejects plans for a major new addition to infrastructure such as an expressway. A major employer leaves the community because of what it considers a lack of cooperation from local government.

Each such crisis will take its toll on the staff who work for local government. The aftermath may be an appropriate time for the city or county to reassess

The level of importance it assigns to communication

The communication training it has given key staff from top management to frontline employees

The way it is organized to handle communication

The way it delegates communication responsibilities

The way communication with the local government's publics is coordinated.

A crisis is a hard way to learn a lesson, but it can provide an opportunity for local government officials to reaffirm that effective communication is absolutely necessary and that the local government has to have the expertise to communicate effectively.

The communication plan

Some local governments understand the value of a written communication plan for specific events such as a vote on a bond issue or the relocation of traffic during construction. But few have written communication plans for their overall operations.

A model master plan

One city with a written master communication plan is Chesapeake, Virginia. Called the City of Chesapeake Public Relations Program, it is prepared by the city's Public Information Department. The written plan was first produced in April 1990. It is updated regularly.

Chesapeake uses the term *public relations* to cover the processes of developing and maintaining effective two-way communication with important target "publics" or audiences. Used in that sense, public relations as a concept is interchangeable with the term *communication* as used throughout this book.

The first paragraph in the Chesapeake plan sets the tone for the document: "Public relations in government, when properly conceived and supported internally, is the most effective tool available to help policymakers and constituents cooperatively formulate and achieve common goals. It is not the job of a single department; it is instead a basic management function relevant to all of the organization's activities." The introduction goes on to note that the public relations (or communication) plan is directly related to and supportive of the following principle from the City of Chesapeake's mission statement: "The employees of the City of Chesapeake are committed to providing quality services to all citizens equitably, in a responsive and caring manner."[1]

The Chesapeake plan, which is more than fifty pages long, has all the components of a good planning document:

It is based on factual information obtained from objective research.

It clearly states the goals of the program.

It defines the target audiences for the city's communication activities.

It lays out the specific strategies and tactics for achieving its goals—including staff assignments, a time line, and a budget.

The plan is discussed in more detail later in this chapter.

Specific communication plans

Although most cities and counties do not have overall communication plans, many local governments develop plans for specific communication projects. Those specific plans are appropriate for occasions when effective communication is crucial. Examples might be the introduction of a new program or concept, the opening of a new facility, the modification or initiation of a service, or an effort to resolve a sensitive public issue.

What results do you want from your communication program?

Before beginning the planning process for a communication program, whether a specific one or a comprehensive one, it is useful to focus on the results you hope for. The following three groups of questions will help you focus on results.

1. *What is the problem?* One way of looking at communication is as a means of solving problems. What exactly is the problem you are trying to solve? How many people does this problem affect? How long has the problem been around? What makes you believe that

---

A comprehensive public relations program: Hanover Park, Illinois
The village of Hanover Park, Illinois (population 31,300), has developed a series of publications designed to keep the public informed and educated.

Resident handbook and village map
Hanover Park's resident handbook and village map are distributed to all new residents, prospective developers, local realtors, and the chamber of commerce. The resident handbook opens with an introduction from the village mayor, who discusses the community's past, present, and future. Quotes from residents on the quality of life in Hanover Park are then interspersed among high-quality, black-and-white and color photographs of community recreational facilities, historic landmarks, public safety facilities, homes, and shopping areas. The publication closes

with an overview from the village manager.

The back pocket of the handbook contains information sheets on state, county, township, and additional services; village services; schools and churches; community organizations; legislators; village permits, ordinances, and regulations; water services; and parks and recreation facilities. The back pocket also holds a map and village directory for municipal administration, emergency services, hospitals, the chamber of commerce, libraries, the post office, churches, schools (by district), community colleges, recreation facilities, transportation services, and shopping centers.

Economic development packet
Hanover Park developed a second 9-by-12-inch package that is used to attract or retain business and development.

The front left-hand pocket of the economic development package contains an introductory brochure that discusses the advantages the village can offer businesses. The postage-paid inquiry response card attached to the brochure enables prospective developers to request information on village demographics and available buildings and sites.

The introductory brochure briefly describes the village's homes, educational system, shopping areas, park and recreational facilities, cultural programs, and health care centers. More comprehensive information concerning each of these areas is included in a descriptive 8-1/2-by-11-inch brochure. A series of separate sheets provide statistical data and information on the village's demographics, health-care and education services, labor force, and transportation and utilities, as well as general information.

Source: Adapted from Michele Frisby, "Public Information: Educating and Communicating," *MIS Report* (March 1991), p. 6.

Figure 7–1 Devising and deploying a communication plan is sometimes depicted as an ongoing, circular process.

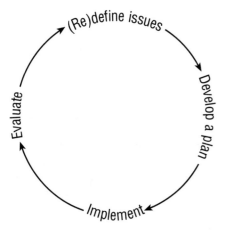

you need to solve this problem, that you need to give it higher priority than other problems? What obstacles are you likely to encounter in trying to solve this problem? How long will it take, and what kind of resources will be needed, to achieve a satisfactory solution?

2. *How do you know it is a problem?* The question is not Why do you *think* it is a problem?—it's How do you *know?* What information do you have that proves that the problem exists? Is this information factual in an objective and scientific sense, or is it based on assumptions and impressions? Does the problem concern identity (what the situation really is) or image (what people perceive the situation to be), or a combination of the two? (For guidance on identity and image, and the importance of distinguishing between them, see Chapter 2.) What are some of the ways of getting the further information you need to define the problem (and the group it affects) more precisely?

3. *What would life be like if this problem didn't exist?* What things would be better? How? Conversely, what things might be worse, and why? Who would be more satisfied, and why? Who would be less satisfied, and why? Envisioning life without the problem can help you gauge its urgency and can also provide insight into possible side effects of trying to solve it. Worse future problems might come from taking action to solve a current problem. It is even possible that solving the problem wouldn't fundamentally change things at all. That would be important to know as early as possible.

The most important part of any communication plan is the thought that goes into defining and deciding on the results you want. To be an effective communicator, you have to know where you're going.

REPACE: Six steps to success

A communication program is a process. That process can be depicted as a circle:

Define issues

Develop a plan

Implement

Evaluate.

Evaluation leads to the redefinition of issues, which prompts redevelopment of the plan. (The process is shown graphically in Figure 7–1.)

Some communicators use a planning model called *REPACE* to guide them through the planning process. REPACE is an acronym for the six steps necessary to develop a successful communication program, whether it be an overall communication plan for a city or county government or a plan for a specific communication undertaking. REPACE stands for

Research

Evaluation of the research

Planning

Action

Communication

Evaluation of the program.

Research   The communication director of a Virginia state agency used to say, "You can act on either what you know or what you think you know. It's all right to act on what you think you know, but you had better be right." Her point was that there is no substitute for *research* as the basis of an action plan. Research can be described as a two-step process:

1. Gather and compile all existing information pertinent to the problem at hand. In this information age, there's always plenty of data available—somewhere. The trick is knowing where and how to look. For local governments, associations such as the International City/County Management Association (ICMA) and the City-County Communications and Marketing Association (3CMA) are good places to start to collect information about local government communication programs. Depending on the nature of the situation, other associations might be of help. Examples are state and national associations of fire chiefs, police chiefs, parks and recreation staff, and communication professionals. (A brief directory of professional organizations for communication professionals is provided in Chapter 6.) Extensive demographic information can be derived from Census Bureau data. Local, regional, and state planning organizations can provide information or sources of information. So can area colleges and universities. The local news media are sometimes willing to help local government staff research a topic.
2. Determine how much additional research is needed. Regardless of how much information is available, it will probably be necessary to gather more, if only to validate findings based on the data you already have. Several informal and formal research methods are discussed in Chapter 2.

Evaluation of research   After you have gathered enough information on which to base a good plan, the next step is to *evaluate* that research. Evaluation consists of the following stages:

1. A careful reading of all the information at hand
2. A determination of positive and negative trends that emerge from the data or opinions gathered
3. An analysis of specific opportunities and problems signaled by the research
4. A list of findings and recommendations that emerge from the process of research and evaluation.

Chesapeake's communication plan includes a section called "situation analysis." It covers (1) historical and background factors, (2) the organization of the municipality, and (3) current issues and problems identified by the city's quantitative and qualitative research. As part of its communication programming, each year Chesapeake conducts a public opinion survey and uses the results to update its communication program.

Planning   The purpose of the research and evaluation processes is to help define the breadth and depth of a problem; then the plan shows how to solve it. In REPACE, the *planning* process involves the following steps:

1. Selecting the target audiences who are to be the focus of the communication plan

2. Setting goals and objectives for the program
3. Developing broad communication strategies to achieve the goals
4. Settling on specific tactics and identifying the time line, budget, and assignments for each tactic or step of the plan.

Selecting target audiences

For the most part there is no such thing as communicating with "the general public." Communication programs are much more effective if they are designed with the express purpose of achieving results with a limited group of people (or target audience)—the more limited the better. Some people share physical, social, and psychological traits. For purposes of communication, we can group them by those traits. (The concept of target audiences is discussed in depth in Chapters 1 and 3.)

Communication programs are more effective if designed to achieve results with a limited group of people.

Chesapeake's communication plan focuses on four major target audiences (called "significant publics" in the city's report): (1) adult residents of the city, (2) news media, (3) business and service organizations, and (4) adults living near but not in the city of Chesapeake. Each of those is divided into subgroups. The first major audience, adult residents of Chesapeake, is divided into eight subgroups, primarily by address. The second major audience, the regional news media, is divided into those based in Chesapeake and those based outside the city. The third major audience, the Chesapeake business and service community, has three subgroups. The fourth major audience, adult residents of the region who do not live in Chesapeake, has no subgroups. The plan notes that many communication activities of the city government affect other audiences not listed in the plan, "such as local school-age children, senior citizens, state legislators, tourists, and many others as the need arises."

In many communication programs, especially community relations programs, it is necessary to deal with a large number of groups: neighborhood groups, interest groups, business associations, civic clubs, and church groups. Therefore, careful identification of all potential audiences is necessary. Priorities must be decided on, to determine which of the groups are appropriate targets for the communication program.

One technique of setting priorities for target audiences is called *AIM*, an acronym for *action, information, and monitor*. The target audiences are divided into three groups, on the basis of the urgency of the need to communicate with them. The *action* group is the top-priority group. It includes target audiences that are essential to the success or failure of the communication program. The *information* group, the second in priority, includes target audiences that need to be kept informed periodically but do not have to be involved on a daily basis. The third priority, the *monitor* group, includes those target audiences that can be monitored periodically to determine whether their priorities, composition, and interests have changed. The priority of target audiences often changes during the communication program, so that an audience that starts out in the "monitor" category may move into the "information" category, or even into the "action" category.

Setting goals and objectives

Effective communication can be equated with getting results. Therefore, the managers of communication programs in local government must state the goals of a communication program in clear terms. The goal statements are crucial to the success of a program, because they define the results the program is designed to achieve.

Setting your goals, then, is the next step. What makes a goal a good one? Good goals have the following three characteristics: They are *ambitious, attainable,* and *measurable.*

Goals should be ambitious

If the purpose of a communication program is to achieve results, the results sought must be worth making the effort. Unambitious goals do not challenge people to do their best work and hence do not challenge the local government and the community to fulfill their potential.

Unambitious goals do not challenge people to do their best work.

Several decades ago, community leaders in Atlanta, Georgia, laid out a series of goals for the community that seemed almost too ambitious. Atlanta's leaders intended the goals to be aggressively ambitious; they were a major part of the leaders' vision for the city. One of the goals was to build a stadium capable of attracting franchises in major-league baseball and football. This was for a city that had never had a major-league team in either sport and had no clear prospects of getting one. The community built its stadium, and the teams did come. Subsequently, the city attracted major-league basketball and other top sports attractions as well. In the years that followed, Atlanta learned to set even more ambitious goals, and the decision to locate the 1996 Summer Olympics there has been one of the more interesting results. But perhaps none of this would have come about without the city's having set itself challenging and ambitious goals.

Goals should be attainable

Do you have consensus on a lofty goal? Do you have the resources to achieve it? Do you have people committed to doing the heavy lifting involved in seeing the task through? If so, you're probably on the right side of that thin line between high ambition and self-delusion, regardless of precedent and the carping of skeptics.

"Ten Commandments" for communication situations

In the December 1991 issue of *3cma,* the national newsletter of the City-County Communications and Marketing Association (3CMA), Peggy Calliham, public relations and marketing manager of College Station, Texas, offered her "Ten Commandments for Holding a Bond Election." The principles she espouses apply to most local government communication situations:

1. Seek grassroots citizen support.

2. Survey your citizens to test the waters.

3. Council agreement on issues is critical to success.

4. Don't place too many propositions on the ballot.

5. Timing is everything. Plan ahead.

6. Plan for the opposition.

7. Get professional help for the campaign if possible.

8. Make it easy to understand.

9. Be careful not to appear too flashy or expensive with promotional tools.

10. Get the voters out to the polls.

Source: Peggy Calliham, "The Ten Commandments for Holding a Bond Election," *3cma Newsletter,* December 1991, p. 1.

Some communications lend themselves more to assessment by measurement than others.

Goals should be measurable

A goal statement must be based on a goal that can be measured either in quantitative or qualitative terms or by a combination of both. One of Chesapeake's goals was "to increase the number of residents who express approval and support for the city's programs and activities." Such a goal statement would be useless if the city government did not know what percentage of residents then expressed approval (which it in fact did know) and did not plan to measure improvement at some point in the future (which it did).

The effectiveness of some communication programs can be measured relatively easily. For example, the communication program for a bond referendum can be measured by answering this question: Did the bond issue succeed or fail? Some communications lend themselves more to assessment by measurement than others. For example, communication programs designed to reduce water consumption or increase circulation of library books lend themselves to quantified goal statements.

Developing communication strategies

After setting communication goals (that is, deciding on the results you want), the next step in the planning process is to develop strategies suited to achieving those goals.

The first task is to list all of the strategies that might contribute to success. Any possible strategy must be weighed on the bases of cost (in terms of money and time) and effectiveness. Three variables are the most relevant and basic in any communication strategy: *time, money,* and *quality.* If you have plenty of time, it is possible to achieve high quality with a limited amount of money. If you have plenty of money, there is no problem producing high quality in a short time. If you demand high quality, then expect to either spend more money or take more time. You cannot expect to develop and implement a high-quality program on a limited budget in a short period of time.

For example, suppose you want to conduct a sample survey of the attitudes of citizens in your community. High quality would undoubtedly be important, since a low-quality survey would be unreliable and therefore useless. If time were short, you could hire a professional research company to design and conduct your research project, and you could expect to pay a top rate for the work. If funds were in short supply but time were not, you might go to a local university and enlist a graduate marketing class to help you with your survey. Given enough time, the class could produce high-quality results on a low budget. The City of Virginia Beach, Virginia, faced with the need to obtain feedback from citizens, worked around a tight budget by empaneling a committee of city employees to oversee the research, with the volunteer assistance of a locally based professional research company.

Goals

It is a good idea to consider each goal area of the program. The Department of Public Utilities in Richmond, Virginia, developed a master communication plan with eight goal areas:

1. Strategic planning
2. Employee relations
3. Customer relations
4. Intragovernmental relations

5. Intergovernmental relations
6. Richmond citizens
7. Special publics
8. Media relations.

Strategies

The department's communication consultant laid out fifteen different strategic approaches, and each of them was analyzed for each of the eight major goal areas. The strategic approaches were as follows:

1. Communication planning
2. Issues management
3. Management counseling
4. Media relations training
5. Damage control/crisis communication planning
6. Annual report
7. Employee relations training review
8. Direct customer communication
9. Customer research
10. Department newsletter
11. Speakers bureau
12. Department audiovisual presentation
13. Ongoing news releases
14. Community relations
15. School communication program.

A useful matrix

The result of this strategic planning was a matrix that listed strategic approaches down the left column and goal areas across the top. Each strategic approach was assessed for each goal area. In the assessment process it became clear that some of the strategies applied to only one goal area, whereas some of them applied to a number of goal areas. For example, the department newsletter applied only to employee relations, whereas an issues-management strategy applied to all fifteen goal areas. The outcome was interesting in a number of different ways. For example, the department's highest-priority goal area was customer relations—fourteen of the strategies applied to that one goal area.

Assessing and prioritizing

After weighing all the strategies, it is possible to assign each of them a priority order to achieve the goals.

Generally it is not a good idea to rely on only one strategy to achieve all your communication goals. An employee newsletter can be a very effective employee-relations tool. But its effectiveness is increased when it is a part of a communication program that includes staff meetings, employee bulletin boards, employee incentive programs, employee training, and other communication strategies. The communication plan for the opening of a new city or county facility could effectively combine a direct-mail brochure, news releases, public service announcements, selected paid advertising, community meetings, and a high-profile opening ceremony. If you select more than one strategy, carefully coordinate the strategies to ensure that they are working together to help achieve the goal.

It is not a good idea to rely on only one strategy to achieve all your communication goals.

Three interlocking strategies

Although a single-strategy approach can create problems, it is better to concentrate the communication effort on a few strategies rather than to try a large number of them at once. With time and money often in short supply, it is generally more effective to focus your limited resources than to spread them thin. Put another way, it is better to do a few things well than do many things poorly. One helpful guide is the rule of three: One or two strategies are probably too limited for you to achieve your goal, whereas more than three probably means that you are stretching your resources too thin. If you were introducing a new health-care plan for employees, for example, you might (1) develop a flier to distribute to each employee, (2) include an article in the employee newsletter, and (3) arrange a series of personal briefings for various city or county department staff members. Concentrating on these three strategies would help ensure achievement of your communication goal.

> *It is better to concentrate the communication effort on a few strategies rather than to try a large number at once.*

Time lines, budgets, and assignments for specific tactics

The goals are in place, and strategies have been identified, weighed, and decided on. The next step is to set up a specific work program within each of the strategic areas. The work program consists of three parts: a *time line,* a *budget,* and *assignments.* In some communication programs, this three-part work program is called the *tactical plan* because it lays out the specific tactics by which the broad strategic plan will be accomplished.

Time lines

Establishing a *time line* entails answering the following questions: When does work on this component begin? When will it be completed? What are deadlines for each of the intervening steps in the work program (drafting material, obtaining management clearance, selecting material, etc.)? Each discrete task within the work program needs to be identified, and a deadline must be set for each. Consider using a PERT (Program Evaluation and Review Technique) chart or other time-planning method to lay out the time line, especially if (as is likely) some of the steps occur simultaneously.

A budget

A *budget* for each component of the communication program will include all out-of-pocket costs, such as travel, telephone, fax costs, and other expenses (unless they are budgeted elsewhere in the organization). The budget is like the time line: it should be tight but realistic. A communication program that is underbudgeted is doomed to failure. In some governments, it may be required that the budget be synchronized with the time line so that projected expenditures are shown by month or quarter during the fiscal year.

Making assignments

The third component of the work program is *assignment* of personnel. Who is in charge of each component of the communication program? Who is going to do the actual work? Who will be expected to assist that person? What outside assistance will be necessary, if any? The work program becomes a useful management tool when it combines the assignments with the time line and enables you to answer this question:

Will the people assigned to complete this work within the specified time period be able to do so?

Action

If the communication program is written properly, its implementation (taking *action* to get the job done) should not be difficult. It is primarily a matter of the administrator of the program making sure the appropriate staff carry out their assignments within budget and on deadline.

It is rare that every component of the communication program gets accomplished exactly according to plan. For one thing, it is difficult at the start of a program to anticipate every possible need and potential glitch. Therefore the time line and budget are really estimates based on the planners' best guesses. Adjustments will be necessary—and should be expected.

Planning for the unexpected

An early-warning system that sends up a red flag when deadlines seem unlikely to be met or budgets appear inadequate is an important part of the process of executing a plan. For example, if one of the components of a communication program is development of a brochure, the manager of the program must monitor progress to ensure that the brochure can be produced within the deadline and budget in the plan. If it becomes clear that more money or more time will be needed, the earlier that is known the better, since delay of the brochure may have a ripple effect on other components of the program.

The need for flexibility

The communication plan is a road map to success, not a rigid master plan that must be followed no matter what. One component of the program may be much more successful than anticipated, for example, so that later strategies may not be necessary. For example, a communication plan to introduce new utility rates might include a news-media briefing, appearances by the utilities director on local radio talk shows, and a utility-bill insert (per the rule of three). The first two parts of that plan may be so successful in informing utility customers and winning their acceptance that the insert becomes unnecessary.

Unanticipated problems may require the local government to reallocate either time or money or both.

Certain opportunities present themselves during the execution of the program, and communicators should be flexible enough to take advantage of those opportunities. For example, the communication program may call for in-house production of videotaped public service announcements, with a budget to support that activity. But a television station may volunteer to produce those PSAs at no cost to local government. This opportunity, if accepted, may free some staff time and money from within the communication program. That time and those funds could then be used to upgrade some other strategic area of the program—for example, a planned newsletter or flier.

Unanticipated obstacles or problems may present themselves during the execution of the program. These could well require the local government to reallocate either time or money or both. For example, a communication program might call for a series of community briefings on a topic, briefings that would involve the top management of the local government. But if there is an emergency, the series of briefings may have to be rescheduled, or replaced with some other strategy, to achieve the communication purpose. The overall communication program should be assessed periodically to determine any adjustments necessary to the work program.

Allowing for managerial review

One of the most common mistakes that local government communicators make when planning communication programs is not to allocate enough time in the schedule to accommodate review and approval of various components of the program by the city or county manager or other administrators. It is unrealistic, for example, to schedule four weeks for a writer to produce copy for the next edition of the employee newsletter and then expect a review and approval from the manager within only one or two days. For one thing, unless the schedule is carefully laid out in advance, the manager may be out of town for a conference or government business at the very time he or she is expected to review and approve the newsletter copy.

In the schedule for a newsletter, time should also be included for rewriting—and reapproval—if those steps are expected to be necessary. The more people required to review and approve communication material, the more time it generally takes. In a communication program, this process is generally called *clearance*. Allocation of ample time for clearance should be based on a combination of prior experience and current expectations.

Communication

During the execution of the program, *communication* is necessary on several different levels. The people involved in executing the program have to communicate among themselves about various components of the program. And the more of them there are, the more complicated that communication process will be. It may also be necessary to keep other people informed during the program. For example, if the communication office is carrying out a community-relations program for the fire department, then the fire chief and other relevant employees in that department should be kept informed as the program progresses.

Along the way, there will be a number of successes, large and small. It is crucial to communicate those successes to everyone who might be affected by the program. For example, the production of a high-quality flier or brochure is in itself an accomplishment, and many people would need to be informed that the brochure was available. A news release describing the brochure, including information on how to get one, would be in order. If the brochure were to win an award or some other kind of accolade, that information would have to be communicated to all concerned. Success breeds success, and people like to be associated with what they consider an effective operation. It is a good tactic to tell "success stories."

The people carrying out the communication program need to be good listeners. They need to constantly seek feedback on the various components of the communication program. Some of the work is just good listening. Some of it will involve actively seeking other people's opinions and ideas as the project progresses. This feedback is invaluable in weighing various parts of the program and making adjustments as it proceeds.

Evaluating the program

The purpose of communication is to get results. Therefore it is important to know whether the communication program has achieved its intended goals. This process of *evaluation* can take several forms. It can take place both continuously during the communication program and after it is over. A program can be evaluated on three aspects: *process, product,* and *outcome.*

Process

The first means of evaluation is to examine the integrity of the *process*. Is each component of the communication program being carried out as planned, on budget and on time? The administrator of the program needs to keep tabs on deadlines and expenditures to ensure that things are going as expected. Problems need to be addressed as soon as possible.

Products

Most communication programs include a number of strategies that result in tangible communication *products:* videotapes, news kits, newsletters, brochures and fliers, annual reports, logos, banners, and buttons, among other things. As each product is completed, its managers and supervisors have an opportunity to evaluate the product from several standpoints:

Overall quality

Quantity

Content

Graphic coordination

Unit cost.

Other considerations also play a part, as do negative factors such as errors and omissions. When the product is not a tangible commodity (for example, a festival, an exhibition, or a ribbon-cutting), there is still an opportunity to critique the event. This critique should be conducted as soon after the event as possible, so that all aspects will be fresh in everyone's mind. The positive aspects of the event should be reviewed first. That should be done first both to build the morale of the team and for another, more practical reason: Critiques that begin with negative factors almost never get to the positive ones. Someone at the critique should make careful notes and circulate them to all participants.

Outcome

The real purpose of the communication program is not to have a good process (on time and on budget) or good products (although they are surely important). The purpose is to achieve some important results with an important target audience. The ultimate test of the program, then, is to ask: Did we achieve the desired *outcome?* As noted above, sometimes the program will have clearly quantitative results (such as the outcome of a bond referendum or the amount of water saved in a conservation program). In other cases, the results may be more qualitative, but they can still be measured by public opinion polling, focus groups, individual interviews, and other means.

The process begins anew The evaluation of the overall communication program and all of its component elements usually leads to changes in the communication plan that produce, in effect, a new plan. This is to be expected, as good communication is a process that requires a continuing commitment on the part of everyone concerned. Occasionally a communication program may be strongly project-oriented, such as one for the opening of a new branch library, and it can be put to bed after the evaluation has been completed. Most of the time, however, the process begins anew.

Checklist

The organization of the communication function within local government depends on a number of factors, including size of the locality and the importance of various communication functions within the local government.

Events that may raise the issue of how the communication function is organized include such changes as the arrival of a new city or county manager, the departure of a longtime director of communication or public information officer, or a crisis or an emergency in the community that is blamed on poor communication.

Although many cities and counties still have a public information officer whose primary concern is media relations, the trend is toward employing a director of communication or public relations who is an experienced professional communicator carrying a number of functional responsibilities.

Everyone within the local government organization has the responsibility to be an effective communicator on behalf of the organization.

Some local governments understand the value of a written plan for a specific communication program, such as an impending bond issue or the rerouting of traffic during construction; few of them, though, have any written communication plan for the overall city or county government.

Three questions are useful in articulating the desired results of a communication program: What is the problem? How do we know it is a problem? What would life be like if we didn't have this problem?

A communication program is a process that can be depicted as a circle: define issues, develop plan, implement, evaluate. Evaluation leads to the redefinition of issues, which in turn prompts the redevelopment of the plan.

REPACE is an acronym for the six steps necessary to develop a successful communication program: *research, evaluation of the research, planning, action, communication,* and *evaluation of the program.*

The planning process involves several steps: selecting the target audiences; setting goals and objectives for the program; developing broad strategies to achieve the goals; and settling on specific tactics and identifying the time line, budget, and assignments for each tactic in the plan.

For the most part, there is no such thing as communicating with the "general public." Communication programs are much more effective if they are planned to achieve results with a limited group of people—the more limited the better.

Good goals share three characteristics: They are *ambitious, attainable,* and *measurable.*

Generally it is not a good idea to rely on one strategy to achieve communication goals. However, it is better to do a few things well than do many things poorly. Using three strategies in tandem is often the best approach to achieving the communication objectives.

One of the most common mistakes communicators make when planning a communication program is not to allow sufficient time in the schedule to accommodate review and approval of various components of the program by the city or county manager or others whose input is required.

As the communication program proceeds, there will be a number of successes, large and small. The successes need to be communicated to everyone who is affected by the program.

The purpose of communication is to get results; therefore it is important to know whether the communication program has achieved its goals. Three ways of evaluating the program are *process, product,* and *outcome.*

Occasionally a communication program may be strongly project-oriented, such as one for the opening of a new branch library, and it can be put to bed after the evaluation is completed. Usually, however, the process begins anew.

8 Interpersonal Communication

Interpersonal communication is the *process* of sharing information and ensuring that the intended message is accurately received. It involves words, actions, feelings, and the environment in which the message is shared. As a matter of fact, words sometimes constitute only a small part of the message. The tone of voice, the style of communication, the working relationship among the communicators, the physical environment in which the message is sent, and past conversations related to the message are some of the factors that determine whether a message is received as intended.

Effective interpersonal communication is crucial to effectiveness in an organization. No single department or unit is responsible for managing interpersonal communication. Nor is it simply management's responsibility to send messages down and hope they are received. It is impossible to delegate communication responsibilities to someone else, even—particularly—if you perceive that you're not an especially good communicator. Effective communication is everyone's responsibility.

Although it is undeniable that extroverted people seem more comfortable communicating in groups, interpersonal communication involves much more than personality. There are distinct skills that you can learn, develop, and hone to improve the way you deal with people in different settings, to strengthen your ability to get your message across, and to improve your effectiveness as a member of your organization. Improving interpersonal communication in organizations begins with learning to understand the way people deal with each other. Equipped with this understanding, you can begin to improve the way you listen, share ideas and feelings, and exchange information.

This chapter examines interpersonal communication with a special emphasis on the way people in local government organizations communicate with one another. Its primary objective is to make the concept of interpersonal communication more tangible, so that you understand what is happening when you talk with people, work with them, or simply pass them in the hall.

It aims to increase your awareness of the important role interpersonal communication plays in organizational effectiveness and to increase your understanding of basic communication processes in order to help you identify obstacles that may interfere with interpersonal communication. It also suggests specific skills you can develop to improve the way you communicate with others.

This chapter covers the following subjects:

Communication theory

Communication and organizational effectiveness

Basic communication processes

Communicating in groups

Skills for improving interpersonal communication.

Communication theory

Although language is a critical element in the effective exchange of information, people who do not speak the same language nevertheless can and do get their messages across. Although a common language makes the exchange of information smoother and quicker, it certainly does not provide any guarantee of effectiveness. The common denominator in communication is the way people interact and behave. For example, a smile followed by a hug says a lot to anyone, regardless of the language he or she speaks.

Interpersonal communication is largely a personal process that involves both the exchange of information (content) and the exchange of

The influence of psychology

on communication theory

cannot be overstated.

behavior (relationships). You probably notice the behavioral side of communication where you work, particularly among the people you deal with regularly. Sometimes what may seem to you a straightforward message is taken the wrong way by someone you work with. That is because more is involved than just the words you are using.

Two fields of study and research have had a significant impact on how we understand interpersonal communication: linguistics and psychology. *Linguistics* is the study of human language as a system, including its structure and characteristics and how it undergoes changes. *Psychology* is the study of mind and behavior.

The marriage of linguistics and psychology has produced several theories and models of communication, including *psycholinguistics, neurolinguistic programming* (NLP), and *syntonics.*[1] These models and theories are concerned with the intricacies of communication processes and (perhaps more important) with the skills required for effective communication.

Some branches of NLP, for example, focus on critical communication skills such as

Sensory acuity, which entails increasing one's intuitive awareness of others, including their skin tone, eye reactions, and muscle changes, all of which send messages about how people respond to messages. Watching how someone's body responds to messages can help the sender determine whether his or her message has been received.

Flexibility, which focuses on reading behavior that sends messages and changing one's own behavior to ensure effective communication. If the return messages—both physical and verbal—indicate a lack of understanding, a skilled communicator makes adjustments to ensure that the message gets across.

Congruence, which emphasizes the importance of agreeing on outcomes and making sure everyone is conscious of those outcomes. Paying attention to defined and shared outcomes leads to better communication.

NLP and related theories of communication emphasize sensitivity to other people's behavior as a key to effective communication. These theories stress that finding the right words to communicate a specific message is only a small part of the process of getting that message across.

The influence of psychology on communication theory cannot be overstated. In his *theory of types,* pioneering psychologist Carl Jung argued that it is possible to discern a consistency in seemingly random variations in human behavior, because people choose to *perceive* and *judge* the world outside themselves in certain basic types of ways. *Perception,* according to Jung's theory, refers to how people gather information and become aware of occurrences, ideas, and other people. *Judgment* refers to how people come to conclusions. How people gather information and arrive at conclusions has a major effect on how they behave and how they communicate.

In the 1960s, Isabel Briggs Myers developed and refined an instrument for determining type in individuals on the basis of Jung's theory. The *Myers-Briggs Type Indicator* (MBTI) is a practical tool for identifying basic preferences by means of a series of questions. Using the MBTI helps individuals become more aware of their own behavior and more sensitive to how different preferences affect day-to-day interaction.[2]

The MBTI identifies four basic pairs of behavioral styles that influence how people act in different situations: *extroversion-introversion, sensing-intuition, thinking-feeling,* and *judging-perceiving.*

Extroversion-Introversion. Extroverts prefer dealing with the external world of action and objects, while introverts are more comfortable with an internal world of concepts and ideas. Extroverts tend to be more comfortable—though not necessarily more effective—as communicators than introverts.

Sensing-Intuition. People are considered "sensing types" if they gather information primarily by relying on information obtained from observable facts or occurrences. By contrast, "intuitive types" rely mostly on meanings, relationships, and possibilities as sources of information. Sensing types use facts to communicate. Intuitive types tend to make leaps of faith, which can create communication gaps if they are dealing with a group of sensing types.

Thinking-Feeling. Some people make decisions by thinking in a detached way about the relevant facts and the logical consequences of a decision. Others, more oriented to their feelings and those of others, take into account values, beliefs, and attitudes related to a decision.

Judging-Perceiving. "Judging types" prefer to act and interact in a decisive, planned, and orderly way. "Perceiving types" prefer a spontaneous, flexible approach to life and events.

The MBTI instrument is an example of a tool that can be used to bring about an understanding of human behavior that will help improve communication processes. Understanding basic differences in people will open channels of communication by making you aware of how behavioral preferences can interfere with communication, by creating an opportunity to talk the language of others whose differences you recognize, and by establishing a climate in which differences are prized as resources for effective total communication instead of being treated as obstacles.

Increasing numbers of local government managers are recognizing the need to build activities into their organizations that acknowledge the behavioral aspect of communication. Instruments such as the MBTI are used in management retreats to help organizational leaders learn which communication style they are most comfortable with, so that they can communicate effectively *and* serve as exemplars of effective communication throughout their organizations. The behavioral tools leaders use to enhance interpersonal communication are generally subtle: for example, communication training for key staff, increased opportunities for interaction, and staff meetings for the purpose of sharing knowledge.

Communication and organizational effectiveness

In 1947, Nobel Prize-winning organization theorist Herbert Simon wrote, "Without communication, there can be no organization, for there is no possibility then of the group influencing the behavior of the individual."[3] A half-century later, despite the subsequent revolution in communication technology, Simon's words still ring true. Basic human communication processes remain essential to achieving organizational goals and getting the job done.

People in organizations communicate for many reasons:

To exchange information about a program, a service, or a complaint so that knowledge may be shared

To give instructions (normally with the expectation that there will be a response to those instructions)

To solve problems and make decisions

To establish themes, messages, and values that define the organization and the people in it

To motivate employees and gain their interest, enthusiasm, and support.

As a local government employee, you communicate regularly with superiors, subordinates, colleagues, elected officials, and citizens. Much of your daily work involves some form of interpersonal communication, such as

Explaining a complicated process or procedure to someone who has little background in what you're talking about

Responding to a citizen who is unhappy about something local government did or failed to do

Giving a specific assignment to a subordinate who may not understand exactly what you want

Meeting with a group of co-workers to discuss a common problem and decide what to do about it.

In all those instances, how well you interact with the people involved will affect your success at getting your message across and getting the job done. You may well supplement the interaction with a written report, a news release, a follow-up note, or a formal presentation to make sure the information is clear, complete, and accurate. But the spontaneous give-and-take that accompanies and highlights the specific information is often what leads to an exchange of meaning among people in organizations. Not surprisingly, some experts have estimated that people in organizations, particularly managers, spend as much as 75 percent of their time engaging in some form of interpersonal communication.

Organizational channels

In all organizations, information is communicated along well-worn channels—some formal and official, others informal, unofficial, and highly variable. These channels of communication can be grouped into three categories: *formal, informal,* and *lateral.* An effective organization relies heavily on all three types of channels to transmit information, make decisions, solve problems, and motivate employees.

Formal channels of communication

Usually running parallel to the hierarchy of the organization, formal channels of communication include reports, memos, staff meetings, policy and procedures manuals, and other documents and activities. Traditionally, information and assignments flowed downward through formal channels; responses flowed upward. The increase in the number of organizations that have moved away from hierarchical structures, however, is changing the way information flows through formal channels.

Employee-involvement techniques such as quality circles and consultative management engage rank-and-file employees in identifying, examining, and solving problems in their workplaces and recommending solutions to management. In a sense, employees in such programs are telling management what is wrong and communicating assignments for solving problems.

If formal channels of communication are to function effectively, information must flow in both directions.

If formal channels of communication are to function effectively, information must flow in two directions at once. More information generally flows downward, because people at higher levels initiate more action and have access to more information. Most of the information that flows up the channels comes in response to the original messages from management.

Communication initiated by subordinates in formal channels is less frequent, except when the manager or supervisor makes it clear that participation and information from the bottom up are not only welcome but expected. Formal employee-involvement programs are a good way to begin and also to maintain the flow of vital communication.[4]

Every message sent through formal channels has one receiver or more. How those receivers react to the message, understand it, and act on it is an important part of the communication exchange. Often the recipients of a message sent through formal channels minimize its importance, or even ignore the message altogether. Meanwhile, the senders assume that the message has been received and understood.

Informal channels of communication

Informal communication is spontaneous, unrestricted, and generally very valuable in an open organization. Informal channels, which supplement formal channels, generally coalesce around social relationships in an organization. This network of relationships provides an informal means of assimilating, analyzing, interpreting, expanding, and adapting information to reflect the interests and needs of various groups. The network manages informal communication channels in order to make sense out of formal communications and ensure cohesion within the organization.

In some organizations, individual employees take on key roles in this informal communication network because of their knowledge, experience, and standing with other employees. Roles such as storyteller, hero, gossip, inside resource, spy, and informal expert may emerge as the network forms and an organizational "culture" evolves. Generally, the stronger the organizational culture, the more powerful the actors in the informal network.[5] Information transmitted through informal channels tends to move quickly and enjoy high credibility.

The informal channels may become busier when formal channels either do not provide enough information or do not provide it when it is expected or needed. Generally it is easier for a manager or supervisor to control and influence the formal channels of communication than the informal channels. No more than a few people decide what information goes into the formal systems, when, and in what format.

Even when a message is originally sent through formal channels, however, it may be reworked, filtered, or distorted as it subsequently makes it way through the informal system. For that reason it is important to be receptive to and involved in both channels regardless of your position in the organization. An effective manager knows that many important messages—some of them accurate, official, and sanctioned, some not—flow through the informal system. By the same token, employees should listen carefully to, participate in, and fairly assess both systems.

You may be tempted to assume that if you heard it first through the informal system it is probably right, and management is trying to withhold the information. But it is not always justified to make such an assumption. The extent to which the organization encourages informal communication, establishes a strong cultural network, and shares important information regularly and completely determines whether the informal network becomes a reliable source of information or a grapevine and rumor mill instead. If people receive a great deal of inaccurate information through an office grapevine, they will be misinformed at best and unwilling to listen to the right information at worst.

Lateral channels of communication

Lateral communication takes place between or among employees who do not work together directly but are at the same level in an organization. Sometimes the lateral channel is considered a part of the informal channel, particularly if it involves little more than social contact among employees or the sharing of marginal information. In recent years, interest has grown in lateral communication as a means of enabling people in organizations to work together more effectively.

Messages that travel through lateral channels move quickly and are considered highly credible.

As public-service programs change and lines of responsibility and authority become less distinct, there may be a need for more regular and even somewhat formal communication across department or division lines without the direct involvement of department heads or managers. Lateral communication helps build links between peers who do similar work, facilitates the exchange of ideas among mid-level personnel with similar specialties, promotes greater coordination, and allows direct contact without forcing a reconfiguration of the official hierarchy.[6]

Because lateral communication tends to be part of the informal system, messages that travel through lateral channels move quickly and are considered highly credible. Modern organizations often require rapid sharing of information—or at least more rapid than the traditional route up and down the hierarchy. An active and legitimate system of lateral communication ensures that people working at the middle and lower levels will develop relationships that will increase the effectiveness of their work.

In some organizations, however, a system of lateral communication can create the impression that the official chain of command is being bypassed. This is why it is important to gauge the credence of the various communication channels in your organization and know how they work. Most managers now recognize that lateral communication will take place anyway through the informal system, so it makes sense to recognize, open up, and otherwise encourage the use of that important channel.

Communication and motivation

Effective communication in organizations involves much more than passing information along. People develop and strengthen relationships through communication. Managers make decisions, accomplish organizational goals, and win the support and commitment of employees through communication. The more employees know about what is important to the organization and what is happening in the organization, the better equipped they are to do their jobs. The ability of a manager or supervisor to give clear assignments, help employees solve problems, and accomplish goals will depend on his or her ability to communicate with others.

Human resource development (HRD) programs in local government organizations can play a crucial role in strengthening organizational communication processes, motivating employees, and increasing organizational effectiveness. Although HRD units are not responsible for interpersonal communication, skilled HRD professionals can increase awareness. And they may assist top managers in designing programs that will respond to needs that employees have expressed.

HRD units can provide employee-orientation programs that define mission, goals, culture, and norms. They can offer skill-development programs that focus on communication. And they can develop performance-appraisal systems that assess how employees get their jobs done as well as what management can do to strengthen the communication environment, motivate employees, and improve the delivery of services.[7]

Basic communication processes

Most communication exchanges involve talking, listening, and actually receiving a message. Talking is generally classified as *oral communication*. Other, wordless aspects of the exchange between a sender and a receiver are classified as *nonverbal communication*. Whether or not the intended message is received will depend on the clarity of the oral communication, the impact of the accompanying nonverbal communication, and the presence or absence of any *barriers* to communication.

Oral communication

Oral communication involves more than just talking. Getting your message across, whether in a spontaneous exchange or a carefully planned presentation, involves thinking not only about what you are saying but also about what is on your mind as you say it, how you are feeling, what you are not saying, who your audience is, and how you can best reach them. Your sensitivity to all the variables that come into play while you are sending an oral message may make the difference between simply being heard and being understood. When conveying an oral message, you need to consider six variables:

1. *The sender.* The person with something to say, whether planned or spontaneous
2. *The message.* The specific information, whether it is data, an idea, a concept, or a feeling that is being transmitted to another person or to a group
3. *The channel.* The format or route used to send the message. The channel may be a speech, a presentation, an informal discussion, or a meeting.
4. *The receiver.* The person or persons who are supposed to be listening to the message. In any conversation, each participant is at times a sender, at times a receiver.
5. *Feedback.* The response, which lets the sender know how well the message is getting across. A request for more information or clarification of a point is an example of oral feedback. Nods and confused looks are other, nonverbal forms of feedback.
6. *Noise.* Factors that affect the way a message is received and heard. These can include actual noises, such as the sound of an electric drill outside a window, or noise in a more figurative sense, such as a personal bias or something unrelated on the receiver's mind that interferes with effective communication.

An experienced public speaker pays attention to all six of these variables. Think about a speech or formal presentation you have attended recently. The person at the rostrum was obviously the *sender*, who had prepared a *message*—the speech—to share with a group of *receivers*—

the audience you were part of. The *channel* was a carefully planned presentation in a formal setting. You may have given the speaker *feedback* in the form of eye contact, a nod, a smile, a frown, or even a catnap. An experienced speaker looks for feedback during a presentation—and may even make "midcourse corrections" on the basis of audience reaction. The presence of a number of catnappers might prompt a speaker to talk faster, shorten the speech, shift to a new topic, or tell a joke.

The attitude of the audience toward a speaker affects the way the speech is received. A speaker who is a controversial figure can expect a lot of internal noise, because everyone will arrive with an opinion that will influence the way he or she receives the message. If the speaker is unfamiliar, audience attitudes are formed the moment he or she appears. This makes the initial contact crucial for the speaker.

In a spontaneous conversation, it is more difficult to identify the variables. Messages are sent and received quickly. In the give-and-take of conversation, it may be difficult to determine which remarks are messages and which ones are feedback. Interpersonal communication often breaks down when nobody is acting as receiver, giving feedback to the first sender. What should be a two-way conversation—a process of sharing information—becomes one-way. Two senders are talking *at* each other, and there is no receiver for either message.

Think about the way messages are exchanged over a two-way radio. Because the sender and the receiver can't see each other, it is hard to tell when the first person has finished sending a message. Therefore, he or she says "over" to indicate that the message is finished and the sender is ready to become a receiver. When two people can see each other, they don't need to say "over," but each sender must at some point become a receiver.

Failure to turn about can turn a conversation, in effect, into two alternating monologues. One speaker goes in one direction and the second goes in another. Instead of sending and receiving, each speaker does nothing more than send a message and then wait for the opportunity to send again.

The presence of a number of catnappers might prompt a speaker to talk faster, shorten the speech, or tell a joke.

Sending a message

One of the keys to getting your message across is choosing words that say what you mean. Choosing words isn't easy, unless you are conveying a simple fact, such as "two plus two equals four." When someone is described as highly articulate, it probably means that he or she is good at selecting, managing, and using words to make messages understood.

When you are the sender, there is something in your mind—an idea, a concept, a thought, or a feeling—that you want to convey. The first step is translating what is in your mind into words that can be shared with someone else. This process is called *encoding*. How well your intended meaning gets from your mind to your receiver's mind may depend on your skill at encoding.

In the process of encoding, you are looking for words that will translate your intended meaning so precisely that the receiver cannot fail to hear and understand exactly what is in your mind. That close a match is difficult to achieve, though, because your idea is flavored, filtered, and defined by your position in relation to the receiver of your message, your role in the exchange of information, your language skills, and even the mood you are in. The same words, moreover, mean different things to different people, so it is important to look for words that not only fit your idea but will also make sense to your audience. You must use the language of your audience if it is to hear and understand your message.

An introductory comment is useful before you begin transmitting an actual message.

Finding the right words for even the simplest message can be difficult, particularly when the message is going to strangers. Think about what happens when you stop someone on the street to ask for directions. There is often a moment when nothing seems to happen. During that moment, the person you stopped is adjusting to the sudden contact, becoming accustomed to your voice, and trying to focus on what you are talking about. Probably the other person will ask you to repeat the question, because he or she has missed the message completely, no matter how clearly you spoke.

You may encounter that moment of adjustment even when you are dealing with co-workers, if you start a conversation abruptly. Even though you and your colleagues may be on the same wavelength, speak the same language, and are accustomed to each other's voices, your message may interrupt someone else's mental processes. The receiver must tune in before beginning to take in your words. That is why an introductory comment is useful before you begin transmitting an actual message.

The base of knowledge you share with your co-workers can be a valuable tool in sending messages—or it can be a serious barrier if you presume too much. It can be a valuable tool for translating your idea into understandable words if you think carefully about the assumptions, knowledge, experience, and background that you already share with those who will receive your message. If you fail to do so, you run the risk of saying too little or using words that do not convey your point clearly and thoroughly. For example, when a manager or a supervisor gives an assignment to an employee, it is important to provide enough information about the specific task so the employee knows clearly what the job is, what your objectives are, and how he or she can meet those objectives.

Supervising across language barriers

Try these tips for helping ESL (English as a Second Language) workers get their points across:

Share responsibility for poor communication. Say something like "It sure is noisy in here," or "I'm sorry it's taking me so long to understand" to take some of the pressure off the speaker.

Invite the speaker to slow down and collect her thoughts.

Repeat what she has said in your own words, and ask whether you've heard her correctly.

Encourage the speaker to write her message down or to spell out difficult words, if spoken communication isn't working well.

Improve your own comprehension by watching the speaker's lips.

Observe body language.

Listen to everything the speaker has to say before you decide whether or not you understand.

Another way to improve communications with non-native English speakers is to learn a few words of their language. This effort will show you respect them. Don't worry about making mistakes—that shows it's okay to try a foreign language even if you don't speak it perfectly. And your effort will give the workers a chance to teach you something, for a change. Just make sure you show the same effort toward all the languages spoken in your department.

Finally, help your ESL workers improve their English by encouraging them to speak it. Smile and look enthusiastic when you talk

with them. If they seem embarrassed at their difficulties, look away for a moment to let them gather their composure. Ask open-ended questions such as, "Tell me about..." to challenge them to express themselves beyond a simple "yes" or "no." And even if they laugh at their mistakes with the language, don't laugh at them yourself. Showing them you respect their effort will reinforce good communication.

Supervising across language barriers isn't easy. But you don't have to settle for a communication gap, waving futilely at non-native English speakers on the other side. Build bridges by using clear English, checking for comprehension, doing your best to understand all ESL workers, and encouraging them to speak English. By doing these things, you'll be developing essential communication skills that will help you reach everyone in your organization more strongly and effectively.

Source: "Supervising Across Language Barriers," *Practical Supervision* (September 15, 1991), pp. 1-2. Reprinted with permission of Professional Training Associates, Inc., 210 Commerce Blvd., Round Rock, Texas 78664-2189 (1-800-424-2112).

That requires a two-way conversation so that words, expectations, and results are exchanged and understood. The manager, in the role of sender, may need to invite questions and check for understanding before assuming that the message has been received. Shared goals, knowledge, and language provide a good foundation for effective oral communication.

But you need to remember that there is more to the receiving of the oral communication than just the content of your message. Bear in mind that your hearer/receiver is an individual—or a group of individuals—with an identity, a background, a specific place in the organization, a particular level of language ability, personal values and preferences, a point of view, moods, and internal "noise." Therefore, the same factors that influence your framing of your intended message will affect the way your hearer/receiver hears and interprets that message.

Receiving messages

Listening doesn't guarantee understanding, but it is a prerequisite.

In the receiving process, someone translates an intended message into a perceived meaning. The message and the meaning can be virtually identical—or completely different. Sometimes the sender and the receiver have no idea how similar or different the original message and the perceived meaning are.

The process of receiving and comprehending messages is called *decoding.* Listening to the words that are used is only part of the decoding process—but it is a vital part. Listening doesn't guarantee understanding, but it is a prerequisite. Although the sender can try to choose the right words and present the idea in a way that encourages understanding, the receiver alone controls whether he or she will listen. When you are a receiver, therefore, your first responsibility is to listen to the words the sender has selected—or admit that you didn't understand or weren't listening and want the message repeated.

Have you ever found yourself involved in a "conversation" in which someone is talking but no connection has been made? When someone is talking *at* you, and you are completely tuned out? The problem may be at both ends: the sender may not be translating the ideas in his or her mind effectively, and you may not be accepting the receiver's first responsibility—to listen. Decoding begins when the receiver hears the words and translates them into something that makes sense to him or her. Usually the process is quick and takes place subconsciously. The receiver may be asking internal questions such as the following:

What does that word mean?

What is he or she really saying?

Is any of this familiar to me?

Have I heard this before?

Is there something he or she isn't telling me?

Do I understand what's going on?

What does all this mean to me?

What am I going to say to him or her when he or she has finished?

If there are obvious information gaps or specific words that don't make sense, the receiver may choose to ask the above questions aloud, as feedback to the sender.

Perception is an important part of the way receivers decode messages into something that makes sense to them. Perception is an individual's interpretation of a situation—not an exact recording of only what happened. No one, of course, sees or knows reality with true objectivity. You only know reality through your brain's interpretation of what it receives from your senses.

Therefore, perception is a critical component of interpersonal communication. Two receivers may hear the same words but decode them into two different perceived messages. It is difficult if not impossible to change the way different individuals perceive the world and interpret messages. It is possible, however, to bring different perceptions to the surface—to articulate what is different about the sender and the receiver that influences the way messages are understood. Clarification of both the information and an individual's perception comes through *feedback.*

Feedback

The crucial link between sender and receiver, feedback lets the sender know whether the receiver has heard the message and whether the intended and the perceived meanings are the same, similar, or totally different. Both the sender and the receiver are responsible for making a connection through feedback. Too often the sender assumes that a lack of feedback means there has been a complete oral-communication connection. Although it is true that the receiver is responsible for initiating feedback, an effective sender seeks feedback to ensure that the message did in fact get across. The cost of failing to do so may be the development of a relationship based on misunderstandings.

When you are the sender, you must be willing to let the receiver influence you through feedback. How the receiver responds may tell you that you need to change your message if it is to be understood and accepted. What happens as a result of the feedback necessarily depends on the relationship between the people involved.

For example, if you are a supervisor telling a subordinate that you are dissatisfied with his or her performance, you will need to modify and clarify your message until it is understood and accepted. The receiver should walk away knowing specifically what the problem is, why you were dissatisfied, and what changes you expect. Your message, in this instance, isn't subject to modification.

By contrast, if you are discussing a specific problem with a co-worker, you may send a message that offers a possible solution. The feedback you receive may tell you that the message has not been accepted because the co-worker doesn't accept your solution. Your choices are (1) to change, modify, or reinforce your message in an effort to convince the receiver that your solution is workable or (2) to become the receiver and see what alternative the co-worker can offer. Your first message in this instance is probably more open to discussion and modification than the one in the first example.

Simply repeating the message in the same words—in a louder voice—will not clarify the meaning.

In both instances, simply repeating the message in the same words—perhaps in a louder voice—will not clarify the meaning. You must be willing to change what you are saying, on the basis of the feedback you receive, to increase the likelihood of being understood. Flexibility in communication fosters shared understanding.

Nonverbal communication

Although words are the most common medium of communication, they are, ironically, sometimes the least effective. Unless your message consists of pure, universally accepted data, you rarely use words alone. All

Nonverbal communication is

continuous, multichanneled,

and difficult to control.

of us consciously or unconsciously send signals, cues, and other supplemental information that influences the way a message is heard and received. Besides what you are saying, other factors (such as the clothes you are wearing, the furniture in the room, the color of the walls, and the temperature) may influence the way your message is received.

These other factors are *nonverbals*. Whereas oral communication is usually precise (you select and use specific words), single-channeled (your words are your sole medium), and under voluntary control (you select the words that come out of your mouth and decide when to start and stop talking), by contrast nonverbal communication is continuous, multichanneled, and difficult to control. If you are a blusher, for example, can you keep your face from turning red when someone says something that makes you blush? Ideally, nonverbal communication will supplement and highlight the oral communication. It can help you send a clearer message.

Sometimes nonverbals stand alone. A scowl or grimace sends a clear message by itself. In the worst case, nonverbal behavior will contradict what you are saying and leave your receiver uncertain as to which message to respond to.

Understanding nonverbal communication better may help you control what else you say when you are the sender. It may also help you understand more clearly the meaning behind the message when you are the receiver. Sensory acuity can enhance the communication process.

Nonverbal communication can be classified into four large categories:

Environment, the setting in which the communication takes place

Body language, the physical reactions that accompany the oral message

Paralanguage, vocal characteristics that influence the way words are understood

Personal styles of the people participating in the communication exchange.

Environment

Environment refers to the physical features of the space in which communication takes place. Physical settings often have a significant effect on the way people respond to messages. In fact, most teachers, speakers, and group leaders spend a lot of time planning the arrangement of the room they'll be speaking in, to make sure that it supports the message they intend to send.

In some instances you will be unable to change the setting in which communication exchanges occur—particularly if they are spontaneous. But you can still be aware of the effect of the physical setting on the message and choose to stop the exchange and resume it somewhere else if you think the environment will interfere with the message. In many instances, you may want to use a specific setting that will reinforce your point. Sitting behind a desk while talking to an employee conveys authority. Is that part of your message? If it is, you're in the right place. If it is not, you might want to pull up a chair and sit on the same side of the desk with the employee.

Another important aspect of the communication environment is personal space—the distance between people involved in a communication exchange. For example, two people huddling in a corner implies an intimate conversation, perhaps a secret. Some people are highly sensitive about personal space and will react negatively to an oral message if

To create an opportunity for participation, look for a setting in which all feel equal.

they feel that the sender is getting too close physically. The meaning of the message can get lost while the receiver is preoccupied with recapturing his or her personal space.

Environment is something you can use effectively to complement your messages. If you want a serious message that reflects your authority, you should choose a setting that conveys authority. If you want to create an opportunity for participation, interaction, and input, you should look for a setting in which all will feel equal. If where they are sitting makes them feel equal, each of the recipients of your message will assume that what he or she has to say carries the same weight as what everyone else has to say. When interaction is desired, it makes sense to take your message to its recipients' turf rather than call them into your office.

Physical settings often have a significant impact on how people respond to the messages they receive.

Furniture also says something about the time you are willing to spend communicating. When you wander into someone's office and lean against the door, you are telling the sender you have only a minute and aren't looking for much feedback. By contrast, if you call people into a comfortable room, it implies that you have time to talk and want involvement and an exchange of ideas and perceptions.

You may also have some control over the way the environment affects the message when you are the receiver. If a subordinate stops you in the hall and wants to talk about "something important," it is not a good idea to have the conversation right there. "Something important" is a signal that the message demands a comfortable environment and a little time. On the other hand, chatting while you're walking down the hall presents a good opportunity for informal exchanges of a more personal sort. You can get to know people better informally in that environment, particularly if you walk slowly and take opportunities to look at each other, even though you are walking in the same direction.

Body language
Usually the most attention-getting and potentially most controllable nonverbal medium is body language—the gestures, facial expressions, unconscious glances, and postures that accompany oral communication.

Gestures often speak louder than words. Many are common parts of everyone's nonverbal vocabulary—like nodding to indicate agreement, wrinkling your brow to indicate confusion, and yawning or stretching to show that you are tired.

The technical name for body language that is part of the regular communication process is *kinesics*. Extensive studies have helped identify many physical signals that carry recurring meanings. For example, sitting back with tightly folded arms and clenched fists usually means that the receiver isn't receptive to the message, even if his or her words say "I agree." You don't have to become an expert and read every physical cue to communicate well, but it is important that you understand how body language affects messages and that you become aware of whether the physical signals you are sending support or deny the words you are using.

Sigmund Freud on body language

When I set myself the task of bringing to light what human beings keep hidden within them, not by the compelling power of hypnosis, but by observing what they say and what they show, I thought the task was a harder one than it really is. He that has eyes to see and ears to hear may convince himself that no mortal can keep a secret. If the lips are silent, he chatters with his fingertips; betrayal oozes out of him at every pore. And thus the task of making conscious the most hidden recesses of the mind is one which it is quite possible to accomplish.

Source: "Fragments of an Analysis of a Case of Hysteria," in *The Standard Edition of the Complete Psychological Works of Sigmund Freud*, vol. 7 (London: Hogarth, 1953), pp. 77-78.

When words do not or cannot convey everything that is on your mind, gestures often can.

When talking, it is important to give equal attention to what you are saying and what you are doing. Often your gestures provide your receiver with clues that go beyond what you are saying. For example, if you are worried about finishing a project on schedule, the visible tension in your body shows that you are worried even though your words may indicate that you are comfortable with the schedule. Or if you are angry at someone yet choose not to express it, your body is likely to give you away whenever you are near that person. Whether you realize it or not, you may avoid looking at the person directly and act remote and withdrawn until that person has left.

Body language that supplements and complements your oral message is a powerful communication tool. When words do not or cannot convey everything that is on your mind, gestures often can—particularly eye contact, smiles or frowns, and hand movement. Sometimes you can use body language to convey—and intensify—the depth of feeling that accompanies your message.

On the receiving end, unconscious body language is often even more telling. How a person responds physically during an oral exchange will provide valuable feedback about how the message is going over. Some obvious physical responses to watch for are fidgeting, excessive movement, frowns, smiles, and nods. If someone is really hearing what is being said, physical responses will more clearly express the way the person really feels about the message than any words used afterward. That is why it is so important to watch and observe body language while you are talking, as well as to think about what your own body is saying while you are listening.

Paralanguage

Paralanguage is what you hear in someone's voice beyond the specific words he or she uses. Vocal characteristics worth noticing include pitch, volume, speed, throat clearing, and sighs. The key to using vocal characteristics as a supplement for oral communication is to be aware of what is normal and typical and what is abnormal and unusual.

If your voice cracks when you are talking, it usually implies that a great deal of emotion is involved with what you are saying, particularly if your tone of voice is usually clear, even, and smooth. Similarly, rapid speech may indicate that the speaker is nervous, tense, or frightened (unless the speaker usually talks fast in any situation). What you want to be aware of in yourself and look for in others are changes in speech patterns that offer nonverbal clues beyond the oral message. Paralanguage is difficult to observe when you are dealing with people you don't know very well.

Personal style

Who you are and how you interact with friends, colleagues, and co-workers will always influence the way you communicate in various situations. A large part of the nonverbal communication process is the impression you send along with the words you use. Much of that impression is based on who you are. Personal style refers to the way a person presents himself or herself and how that affects what that person is saying. It can be a reflection of preferences such as those indicated in the Myers-Briggs Type Indicator. One's style of communication (and of responding to communication) can also be affected by ethnic or cultural background.[8]

Sensitivity to the variety of backgrounds and preferences that shape people's communication styles is essential to effective organizational and social communication. Some people are naturally outgoing and readily engage in warm, spontaneous conversation. Others are shy and a little uncomfortable around people. Outgoing people sometimes supplement their conversation with touching—a hand on the shoulder to express warmth and understanding, for example. Others are anxious about preserving personal space and avoiding any physical contact.

You can't change who you are, but you can be aware of the way certain aspects of your style and personality affect what you are saying. And you can recognize how the personality and style of the people you work with influence the way they communicate with you. Sometimes you may have to adjust your style to accommodate the styles of those with whom you are communicating.

Barriers to effective communication

Everyone is familiar with the telephone game. A group of children sit in a line and pass along a whispered message. When the child at the end of the line announces the final version of the message, it is rarely more than remotely related to what the first child said. The telephone game is an example of the way messages become confused and lost when there are barriers to communication.

In the telephone game, there are many barriers to clear communication that the children are not aware of. For one, it is hard to be articulate when you're whispering. The child who is receiving the message is already worrying about passing it on to the next child, so he or she probably isn't listening carefully. Second, there is no opportunity for feedback to make sure the message got across. There are probably noises and other distractions in the room, and there is pressure to keep the message moving quickly. No wonder it gets lost early in the game.

You will find similar barriers to effective communication whether you are working in an organization, chatting at a social event, discussing a problem at a meeting, or eating lunch with a friend. Regardless of the communication setting, it is important to be aware of possible barriers, to maximize your chances of getting the message across. It is particularly important to be aware of barriers to communication in your organization and try to minimize them, because getting your message across and receiving clear messages in response is an important part of getting the job done.

Common barriers to effective communication can be grouped into three categories—*noise, gaps,* and *personal behavior.*

Noise

The most obvious barrier to effective communication is actual noise. If you can't hear the words, you can't understand the message. Background noise can interfere with effective communication because it is distracting.

Background noises can be hypnotic, particularly if you are only marginally interested in the message.

Sometimes a minor noise can be more distracting than one might expect. Have you ever been listening to a discussion when a noisy air conditioner suddenly turns off? You hear the noise stop, even though you may not have noticed it or its impact on your conversation. Similarly, background noises can be hypnotic, particularly if you are only marginally interested in the message or aren't in the mood to listen. The hum of an air conditioner or the buzz of a fluorescent light may gradually capture your attention and relegate what the speaker is saying to the status of background noise.

Though you can't always eliminate noise, you can call attention to it to minimize the distraction; or, if the noise is overpowering, you may be able to find a different place to talk. Pretending that noise isn't there won't eliminate the barrier. If there is no choice, it is best to acknowledge the noise and make sure that the speakers talk loudly enough and that the listeners pay full attention.

Semantic noise

Another common barrier to effective communication in organizations is *semantic noise.* Semantic noise is generated by the use of words that are not widely understood or that have different meanings for different people. To ensure effective communication among people who work together regularly, it is the sender's responsibility to choose words that will be understood by the receivers. At the same time, receivers must be willing to "turn down" semantic noise—to ask what a word or phrase means, so that the speaker will know that the message isn't clear. Complex, technical language is rarely appropriate and easily misunderstood. It is difficult for even the sharpest minds to process long words and absorb the message.

Jargon

Jargon is another form of semantic noise that appears in many conversations. Jargon is shorthand expressions, acronyms, words, and phrases that are peculiar to an organization or profession. Although it is supposed to simplify speech and facilitate communication among people with a common frame of reference, often the opposite occurs. Not everyone involved in the exchange knows or uses the same jargon, so messages get lost.

Organizational jargon is useful when it fits the situation and clarifies the meaning of the message. Like technical language, however, jargon

Don't send signals that

say everything is clear

when it isn't.

may have a serious effect on effective communication beyond missed messages. If people frequently don't understand what is being discussed, they will feel left out, both organizationally and semantically. It is difficult to admit that you don't understand a word or phrase when you are in a group of people who act as if they all do understand.

To minimize semantic noise, you should analyze your message, its intended receivers, and the words or style they will understand and identify with. Clear, simple, direct words are usually your best tools. When you are on the receiving end of a noisy message, it is important to let the sender know you don't understand. Ask for clarification.

Don't send signals that say everything is clear when it isn't. Try not to take semantic noise personally. Even the best-read scholars or leaders in technical fields don't understand every word, phrase, or acronym. If you ask a sender to clarify a message, you will help eliminate misunderstandings, and the sender may get the message that he or she should use more commonly understood language in the future.

Gaps

Communication gaps generally occur because the sender and receiver have different backgrounds, experiences, or points of view. Differences in age, social norms, or cultural background can lead to communication problems. Gaps also may occur because the sender isn't saying everything that is on his or her mind. When the sender and receiver have different points of view, they may have trouble understanding the meaning of messages even if their words are well chosen and they are both trying to send and receive a clear message. An effective exchange may require extra background discussion to get participants on the same wavelength.

Communication gaps sometimes appear, however, because the participants expect them to appear. If you assume that the receiver won't understand your message, you may create a communication gap even before you begin talking. If you start a conversation with "You probably won't understand this, but . . . ," a huge gap suddenly opens up. The receiver has several choices:

To listen carefully and try to understand despite your skepticism

To try to convince you that he or she does understand the message, even it if isn't clear to him or her

To tune you out completely.

The problem of perceived communication gaps is most likely to occur in organizations when people from different backgrounds, at different levels in the organization, or with different types of expertise are sharing information. In such instances, it is important for the sender to minimize the differences and try to bridge what might be a communication gap. Here are some specific ways of dealing with communication gaps in organizations:

If you are sending a message that may involve a knowledge gap, try to bridge that gap by using examples rather than technical language and by providing extra background to make sure everyone is on an equal footing.

If your message doesn't seem to be getting across, try to find out whether there is a gap, determine what is causing it, and modify or adapt your message to bridge the gap.

If the gap between you and a potential receiver seems insurmountable, try to bring other people into the information exchange who might be able to help bridge the gap by adding information, participating in a discussion, or clarifying concepts.

If you are receiving a message and sense that there is a gap, let the sender know you are missing something and work together to bridge the gap.

Communication gaps become most destructive when they are ignored. A gap may be ignored either because the interlocutors don't realize that there is one or because they assume that the gap is unbridgeable.

Communication gaps also occur when a speaker says one thing while thinking and feeling something completely different. In such an instance, the speaker is said to have a *hidden agenda*. A hidden agenda is a reason or motive that the speaker has not shared with others. Usually a hidden agenda is more discernible than the speaker thinks or wants, even if its exact details are not clear.

Sometimes a sender may have a good reason for not saying everything on his or her mind. For example, if an employee seems troubled, there is no need to bluntly ask, "What's wrong, Michael?" A perceptive supervisor may instead engage the employee in a casual conversation to collect information. The hidden agenda beneath the conversation is the effort to figure out what, if anything, is bothering Michael, and whether there might be anything the supervisor could do to help.

Even when the intentions are good, however, hidden agendas cause gaps that interfere with effective communication. Michael's reaction to the conversational attempt might be to respond that he has a lot on his mind and a pile of work to do, and he doesn't have time for a chat.

The most effective way to deal with gaps caused by hidden agendas is frankness. Hidden agendas are rarely as hidden as the speaker thinks, and what is vaguely perceived as present but left unsaid is always threatening. The strength of the communication relationship will determine how easy it is to be open and how risky having or revealing a hidden agenda might be. If people involved in the regular communication loop too often sense hidden agendas, they will be on guard, even when everything is open and above board.

Hidden agendas are rarely as hidden as the speaker thinks.

Personal behavior

Just as personal style can enhance your ability to transmit messages, inappropriate personal behavior can create communication barriers. Sometimes you may unconsciously say or do things that have a negative effect on the way people respond to your message. Here are some suggestions to alert you to personal behavior that may inhibit or interfere with effective communication:

When sending messages, avoid words that create the impression that you are on the defensive or that will put your audience on the defensive. Judgmental or dogmatic words, such as *stupid, incompetent,* and *lazy,* create a confrontational environment that interferes with the message. You can minimize defensive reactions by projecting an attitude of equality rather than superiority and by making an effort to uphold the self-esteem of the people you're talking to.

Refrain from interrupting or finishing someone else's message. Putting words in other people's mouths—even when you are in a hurry or the speaker's pace is slow—implies that you already know what the speaker is going to say and do not care to listen. However, your conclusion might not be the same one the speaker had in mind.

Be particularly sensitive about the use of jokes and humor in your communication. Sometimes, when humor is inappropriate, it can close the channels of communication. For example, off-color jokes are never appropriate and may interfere with future communication. Puns can be useful if they enhance your message, but people eventually stop listening to punsters who overdo it.

Take the time to get to know the people you work with and to talk with them. Important messages that you try to pass along on the run may be ignored because you did not stop to make contact.

Don't spend too much time worrying about what someone didn't say. Sensitivity to the possibility of hidden agendas can be valuable, but suspicion about what *isn't* being said at the expense of hearing and understanding what *is* being said is a serious barrier to communication.

Be careful about appearing to agree too readily, nodding too much, or mouthing what other people are saying. Although it is sometimes an unconscious response to show support and understanding, it may have the opposite effect. The sender may feel that your instant and overwhelming agreement means you aren't listening.

Don't fidget, doodle, or continue doing your work when someone is trying to share a message with you. If you don't have time to talk, say so, but don't invite a person to share something with you and then continue to do what you were doing. Effective communication requires attention and contact.

Don't "disappear" mentally during a conversation, even if you have something else on your mind or you are upset by what the person has said. When a person senses a conflict or is hurt by something someone said, he or she may disappear psychologically from the conversation. It is more effective to react to the hurt and to discuss it than to withdraw from the conversation.

Personal behavior can erect barriers that will create problems in the future. If you react one way, people may expect or look for that reaction the next time they encounter you. That is why it is important to be alert to things you may be doing that might interfere with effective communication in the future.

Sexual harassment   Although in many ways the public sector has led the way in creating an environment where women and men can work together with mutual respect, sexual harassment remains a problem in the government workplace, as elsewhere. Whether it is the result of a communication gap, a lack of understanding of what is appropriate behavior in today's workplace, or actual outright antagonism toward a co-worker on the basis of his or her gender, sexual harassment (which the federal government's Equal Employment Opportunity Commission has defined as "unwelcome sexual advances, requests for sexual favors, and other verbal or physical conduct of a sexual nature"[9]) can undermine an organization's ability to perform its mission. Just as important, sexual harassment can wreck careers and emotional well-being.

Communicating in groups

Most local government organizations rely on groups of people working together to get things done. It might be a committee of two or three people from different departments who are responsible for organizing special events for employees. It might be a group of employees working together to identify problems in the office and recommend solutions. Or it might be a special committee or task force of local volunteers examining a community problem. Generally, small groups are created to solve problems and make decisions. In order to make decisions in groups, participants must be able to communicate effectively and interact in a group setting. The effectiveness of decision-making groups requires attention to three aspects:

The mandate of the group

Roles people play in the group

The evolution of the group as it carries out its task.

These factors are all directly related to how members of the group communicate with each other.

Variables in group communication

In their book *Decision-Making in Group Interaction,* Bobby R. Patton and Kim Griffin identify eight variables that directly affect communication processes in groups: *member status, group size, group norms, cohesiveness, power structure, roles, member personality,* and *group tasks.*[10]

Is it harassment?

Is all sexual conversation inappropriate at work? Is every kind of touching off limits? Consider the following examples. In your opinion, which, if any, constitute sexual harassment?

A male manager asks a female subordinate to lunch to discuss a new project.

A man puts his arm around a woman at work.

A woman tells an off-color joke.

These comments are made at the workplace:

"Your hair looks terrific."

"That outfit's a knockout."

The answer in each of these cases is, "It depends." Each one *could* be an example of sexual harassment—or it could be acceptable behavior.

Take the case of the manager asking a female subordinate to lunch to discuss a new project. Suppose this manager often has such lunchtime meetings with his employees, male and female. Everyone is aware that he likes to get out of the office environment in order to get to know the associates a little better and to learn how they function—for example, whether they prefer frequent meetings or written reports, detailed instructions or more delegation of responsibility. The female subordinate in this case may feel she's being treated just like other colleagues and be glad to receive the individual attention.

On the other hand, suppose this subordinate has been trying for some time, unsuccessfully, to be assigned to an interesting project. The only woman who does get plum assignments spends a lot of time out of the office with the boss; the two of them are rumored to be sleeping together. The lunch may represent an opportunity to move ahead, but it could mean that the manager expects a physical relationship in return. In this case, an invitation to lunch with the boss is laden with unwelcome sexual overtones.

An arm around the shoulder, an off-color joke, comments about someone's appearance, or even sexual remarks may or may not be offensive. What matters is the relationship between the two parties and how each of them feels.

"Your hair looks terrific," for instance, could be an innocuous compliment if it were tossed off by one co-worker to another as they passed in the hall. But imagine this same phrase coming from a male boss bending down next to his secretary's ear and speaking in a suggestive whisper. Suddenly, these innocent-sounding words take on a different meaning. The body language and tone of voice signify something sexual. While the comment itself may not amount to much, the secretary is left to wonder *what else the boss has in mind.*

Source: Ellen Bravo and Ellen Cassedy, *The Nine to Five Guide to Combating Sexual Harassment* (New York: Wiley, 1992), pp. 8-10. ©John Wiley & Sons. Reprinted by permission.

Member status

Who talks to whom and how often is affected by the way members of the group view each other. Even if all the members of the group are from the same level of the organization, when they become members of a small group a sorting process takes place. Some emerge as leaders, whereas others are viewed as having (or view themselves as having) a lower status in that group. People of perceived high status tend to talk more in meetings and may therefore control the decision-making process.

Group size

The smaller the group, the more nearly equal the communication. Three people will have less difficulty sharing the floor than ten. Generally, as groups become larger, fewer people dominate the communication process and feedback among the members decreases.

Group norms

Most groups establish group rules, or *norms,* for participation. Norms identify what is acceptable within the group. If some members do not follow the ground rules, much communication time is spent in bringing them into line. If the nonconformists do not come around, they may be left out of the communication process entirely.

Cohesiveness

Groups are likely to experience a high level of cohesiveness if the members appear to work well together, enjoy being together, and value the accomplishment of their tasks to everyone's satisfaction. The more cohesive the group is, the more effective the communication among its members will be. In a highly cohesive group, everyone participates actively in the communication process—not necessarily by talking a great deal but by sharing meaning with each other by using all the components of communication, both oral and nonverbal.

Power structure

Power structure within a small group often reflects the members' relative status outside the group. Generally, the more powerful members of the group will talk more, direct conversations, and sometimes act as if they alone spoke for the group.

Roles

People who work together in a group over a long period begin to define specific functions for themselves, in effect carving out a niche, in the group. Someone may emerge as leader—if no leader was officially appointed. Someone may regularly serve as summarizer at the end of meetings of the group. Other roles may emerge.

The roles people play in groups may be directly related to their functions in the organization. They may well be extensions of the roles they generally assume in social settings. Or they may be radically different. Some people who communicate well in two-way conversations or informal settings may behave very differently when working in a small group over an extended period. The roles people assume in groups affect the communication process significantly, particularly if the group has a long life. Some of the typical roles people play in groups that affect communication within the group are summarized in Figure 8–1.

Figure 8–1 Some of the typical roles people play in groups and how they affect communication within the group.

Task roles   Roles that help the group get its work done.

Information or opinion giver provides for the discussion.

Information seeker asks questions to make sure the group gets the data it needs.

Expediter helps the group stay with the agenda and focus on the problem at hand.

Idea person thinks originally, rattles off alternatives, and comes up with new ideas.

Analyzer helps the group get to the core of the problem and examines the suggestions of other group members.

Maintenance roles   Roles that facilitate good interpersonal relations among group members.

Active listener gives feedback to group members and helps them feel better about their participation.

Game leader helps the group lighten up when the work or group process gets too intense, too boring, or too exhausting.

Harmonizer reduces and reconciles misunderstandings, disagreements, or conflicts.

Gatekeeper helps keep the communication channels open and facilitates interaction.

Compromiser senses when two different views can be brought together with minor modifications.

Public relations person develops channels of communication with other people who have some role in, or will be affected by, the group's work.

Negative roles   Roles that interefere with group communications, interaction, and decision making.

Aggressor works for his or her own status by criticizing and blaming others.

Blocker goes on tangents or argues continuously in order to slow group action.

Competitor rivals others for attention.

One-track mind has one or two pet ideas that get worked into every group discussion.

Joker disrupts group work by clowning, mimicking, and joking about everything.

Withdrawer refuses to be part of the group and acts as a mental dropout.

Monopolizer needs to talk all the time to impress the group.

Floater does not stay with the discussion, going from one side to the other and one point to the next, creating confusion among the group members.

Member personality

People come to groups with individual personalities that affect the way they participate. They may also develop different personalities as a result of what happens in the group. Changes in situations in the group affect the way people behave and interrelate in the group. Behavioral changes that take place include the frequency with which members communicate and the nature of their participation—supportive, defensive, positive, or negative. The personalities of the individuals in the group will always have a significant effect on the way people work together to reach decisions.

Group tasks

The purpose for which the group is organized affects the way members work together. If the group is supposed to be dealing with a difficult issue that people feel strongly about, the group process will require intensive communication and interaction. By contrast, if the group is organized to collect specific information about a specific problem, the members may decide to distribute assignments and meet only to compare notes. The more personal contact is required in dealing with the issue or solving the problem, the more important group communication will become.

Groupthink Some groups work together too well. They may, in fact, carry the process of working and thinking together so far that they begin to make poor decisions and support each other in making them. The phenomenon is called *groupthink.*

According to Irving L. Janis, who popularized the term with his 1972 book *Victims of Groupthink,* people who work together regularly in groups sometimes reach the point where they are more concerned about supporting the group than about thinking carefully and critically. Janis studied several foreign policy "fiascoes," such as the Kennedy administration's decision to proceed with the 1961 Bay of Pigs invasion and the Johnson administration's escalation of the Vietnam War in the mid-1960s, and concluded that poor decisions were made by highly cohesive groups that discouraged disagreement or criticism—without even realizing it.

It is unlikely that your work group will ever face the kind of life-and-death decisions that Janis studied in defining groupthink. However, it is important to be aware of the way groupthink affects the communication process, particularly if you are part of a permanent decision-making group. A well-functioning group allows and encourages disagreement and criticism, thereby ensuring that the group decision is based on the collective knowledge and wisdom of the members.

If all the members of a problem-solving group think alike, the benefit of applying many heads to a problem is lost. Groupthink is likely to occur when members of a group are reluctant or unwilling to express disagreement. Good feeling among the group becomes more important than good decision making, and consensus, rather than open communication, becomes the primary goal. Or, in some cases members are hiding behind the group when it makes a decision about which all of them have misgivings.

Open communication is what makes work groups function effectively. The exchange of feedback remains the vital link among people involved in the communication process. If the channels of communication are open and functioning well, the risk of groupthink is minimal. Observation is your best tool. If you are participating in a decision-making group, ask yourself the following questions:

How does the group make decisions?

Are decisions reached too easily?

Does everyone become involved in deciding what to do or how to proceed?

Am I always fairly comfortable with what the group decides?

Do I always say what's on my mind, even when I disagree with most of the others in the group? If not, why not?

What would happen if I shared my disagreement or criticism?

Is my reluctance to express my ideas encouraging groupthink?

Skills for improving interpersonal communication

Understanding more about the way people communicate and recognizing some typical barriers to effective communication will help you improve your communication skills. In this section, some additional skills are highlighted that can enhance your ability to communicate, both on the job and in social settings. Four activities to think about implementing are *listening, giving feedback, paraphrasing,* and *describing feelings*.

Listening

Sometimes what may look like a problem in interpersonal communication—nobody seems to be getting his or her messages across—is simply a matter of poor listening habits. Many people assume that listening is passive—that it happens automatically when someone starts talking.

Simple messages are often misunderstood because someone was sitting back and relaxing rather than working at listening. To improve your listening skills, think about these steps:

Get ready to listen. Effective listening doesn't always come naturally. When you are supposed to be receiving a message, take time to clear your mind and begin to listen. Effective listening requires a focused, active, alert mind—not just open ears.

Make the shift from speaker to listener completely. When you are involved in a conversation, think about changing functions, as if you were to say "over" when you were ready to start listening. Forget about the message you just sent. And don't start formulating what you want to say next. When you shift from sender to receiver you are in a different position, for which different skills are required. Be sure to make the shift completely.

Focus on the message. Look for main ideas, significant points, and a purpose for the message. Try to absorb what the sender is saying, process it, and think about it. When you are really listening, your mind should be working as hard as it does when you are preparing or sending a message. Effective listening is *not* passive.

Give feedback that is based on the message. Your feedback should be based on what you heard rather than on what you planned to say beforehand anyway. If the message is complicated, you may need some clarifications or perhaps a few minutes to think. Don't move on to your next message until you are sure you have listened carefully to what the sender has said.

Effective listening is sometimes more difficult when you are listening to a speech or presentation in a large group. Because you are less personally engaged in the exchange, you will have to work harder at listening. Here are some guidelines to help you listen effectively during formal presentations:

Don't daydream. Keep your mind focused on the message. Use the time to ask yourself questions and to think productively about what the speaker is saying.

Don't jump to conclusions. Listen first, and draw conclusions only after you have heard what the speaker has to say.

Take notes. If you are in a large group, taking notes will help you capture main ideas and keep your mind on the speech. In smaller groups, though, speakers are sometimes uncomfortable if someone is taking notes, so you may have to rely on mental note taking.

Plan to report what you heard to someone else. If you know you have to report what you heard, you will have a strong motive for listening. If you don't have a specific reporting responsibility, assign it to yourself. It will help you focus on the information.

The quality of your listening should not be based on *your* perception of the importance of the message. You may be tuning out important messages because you think they won't be important. You may also develop poor listening habits if you begin tuning people out. If you work hard at it, though, you will develop good listening habits that will make it easier for you to capture and retain messages in the future.

Giving feedback Because feedback is the vital link between the sender and the receiver, being able to give clear feedback may be the most vital communication skill at your disposal. Many of the other skills used to improve interpersonal communication are variations on giving feedback. How well you express your reaction to a message, both orally and nonverbally, is a function of your ability to send and receive messages. To be able to give feedback, you must listen to what the sender is saying first. And you must be able to express what is on your mind clearly on the basis of what you heard and your understanding of it. Here are some guidelines to help you hone your feedback skills:

Try to be descriptive rather than judgmental. Make sure you heard the message correctly before you evaluate or criticize it. If your immediate feedback seems to evaluate the message, the sender may become defensive before you have even begun to understand each other.

Be specific about what you think you heard, even if the message was fairly general. Specific feedback will help the sender clarify an unclear message and bring it into focus.

Make sure your feedback is helpful. Your feedback should be framed so that it helps clarify the message and helps you develop a communication link to the sender instead of confusing the issue or challenging the message.

Try to focus on the sender's point of view first. This approach will give both you and the sender a chance to move toward a match between your respective points of view. It will also decrease the possibility that you will jump to conclusions in your response to the sender's message.

When in doubt, ask a question rather than make a statement.

The amount and quality of feedback exchanged by the sender and receiver will depend on the clarity of the messages, the links between sender and receiver that already exist, and the time they both are willing to spend in clarifying the message. If the issue is important and complicated, both must be willing to spend time giving and receiving feedback. A great deal of feedback can slow the communication exchange, but if the result is a close match between intended and perceived messages, the time will have been well spent.

Paraphrasing

A feedback tool worthy of special attention is *paraphrasing*—feedback you can use to check your understanding before the conversation continues. Paraphrasing involves restating the intent of the message as you heard and understood it. When you paraphrase, you are putting someone else's message into your words or symbols to make sure that what you heard is close to what the sender meant. Paraphrasing is not just repeating the sender's words. Here is an example:

Jackie: I think we need to change our work schedule around here.

Carlos: Well, right now the official work hours are 8:30 to 5. You mean you want to change the hours we all work?

Jackie: No, I was thinking more about coordinating work breaks so that someone is always in the office.

Carlos: Oh, you're saying we'd still work the same hours, but we need to agree on who will go to lunch when, so that the telephones and the office are always covered.

Jackie: Yes. It seems that we all end up leaving at the same time, so there may be no one here between noon and one.

Jackie's first message was brief and unclear. She said "work schedule," and Carlos thought she meant "daily work hours." What she meant was "schedule coordination." Paraphrasing helped expand and clarify Jackie's message.

Usually paraphrasing is focused on the facts, although it can be used to probe beneath the surface. For example, something specific may have happened that made Jackie notice that the office was empty during certain hours. She may have become angry when she discovered an empty office. A client, customer, or patron may have come in and found no staff people. Although Carlos didn't probe for feelings, once he understood the message he could have pursued the details to uncover the feelings—assuming Jackie had been willing to talk about them.

Paraphrasing is a good way of checking your listening skills and improving your sending skills as well. Often, what the receiver sends back to you in a paraphrase is a better way of saying what you had in mind in the first place. It can help you be more precise the next time.

Describing feelings

An important part of sending clear messages is being able to say both what you mean and how you feel. Few messages are purely factual. Most people concentrate on finding words to convey the facts, however. What leads to confusion and mixed or missed messages is what else is going on in your mind besides the facts. It is difficult and sometimes uncomfortable to describe your feelings about a message or general feelings that influence what you are saying. And it isn't always appropriate. When it is clear that how you feel is an important part of what you are saying, however, you must find words that will help receivers understand your point of view.

Most people aren't inclined to let a receiver into their inner world unless he or she is a close friend and the message is clearly a personal one. As this chapter has already shown, however, even if you don't talk about your feelings, they are likely to show and to influence the way people read your message. So you need to decide how to handle how you express them. Here are three major steps you can take to help you understand when and how to describe your feelings:

Understand your feelings. Make sure you are aware of the meaning behind the message before you send it. If you are angry, confused, hurt, happy, unsettled, or confused, think about why you feel that way and what effect it will have on your message. Your feelings, in fact, may be your message, and you may simply be searching for facts or examples to explain or clarify the reason you feel the way you do.

Translate your feelings into words. If you decide that what you are feeling is your message or is an important part of it, try to find words that express your feelings. Make sure you focus on *your* feelings—"*I* am angry because . . . "—rather than shift your feelings onto your receiver—"You probably think I'm angry because . . . " or "You made me angry when . . . "

Link the feeling to the message. If you are planning to change the way your division fulfills part of its responsibility, try to figure out how the feeling and the message are connected. Are you worried about making the change, or are you making the change because you are concerned about how the unit is functioning? Try to ascertain whether there is a connection between what you are feeling and the message you want to send, then organize your message to express both.

Being able to describe feelings is an important communication skill to which few people give much thought. Knowing *when* to express your feelings as part of your message is a skill that is even more important to understand and more difficult to master.

There are two extremes to avoid. You can ignore your feelings completely and hide behind the factual message. Or you can overemphasize your personal feelings at the expense of your message, so that co-workers feel as if they were in therapy every time you talk with them. There is clearly a middle ground. When the message and the feeling are closely linked and *not* describing your feelings will lead to confusion or a communication gap, *say it.*

Conclusion   Interpersonal communication involves much more than passing information along. People develop and strengthen relationships through communication. Strong, open relationships foster effective communication. It is likely that you can communicate more effectively with people you know well and trust and with whom you have much in common. There is an unspoken bond there that adds meaning to the messages.

You can also use interpersonal communication to develop better working relations with people you don't already know well. Taking the time to talk, to listen, and to exchange information will develop bonds of understanding that can facilitate the communication process. The ability of a manager or supervisor to give clear assignments, help employees solve problems, motivate employees, and accomplish goals will depend on his or her ability to communicate with others.

It is a cyclical process: If you communicate well with others, you will develop good working relations that will enhance your overall ability to communicate. John Ingalls, in his book *Human Energy,* says that patterns of communication in organizations create "powerful bonds of inclusion and exclusion" that significantly affect the way people work together.[11] That is why it is worth the effort to become an effective communicator in your organization. You must learn to speak the same language as the people you work with, in more ways than one.

Checklist

Pay attention to how people deal with each other in the organization. Different people may use different channels of communication to get messages across.

Stay tuned to both the formal and informal communication networks in the organization, and weigh information equitably before deciding what is fact and what is fiction.

Choose words carefully to make sure that you mean what you say and that the people you are talking to will be familiar with your language.

Remember that what you think, know, hear, and understand is based on your perceptions of the world. And your perceptions may be very different from those of the people you are talking with.

Look for nonverbal behavior that may tell you more about what people are thinking and feeling than their words do.

When working in small groups, observe the way people interact and exchange information. Become self-conscious about the role you play in groups and its effect on how the group gets its work done.

Don't try to bridge a communication gap that may not exist yet. Assuming the existence of a gap can create one.

Develop a personal style for sending and receiving messages that is open, honest, direct, and flexible. Your style and behavior will affect people's understanding of your message.

Acquire the habit of paraphrasing messages to make sure what you heard is what the speaker intended. Listen when people paraphrase your messages, so that you can learn to be more precise and direct the next time.

Listen! Even the most carefully presented messages will be missed completely if you and others aren't listening carefully.

9 Effective Presentations

Regardless of the level at which you manage, your schedule includes challenges and opportunities to speak in public. Make the most of them. Work toward a mastery of the whole process of effective presentation, making the art of speaking a creative and refreshing part of your professional life.

This chapter focuses on the dynamics of presentations. As you read, consider your needs, goals, approaches, strengths, and challenges, and your overall attitude toward public speaking and public management. Think, too, about your style of speaking, your voice, your appearance, and the way you approach and communicate with others as you speak.

In the public sector especially, where many of the traditional resources managers once depended on to motivate employees are now often in short supply, the ability to communicate in an inspiriting way is an asset. As your most direct communication tool, your public speaking must be—and can be—clear, concise, precise, and compelling.

Think of the talks you've given as a manager in local government. Consider those that were successful, and others that could have been better. As you reflect, you

may realize that your more successful efforts were often the ones that were preceded by decisive planning and research. This chapter suggests practical speech-planning ideas, methods, and choices that will enable you to manage and enjoy developing speeches and other spoken-word presentations.

"Come," Shakespeare exhorted—"a passionate speech." As those who serve in the public sector make the transition from a bureaucratic mind-set to one based on teamwork and innovation, your words and manner will take on an unprecedented importance. Someone once chided President Reagan by asking, "How can a president be an actor?" To which Reagan replied, "How can a president *not* be an actor?" In reading this chapter you will come to see the power of taking passionate and dramatic approaches to your spoken message. You will have a foretaste of the enjoyment you and your audience will experience when you share a thoughtful, powerful, and occasionally humorous presentation.

As a public manager, you are always in the spotlight— whether at a staff meeting, at a public function, or during a formal talk. This chapter will help you become more aware of your facial expressions and the other body movements you use when you speak.

Timing is a key to success. This chapter includes guidance on when to make an oral presentation and when not to. You will also find guidance on how to manage your time, whether you are giving a briefing on a complex topic or an after-dinner speech to a well-fed, drowsy audience.

A commitment to sharing accurate, helpful information will empower and strengthen your approach to speaking. It will enable you to provide better service to the people in your city or county.

This chapter addresses the following topics:

Public speaking as an opportunity

Types of presentation

Preparing for speeches

Humor

Assembling your presentation

Time and location

Audiovisual equipment

Audience involvement

Speaking on television and radio

Self-evaluation afterward.

What makes public speaking effective

Public speaking is one of the most potentially effective and persuasive communication tools at your command. Although great speakers from Abraham Lincoln to Martin Luther King Jr. have all recognized the value of various forms of communication, they are best known for their command of the spoken word. Their ability and willingness to speak creatively and persuasively moved nations.

Dynamic speakers are made, not born. It is true that some seem to have a gift to wing it on any occasion. But look more carefully and you will find that most great speakers really work at their craft.

On "winging it"
Always be prepared. Never, ever wing it. In being prepared, even if you find yourself in a spontaneous situation, your preparation will guide you through, much like an athlete in "the zone." When you think about an athlete in the zone you might ask, "Well, O.J., why did you turn left instead of turning right then?" He really can't explain it, but all of his years of training have put him in a position where the information that he processes is processed so quickly that his action occurred on something other than a conscious level. Therefore, he can't explain it. That happens to us sometimes. Even if you encounter something you did not anticipate you can process it and respond to it if you are thoroughly prepared.

Source: V. Wayne Orton, city manager of Portsmouth, Virginia.

The successful speaker combines thought and performance, substance and style, matter and manner. Although the content of your message is paramount, its impact depends almost entirely on how you prepare, sound, look, and act.

Public speaking as an opportunity

The arena of local government abounds in opportunities and responsibilities for demonstrating leadership by making speeches and presentations before an audience. Some are internal opportunities, such as a briefing of the city or county council. Then there are the external speaking opportunities, which range from testimony before the state assembly to informal addresses to the local civic club. The nature of the occasion should dictate your approach to an event. Also keep in mind the presence of the news media and possible video and audio coverage. The event—not the platform—is your real stage.

View your staff as a dynamic speaking team or speakers bureau. Key support staff can provide vital information (and advance their careers) by sharing their expertise with various select audiences.

Consider these suggestions when setting up a speakers bureau within your local government:

1. Choose the members of your bureau carefully. Make sure they are coached by an experienced speaker.
2. Choose topics that both meet the needs of potential audiences and articulate your local government's message or stance on important public issues.
3. Make sure your speakers have access to visual aids such as flip charts, slides, overhead transparencies, films, and video.
4. Publicize your speakers program among appropriate groups.[1]

Speakers who are trained well have the edge. Include your staff in support activities, from speechwriting to logistics. Be alert for training opportunities for your staff—and yourself. Some local governments contract with communication consultants for speech training. Toastmasters International, a nonprofit, chapter-based organization, has also helped countless government employees develop their public-speaking skills (check the telephone white pages for a chapter near you). The names of other organizations that might be of interest to public sector speakers and would-be speakers are given in the accompanying sidebar.

Speeches and speakers bureaus: Dubuque, Iowa

As part of its public information and education efforts, the city of Dubuque, Iowa (population 60,200), developed a comprehensive speakers bureau to communicate information to citizens about what city employees and the local government do to maintain the quality of life in Dubuque.

The program, which makes available names and background information for speakers from all walks of city government, includes more than 50 contacts in more than 100 topic areas, ranging from city finances and zoning enforcement to book talks and gardening. Program listings are packaged in an attractive booklet, available to citizens upon request. The booklet is organized by 23 city areas, and each listing includes the primary contact, his or her title, a brief description of each individual's professional and educational background and interests, and the topics on which the individual is qualified to speak. Some listings also include suggested target audiences and information on speaker availability.

Source: Michele Frisby, "Public Information: Educating and Communicating", *MIS Report* (March 1991), p. 5.

Types of presentation

Most presentations fall into one of four categories: *impromptu, extemporaneous, from manuscript,* and *from memory.* Some speeches are mixtures of two or more categories. The four types are described below.

The impromptu presentation

Given with few if any notes in a seemingly spontaneous manner, *impromptu* remarks can add energy and intimacy to otherwise routine luncheons, ceremonies, and meetings.

The key to making successful impromptu presentations is to anticipate and be prepared. Mark Twain once said, "It takes about three weeks to prepare a good ad-lib speech." Although you probably won't need three weeks, give some thought to possible comments if you expect to be attending a luncheon or ceremony where your position in the community or your relationship with those hosting the event create the possibility that you will be called to the podium.

Perhaps the single most useful thing you can do to "prepare to be spontaneous" is to think of an anecdote that in your mind characterizes the people providing the occasion for the gathering or sums up your relationship with them. If the gathering is a celebration, cast the anecdote in a humorous light. (Most requests for spontaneous remarks are made at celebratory events.) If the event is more serious, emphasize the motivational or inspirational elements of your story. Some sources of anecdotes:

A first encounter

A shared moment of disappointment or triumph

An embarrassing moment (that turned out happily).

If you can't come up with an anecdote, get an anthology of quotations (they're arranged by subject and author) and find one to serve your purpose.

If you use an anecdote, go over it in your mind until you feel comfortable telling it without notes. If you base your remarks on a quotation, no one will mind if you pull a scrap of paper out of your pocket at the podium while saying something like "I ran across this remark by Thomas Jefferson the other day while thinking of all the great years of public service my boss has given this county . . ."

Never be afraid to improvise. Just remember to keep it short, tasteful, and appropriate. One final, but vital, bit of advice: If asked to speculate or provide information on a project or situation, beg off gracefully unless you have a firm grasp on your facts. Any embarrassment you feel at declining will be quickly forgotten by everyone but yourself; conversely, the problems you'll cause yourself and your local government by speaking out of ignorance will last a long, long time.

Organizations of interest to public sector speakers

American Society for Public
  Administration
1120 G Street, NW
Suite 700
Washington, DC 20005

City-County Communications and
  Marketing Association (3CMA)
409 Third Street, SW
Suite 206
Washington, DC 20024

Government Finance Officers Association
1750 K Street, NW
Suite 650
Washington, DC 20006

International City/County
  Management Association
777 North Capitol Street, NE
Suite 500
Washington, DC 20002-4201

National Association of Government
  Communicators
669 South Washington Street
Alexandria, VA 22314

Extemporaneous presentation

Extemporaneous talks are carefully planned, practiced, and timed. You follow a skeletal outline only, listing vital facts and points in the most logical presentation order. The spare structure of the extemporaneous speech enables you to follow your notes while maintaining eye contact with your audience. Extemporaneous talks give you both the security of structure and the freedom to improvise.

From manuscript

Formal presentations are best delivered *from a manuscript*. This type of speech should be clearly structured. Appropriate occasions include legislative testimony, sworn statements, statements to the media, and official proclamations. On such occasions, the presenter simply cannot afford to stumble. Practice reading your speech aloud. Clock your practice runs so that you can trim or add if time limits will be strictly controlled. Vary your emphasis to find the best combinations of thoughts, sounds, and pauses.

From memory

If you lack theatrical experience, delivering a speech *from memory* can spell disaster. But if you have the knack—and the time—for memorization, make full use of the advantages of memorized speech: an unbroken rapport with the audience and freedom from notes.

Even a little memorization will go a long way, though. In preparing for any speech, learn your favorite lines—particularly at the talk's beginning and end, and when stressing key points. This technique is useful for impromptu, extemporaneous, and from-manuscript speeches; it reduces your stress and allows you to make valuable eye contact with your listeners.

President Wilson's inverse law of speech writing

Someone once asked Woodrow Wilson how long it took him to write a speech. He replied, "It depends. If I am to speak ten minutes, I need a week for preparation. If fifteen minutes, three days. If half an hour, two days. If an hour, I am ready now."

Source: Gilbert Gude, *Respectfully Quoted: A Dictionary of Quotations Requested from the Congressional Research Service,* edited by Suzy Platt (Washington, DC: Library of Congress, 1989), p. vii (Foreword).

Meetings and panel discussions

Public speaking skills are used in meetings and panel discussions, although you will not be making speeches per se when you lead one. These are opportunities to show leadership by getting the members of a group to open up and really speak their minds on a topic.

When you are called on to lead a discussion group or facilitate a meeting, envision your role as being that of a generator of ideas: pose questions, repeat points for emphasis, and list key issues and findings. Strive to encourage comments from every participant—people who seem introverted sometimes provide the most creative contributions. One of the most effective ways of helping a reluctant discussant break the ice is with a sharply focused question that shows regard for his or her area of expertise. Instead of posing an open-ended—and hence intimidating—question along the lines of "Well, Michael, what do you think of privatization?" try something like "Michael, since we contracted out school-bus operations last year, has the Education Department seen much of a change in the number of complaints about service?"

Always take the measure of your audience. Who are your listeners? What are their interests and lifestyles? Why are they present? What are their expectations? Most important, ask yourself, What do they need or want to know? Two good ways of answering these questions are (a) to ask the audience itself and (b) to role-play by assuming its perspective. Work to forge a bond with your listeners and convince them of the value of your message. If time allows, welcome questions. They connect you with your audience, provide material for discussion, and add up to useful feedback for you.

Make room in your management schedule for panel-style presentations that can advance your leadership mission. But don't leap at every opportunity yourself. As a good leader, you'll want to give qualified members of your staff opportunities to speak and turn down speech requests that may conflict with the objectives of your office.

Preparing for speeches

As you prepare any talk, be it a major public address, a civic-league discussion, or a staff briefing, always ask yourself these questions: Why am I speaking? What do I want to achieve? What's my major point? Which point or points are absolutely vital to my audience? Jot your answers down quickly, like a brief shopping list. Ponder and rearrange them, eliminating or adding points as you see fit. At this early stage, be receptive to new and different ideas and approaches. Author and speaker Charles "Chic" Thompson suggests visualizing a problem as having been solved before setting out to take care of it. Then follow the imagined trail back from the future, step by step, to envision the best solutions.[2]

Bring in enough content

Discuss your subject with others as you develop your speech. Buttress the points you intend to make with pertinent observations. Use solid facts, cases, and examples.

Choosing your main point or points is one of the most important decisions you'll make in planning your speech. Being sure of your main points (select only a few) helps you aim, organize, and reduce clutter. As you decide on your main points, you're laying a foundation for a successful talk.

Brainstorm to identify the goals of your presentation. Keep in mind that presentations can serve several functions, from providing information to provoking discussion.

Former presidential speechwriter James C. Humes stresses Winston Churchill's advice: to write out a statement that sums up the message of one's talk. Keeping what Humes calls this "umbrella statement" in mind, focus your research and design your talk. This touchstone will keep your talk on track and help you drive out the extraneous.[3]

Create a vision

Next, initiate the three steps to successful preparation: *research, analysis,* and *creative reaching.*

Research—and *over*research. You want to be both comfortable with and masterful on your subject. Save ideas, notions, and all materials that may relate in any way to your talk.

Always be prepared to catch your thoughts. Be ready to list or dictate your ideas, views, and observations anywhere, any time. Have a pad and pen or tape recorder handy, even in the car and on the nightstand.

Clip news and magazine articles, reports, jokes, stories, and even advertisements that spark your interest—anything that might be useful later in a speech.

Personal touches

Review your information. Select and arrange the most relevant items. Then ask yourself, What do I think of my initial design for this speech? Try to consider the message and plan delivery from each listener's point of view.

Next, train your thoughts on your personal position on the topic of your speech. This will help focus you on your conclusions. Your thoughts and feelings are the spark plugs that can make your talk personable, persuasive, and memorable. It's *your* presentation, so shape *your* views. Dale Carnegie called this the "brooding and hatching" process.[4]

Developing a demeanor

The wonderful thing about your voice and manner is that both can be continually improved. Yet many local government managers have no idea how they sound or look to others. So videotape and audiotape your next presentation. Watch and listen for your strengths and for the areas that need improvement.

Pay close attention to your tone. A message may be positive and well meaning, but a boorish tone can turn it into a demeaning put-down. Monitor how fast you talk, and notice the length of your pauses. Many people speak too quickly and pause too briefly. Do you enunciate, or do you slur some words and phrases? Do you ramble, or do you get right to the point? Do you notice any repeated pet phrases that you should eliminate? Does an occasional *uh* or nonessential comment cloud your message? Do you hear spirit and enthusiasm in your voice?

Assess your body language. Are your gestures natural and helpful? Do you appear open, receptive, patient, and caring? Do you stand and move comfortably, or do you project a rigid image? Are you making eye contact and developing rapport with the audience? Are you aware of your facial expressions? Do they support your message or do they undermine it?

Are there any "down" times, or moments when you stumbled? Go back and analyze them again to figure out why. Were you rushing to get to another topic? Trying to share an aside? Trying to make a transition to a different idea? Polish those trouble spots to avert a repeat performance.

The art of leadership is the art of being human.

Finally, do you discern a spirit of leadership? Are you projecting the dynamic, sincere, caring self that you envision? Leadership guru Warren Bennis advises that "the art of leadership is the art of being human."[5] Strive to be *comfortably theatrical* and *passionate*—and be yourself.

You have now entered the phase of "speaking awareness." Your potential is unlimited. Go ahead and make your changes, emulating the qualities of voices you admire, adjusting your pace, polishing your pronunciation, mustering the courage to infuse more spirit into your communications.

Remember to match your new speaking skills to your venue. A large auditorium will call for masterful, occasionally thunderous oratory. A staff briefing or television interview, on the other hand, will call for a quieter style.

Humor

One of the most delicate decisions you'll make in preparing your presentation is whether—and how—to use humor. Though invigorating when appropriate and well-presented, humor can chill or even alienate an audience if it misses the mark. There's a fine line between the quip and the wisecrack.

First and foremost, remember never to joke down to people. A hint of ridicule and a superior attitude alert an audience to a speaker's insecurity—and possible insincerity. Be particularly aware of humor attempts or remarks that might be perceived as sexist, racist, or otherwise offensive. Even indications regarding a positive grouping or stereotyping can be wrongly perceived. Be aware of different perceptions of language among your audience that might lead to misinterpretation.

The wonder of humor is its potential power to unite the speaker with the audience. The safest, and often the most effective, way to do this is to let the laughs be on you, the speaker. Self-effacement signals that you are warm, mature, and don't take yourself too seriously. Former U.S. senator William Proxmire once shared a great opener at the National Press Club: "I was really delighted when I arrived today to see that my reputation had preceded me. [Pause] I was in the rest room washing up, and when I went to use the hand dryer I noticed, just above the button, that someone had written, 'Push here for a speech by Bill Proxmire!'"

You can turn a shared experience into a laugh. When then-vice president George Bush visited Norfolk, Virginia, for a major maritime address, the minister preceding him seemed destined to set an invocational record by praying eleven minutes. Bush, noticing that the audience had become testy as a result, took his cue, paused at the microphone, and said, "I believe the preacher covered just about everything I was going to say, so are there any questions?" The audience roared.

Use set-ups and groundlayers: "Driving over today . . ." "Entering the auditorium tonight . . ." "I was just talking with . . ." Keep an active list of safe targets of humor you can use with most audiences: the economy, the weather, etc.

Used at the end of your talk, humor can reward the audience and drive the message home.

Appropriate humor can serve you throughout your speech. At the beginning, use it to win the audience over and build energy, or to sum up the situation. Within a speech, it refreshes the audience during natural breaks. Humor can also be used to make a point. Humorist Gene Perret advises speakers to make the point, highlight it with humor, and then repeat the point.[6] Used at the end of your talk, humor can reward the audience and drive the overall message home.

Humor often involves exaggeration. Humor-writing guru Mel Helitzer explains that comedy writers have long developed gags by "associative brainstorming".[7] It can work for you as well.

First, pick a topic—say, your local government's motor pool. Next, pick a slant to describe the motor pool. It may be old, or small. Now make lists of things associated with those two characteristics. For old, you might list Roman numerals and the horse and buggy, among other things. Finally, make connections: "Our cars are so old the speedometers have Roman numerals."

And remember small? You could say, "Our motor pool is so small that the mice take turns going in there. It's so small that if a mechanic drops a tool he has to kick it out the door before he can bend over to pick it up."

You can use association to make the transition to meaningful comments. Remember, aim at the shared need, not the motor-pool staff. You want to spotlight a need *and* build morale.

Anticipate questions. And be ready with zingers, one-liners, analogies, comparisons, and funny stories—and, of course, serious, well-considered replies. This means thinking ahead.

Don't overdo humor. Helitzer cautions speakers to heed the "rule of three": Never use more than three successive jokes on the same topic. And remember timing: Stop talking and listen as they laugh. Then, just as the laughter begins to die down, begin your next laugh line.

When you get to a punch line, punch hard. Don't rush it. Take your time, articulate, and really draw it out. Never diffuse a potential laugh by announcing it with the prefatory, "Hey, this is funny." Remember, surprise is what ignites humor.

Assembling your presentation

In putting together a presentation, the first consideration is to establish and maintain a clear theme throughout. Though your address on the budget, for example, may include a detailed review of every department, your main point or theme—be it hailing a surplus or girding for revenue shortfalls—should underlie your entire talk.

Write the way you speak. Peggy Noonan, the veteran broadcast writer who created many remarkable addresses for President Reagan, succeeded because she wrote for the ear. To get your ideas across, avoid bureaucratic jargon and try for a natural, conversational flow. Practice speaking your best lines. Do they sound good? Do they feel comfortable as your speak them? Revise repeatedly until they sound and feel right.

Naturalness is powerful

Share your notions. Saying *I* is fine, but consider the leadership power of *we, our, us,* and *you.* Include and involve your listeners. You want your message to touch their minds and hearts.

Make your message direct. Take it to your audience. Share it with them in their terms. It is best to use a natural, comfortable vocabulary instead of long, official-sounding words. Simplicity and a dynamic delivery make it easier for your audience to understand—and later recall—your message.

The senses and the facts

Recently researchers have categorized the avenues of perception on the basis of the three major senses. They stress that most of us perceive through the senses of seeing, hearing, or feeling. A given person favors one or two of the three avenues. Help your audience *see* a condition by peppering your comments with visual terms and description. Help them *hear* by explaining with sound-oriented images and descriptions. Help them *feel* by using metaphors and other expressive tools relating to the emotions and physical sensations. Some master speakers blend the three concepts to ensure that they reach all types of listeners.

Back up your opinions with the facts you have gathered via research. Make sure to present the information so that it clearly supports your conclusions and recommendations. Use comparisons that are graphic and dramatic: "Ladies and gentlemen, that amount of money would fund four new high schools."

Structuring the components

Outline by listing your main points as you think of them. Then arrange them. Next, list each section. Every speech has at least three sections: an *introduction,* a *body,* and a *closing.* Now use the data you have collected to brainstorm for each section, listing possible points, comments, and subjects in any order. Then outline each section: arrange and rearrange, add new ideas and remove ideas until each one is sharp and clear. Then your outline—the framework of your entire speech—will be finished. But don't necessarily consider it carved in stone. Be flexible; always be willing to add, delete, or rearrange at any point until you've finished speaking.

It's often easier to plan your whole speech if you can see all of your components together. One simple way to do that is to brainstorm and outline with a large art tablet, or a sheet of poster board, or stick-on notes and a tabletop or wall. This system gives you an overview of your talk and allows you to make changes more easily than if you were flipping through a note pad.

The many ways speakers can make a point
When making points . . . use effective:

Examples	Humor
Analogies	Appeals to the senses—seeing, hearing, feeling
Depictions	Facts
Stories	Contrasts
Questions	Quotes
Comparisons	

Expressions and body language

Plan to emphasize your key points. One way of doing this is to pause. That gives you an opportunity to set up your next thought. Pausing is also an effective way to show that you are thinking about an audience member's question or comment.

If time allows, videotape or

audiotape your rehearsals.

Voice, too, is a part of your expression. Vary your speech rate and pitch, so that you sound natural and not monotonous. That will net you an alert, involved audience.

Enjoy and manage your eye contact with the audience. One of your goals should be to seem to visually "speak with" everyone in the audience. There are ways to achieve this without seeming to roll your eyes up and down each row. You don't have to gaze at every face, just every section of the audience. One way of doing this is to visually divide your audience into sections and challenge yourself to speak comfortably and naturally with each one in turn.

Be conscious of your facial expressions and the "language" of your head and body movements. Use comfortable, natural gestures. An open palm is a friendly gesture; tight-fisted pointing may appear threatening. If time allows, videotape or audiotape your rehearsals. Make sure you avoid nonessential comments and rambling statements. They will distract the audience from your main points. Trim to keep your message tight. And look for points where illustrating via stories or explanations would help to enliven your talk.

Once you are comfortable with your message choices, you will be ready to shape them into an excellent presentation.

The introduction

There are many effective ways to begin. Humor (which was discussed earlier in this chapter) is effective when it is used appropriately. An anecdote or a shared experience can connect you with your audience. Or you might raise a question or challenge that prompts your audience to respond or ponder a problem. The important thing is to tailor your introductory remarks to the particular occasion.

One of the safest and most gracious approaches is to start by emphasizing the occasion or praising your host group. Then clearly and directly make the transition to the subject of your talk: "It's always a delight to speak with the Civic Affairs Council, a group that has shared strategic vision and leadership in our town. I'm especially delighted to be here tonight, to share with you our staff's latest economic projections and some very good economic development news . . ."

Your first remarks should put your audience at ease, convey your likability, and stimulate interest. Don't take your initial remarks lightly. As the saying goes, you only get one chance to make a good first impression. A tasteful, lively greeting can reduce tension, convey warmth and sincerity, and unite you with your listeners.

Most experienced speakers agree that you should avoid opening a speech with an apology. It's awkward and seldom impressive. An apology should be used only to address an immediate crisis. You're trying to win your audience over, not plant seeds of doubt.

The body of your speech

Plan a brief transition from your opening messages—it can be as simple as a pause—and proceed to the point of your talk. Share your focus, your perspective, and your interest in the subject. Then present your observations, findings, and conclusions in the order that you think is most effective and convincing.

You may wish to frame the body of your talk in what is termed a *positive sandwich* style. Begin with a sincere and positive message, state your main theme, then end with a second positive or constructive thought.

The body of your talk may be divided and arranged in various ways: logically, chronologically, by sharing related observations or factors, or by depicting challenges and solutions, to name a few. The method should suit the type of topic. Cite facts and sources to support your opinions.

When sharing good news, try *induction*. Announce the good news first, then support it with reasons and a sound explanation. If bad news is on the agenda, avoid dropping a bomb. Instead, use *deduction*. Share the accumulation of findings and reasons that led to the bad-news conclusion. Share possible solutions. Negative news requires leadership that offers a positive response.

Phrase your main findings, your main conclusions, and your central point or points concisely. That way they'll be easier to comprehend and remember. Use the power and the connective capacity of parallel construction and repetition to bring your theme to life. Remember the galvanizing effect of the resounding—and *re-sounding*—phrase "I have a dream" as used by Martin Luther King Jr. in his speech at the 1963 March on Washington.

Good stories will engage the most inattentive listener.

"I have a dream"

Ralph Abernathy describes the effect of Martin Luther King Jr's "I Have a Dream" speech on his audience at the Lincoln Memorial on August 25, 1963, as follows:

It is the usual custom of a preacher as he finishes a prepared text to say some other words. Here he establishes eye contact with his audience. On this day, Martin Luther King's speech really began when he left his text. He said, "I have a dream," in a very musical voice, and he lifted his hands in oration. As he lifted his hands, the audience lifted theirs, and he went on.

"I have a dream that one day on the red hills of Georgia, the sons of former slaves and the sons of former slave owners will be able to sit down together at the table of brotherhood . . . I have a dream that my four little children will one day live in a nation where they will not be judged by the color of their skin but by the content of their character." People were standing on their seats, yelling "Amen!", and those who were not standing began to applaud . . . He was expressing the longings, hopes, and dreams of every person in that assembly of 250,000 people. He took the audience higher and higher, and as he left, the entire group rose to its feet.

Source: Ralph Abernathy, "Martin Luther King's Dream," *The Sixties*, edited by Lynda Rosen Obst (New York: Random House, 1977), p. 94. © Straight Arrow Publishers, Inc. All rights reserved. Reprinted by permission.

When trying to persuade people, you should stress an appeal or a need that is central. State this clearly, appealing to your audience's values.

Storytelling is an effective, enlivening way to make a point at any stage of your speech. Good stories and vignettes will bring back or engage even the most inattentive listener. Make them brief, compelling, relevant, and pointed.

Your voice should shift gears when you begin a story. Slow your pace; pause more frequently. Be conversational rather than oratorical in your delivery.

The closing

The closing gives you an opportunity to summarize your talk by restating your main points. (Keep a checklist handy.) The closing is also an ideal time to encourage your audience to take action. This is your chance to motivate.

At the very end of your closing come your final comments. Just as you only get one chance to make a good first impression, you only get one chance—your speech's closing—to make a good last impression.

Speechwriter Joan Detz encourages speakers to consider an array of possible endings: a quote, an anecdote, a call to action, a reference to points brought out at the beginning, a realistic assessment, a sincere and optimistic thought, or a rhetorical question.[8]

To let the audience know when the end of your speech is near, vary your tone or use a direct transition or even an announcement. Listeners are at their most alert at the beginning and end of a speech, so let them know when you're nearing the conclusion. Plan it, remember it, and project it with passion.

Thanking your audience, and wishing its members well, is a gracious way to make your final remarks. It's also correct to walk to your chair and be comfortably seated during the post-speech applause.

Using your notes

The notes you use to speak from may range from a single checklist to note cards to a typed manuscript. Use whichever you find to be most comfortable and useful for you. Make certain that the print is double-spaced and large enough to read at arm's length (using capital letters works well), and that it has wide margins. The margins will not only brace a narrow and easily read text column but also provide space for last-minute insertions. Plan to use notes sparingly. Recall grows with familiarity; the best delivery comes with practice, practice, practice.

To summarize: Write and rewrite, edit and rearrange, and say your speech aloud (both in private and to others whose opinion you value). When revising, ask yourself, Is this the way *I* would say it? Use pauses for emphasis and to build interest. Make notes on your text. For example, underline for emphasis. Use ellipses or vertical lines to indicate pauses. Finally, rehearse your presentation until it becomes almost second nature.

Keep the message consistent

Once you have developed and refined your message or position, immediately share it with your organization's public information staff and other key members of your team. That will ensure consistency of message. Consistency is essential to high staff morale, good information management, and a favorable public image.

Many local governments require public addresses on policy-related matters to be cleared with the public information office or with the office of the mayor or executive. Make sure you understand and apply your local government's policy on public speaking.

Time and location

First you needed to analyze your audience. It was then vital to decide your type of speech and its goal. You proceeded to inject some humor and to organize your speech. But your temporal and physical limitations also affect the success of your speech. When you can't control them, work *with* them.

Time

Everyone has prime times and down times. Remember that your speaking performance, and the audience's attentiveness, can be influenced by your biological clock and theirs. Learn to adjust your clock. Modify your diet, your energy output, and even your sleep schedule so as to be at your best when you speak before an audience.

Time also largely determines what kind of speech will be called for. The unscheduled talk has a very different approach and structure from one for which you set the time in advance.

Presentations by local government officials can be grouped into three categories: (1) immediate responses to crises, (2) scheduled or routine talks and meetings, and (3) special speaking opportunities you or your staff create. Be ready to do your best in each of these circumstances by adapting and being flexible.

Whether you are running a meeting or serving as a guest speaker, insist that the preliminaries be trimmed to the bone to make way for the main talk. Otherwise you invite disaster. A local government official once spoke at a service-club meeting that began with a heavy lunch, followed by fifty minutes of club business. Finally, with only fifteen minutes of the time allotted for the whole event remaining, one of the oldest members stood up and tearfully told the group that he was facing heart surgery the following day. With that announcement having taken the heart out of whoever had not yet succumbed to digestion and exhaustion, the master of ceremonies rose up to introduce the speaker, as follows: "And now here's [name of luckless speaker] with some great humor!"

Take note: listen to your instincts. When in doubt about the setting, the occasion, or the arrangements of a speaking opportunity, don't hesitate to decline gracefully. Offer to speak at a later date only if you'd really like to do so.

Location Just as is the case with real estate, it is true that location can either make or break a talk. Assess—and if possible, manage—your speech setting to gain an edge. Try to match the room with the expected size of your audience in order to generate energy within it. The room should not be too large or too small. If you find yourself facing a large room with a small, scattered crowd, ask everyone to join you at the front. Physical proximity sparks rapport and candor.

Time is also a paramount consideration in analyzing a speaking location. If you hope to have a large business community turnout for your luncheon talk, schedule it near the offices of your likely audience. Arrive early, so that you can meet audience members and get a feel for their mood and the setting. Although a just-in-time arrival may raise the room's energy level, it may also rattle your—and your host's—nerves.

Make sure that you (or, preferably, a trusted colleague or staffer) check the room and stage lighting, sound system, seating arrangement, and room temperature to ensure that the setting will encourage comfort and attentiveness among the audience. If no public-address system is available, consider the acoustics when arranging seating and choosing where to speak. Proper stage and room lighting is a must. A spotlight draws attention to the speaker; full stage lighting may diffuse people's attention. If you are speaking outside, the echo may interfere with the audience's understanding, so be sure to speak in short sentences.

The stage, like your speech, should be simple.

If you notice something distinctive about the setting, keep it in mind as a groundlayer for comments or quips that can serve as transitional devices or opportunities for short, lively diversions from the main message. Such localizing comments help connect you to your audience. Connecting is a major boost to your talk.

The stage, like your speech, should be simple. Too many plants, chairs, tables, and decorations can create a busy, messy impression. Get unneeded items removed ahead of time.

If possible, avoid the dais or simply use the lectern or table on it to hold your notes. Your goal is to establish rapport with your audience, and a podium can seem like a barrier. Assume a relaxed, friendly stance, perhaps moving around from time to time.

If you plan to use printed supporting materials or other handouts, make sure they are easy to read. Materials circulated before you speak may help clarify your talk but they may also distract your audience. During your talk, they may generate interest and help the audience follow along—or they might cost you listeners as the audience noisily peruses the materials. If your talk is long, printed matter can provide a refreshing break. You need to consider the tradeoffs.

If you distribute materials after your talk, have them readily available at the door or entrance. You might have them spread out on tables outside the speaking hall. This method often prompts discussion among audience members, thus reinforcing your message.

Special occasions

If you are serving as master of ceremonies at a special dinner or program, be sure to equip yourself with notes and an agenda. You want to keep the program moving and make it enjoyable. Use the program as a guide in planning the agenda. Once the event is under way, pay close attention to the proceedings for both inspiration and timely ideas. Always be aware of your manners, mannerisms, and expressions.

If a meal precedes your talk, eating lightly will keep you comfortable and alert. Sometimes you will share the program with key elected officials or business leaders. Be aware of your role as a gracious, supportive public servant. You will serve the local government's interests and your own by doing your best to honor and focus attention on everyone's presentation.

Audiovisual equipment

Equipment should contribute to your talk without being noticed for itself. Check in advance for what the location has already and what you'll need to bring. Finally, suit the use of equipment to the place, occasion, and audience. Audiovisual (AV) equipment can enhance your presence and message. A picture can be worth a thousand words. But use it only if it fits the topic and your message lends itself to graphic presentation.

Remember, AV equipment is there to serve *you.* If your use of it is motivated by guilt ("Gee, our agency spent a lot of money on this thing: I guess I ought to use it") or by me-tooism ("She uses computer graphics in all of her presentations; maybe I should too"), you may find that the equipment is working against you instead of for you. Do learn about new AV options, but remember that they're a means to effective presentations, not an end in themselves.

Basic tools

Keep charts, graphs, and illustrations simple. Make sure that they are easy to see and understand. And keep them organized.

Flip charts and chalkboards are basic, time-tested speech tools. Keep a few markers and pieces of chalk in your briefcase. In some presentation settings, two flip charts fill the bill: one for messages and drawings prepared earlier, and one that allows you to write and draw during the talk. Make the writing large. And don't crowd or clutter. Take along a roll of masking tape to post completed charts, lists, and graphs.

Projectors

An overhead projector allows you to show and discuss a wide range of previously prepared transparencies and to write on clear transparency sheets. The latter keeps the audience alert and fascinated. Computer graphics and color transparencies can provide impressive images. Also consider using the potential drama and effectiveness of transparency overlays to illustrate change.

Practice using projection sets to find the equipment you like best and the way of using it that makes you feel the most comfortable. Before your talk, test and focus your equipment. Tape an index card to the top of the projection arm, then casually flip it to block the projected image when you want the audience to focus on you.

Make certain your screen is large enough to give a clear picture to your audience—often a white wall provides a larger and better surface than a screen. Make certain that neither you nor anything else—head table, podium, or flag—is blocking the audience's view. Overhead projectors are increasingly favored for their flexibility and ease of use.

Slides without slips   Always carefully plan, arrange, and practice your presentation if you use slides. Once you've chosen the best sequence, *lock* your slides into a portable slide tray for mobility and convenient use and storage. For effective timing, mark the slide-change "moments" in your speech notes. Project each slide only long enough to convey its message. One impressive approach is to include multiple projectors with a mixer, producing fade-in effects with sound.

Advanced technology   Computer-generated graphics and sound can give you virtually unlimited audiovisual flexibility. Precise data depiction and manipulation can provide stunning visuals. To achieve an impressive high-tech aura, combine a personal computer, advanced desktop graphics, an overhead projector, and a projection pad. But use these techniques only if they fit the content of your message and the personality of your audience.

"Tell your organization's story with slides"

What do good shows have in common?

1. *Brevity.* They usually last just six to ten minutes. Communication in this form is essentially visual. Your audience will absorb only two or three major ideas or facts from your soundtrack—but they will absorb an immense amount of more subjective information from the visuals and from the feel of your show—the audio and visual combined.

2. *Visual integrity.* It's best not to mix images from many different sources and with very different photographic quality. Doing so can give your show a patched-together look, unless you have the budget to hire a specialist to make all the images fit together through special mounting and graphic design.

3. *A good script.* A wordy, boring narrative with lots of facts illustrated by pictures will send your audience to sleep. Try a shorter script, and use different voices (interviews, for instance, or taped conversation, if it's clearly audible). Music and sound effects add impact. But remember: good-quality sound is just as important as good slides. And every time you add a sound element to your audio mix you are adding time and expense. A one-track narration well done is much more effective than a multi-track recording that is poor.

Source: Reprinted from Emily Caperton, "Tell Your Organization's Story with Slides," *Nonprofit World* (January-February 1988), p. 29. 6314 Odana Road, Suite 1, Madison, Wisconsin 53719 (800-424-7367).

Using video effectively   A video recording can also enhance your presentation. Pay careful attention to quality of production and editing. Audiences that have grown up watching TV expect high quality. Keep your video presentations brief—two to ten minutes seems to work best.

Recording your talks   The tape recorder may be of limited value as an AV speaking aid, providing sound effects and other unobtrusive assistance. It is more valuable in helping you to assess yourself. Make a tape recorder with fresh batteries your constant companion. Record every talk you give, and learn from what you hear. Use recordings to improve your techniques. A tape recording also can be quite useful as a record in case you find yourself misquoted or misunderstood.

Microphones

Microphones are now so much a part of our speaking equipment that we often take them for granted. A word of caution: Don't. An excellent microphone setup can help you project a personable, sincere message and image. But if overlooked or mismanaged, a microphone system can distort or sour your presentation, accentuating even the slightest miscue. It's a good idea to practice with the microphone that you're likely to use. If that's not possible, carefully watch and listen to the preliminary speakers to get a feel for how you'll sound.

Fixed podium mikes limit your mobility. Head-turning can vary your volume dramatically; be sure to center your voice on the mike. When you want to look from side to side, shift your body while keeping the mike centered. Adjust the height quietly by handling the stand or the neck, not the mike itself.

Hand-held mikes allow you comfortable movement on stage. But make sure you have enough cord before venturing away from the mike stand. When holding a mike, use a secure yet comfortable grip. Change hands casually. If time permits, practice to find the best distance between your mouth and the mike. One way to keep the mike centered is to rest it on the thumb of the hand holding it on your chin. And don't overlook the mike stand. It can free your hands or provide a comfortable hand rest. Practice casually setting it aside after you remove the mike. Be aware of the trailing cord. If a wireless or broadcast mike is available, it will free you to roam your audience like the most experienced talk show host.

Lavalier microphones (which are hung around the neck) and broadcast mikes provide the greatest mobility. They are especially favored by speakers who work with overheads or flip charts. Because these mikes are so sensitive, though, be sure to cover them when coughing or clearing your throat.

When speaking outside, cover your mike with a wind sock made of foam. A wind sock can also serve as a helpful muffler during inside appearances to rid your talk of popping *p* and hissing *s* sounds.

Finally, the most important AV tip of all: Always remember to look at your audience, not at your screen or blackboard.

Audience involvement

When speaking, be flexible. Be willing to modify your talk—or even cut it short—for the sake of the success of your message. Welcome feedback. Accept questions and comments as opportunities to restate or refine your message rather than as attacks on yourself or your position. Restate the essence of each question if it's likely the audience didn't hear or understand it. It is polite, and it gives you valuable time to frame a response.

Managing audience participation

Control audience participation patiently but directly. It's your stage, so manage it well. First, always take the higher road, conveying a positive, hopeful tone. Use the power of transformational reasoning: a problem is a challenge that may also be seen as an opportunity.

The Socratic method is excellent for posing effective questions and counter-questions, raising points, and playing devil's advocate on issues that warrant exploration. You may need to limit the discussion for the sake of both time and topical focus. If you are blindsided by a question or comment on an unfamiliar topic, be candid: "I'll look into that and get back to you." Urge longwinded audience members to streamline their remarks so that others may have a chance to participate.

Pay attention to your posture and facial expressions. Remember that question-and-answer sessions often attract the best attention from an audience. Maintain eye contact with questioners as they speak—it shows respect. Continue the eye contact when you begin your answer, then comfortably make eye contact with others as you continue.

If you are heckled, stay "in character." Ignore brief catcalls. If a heckler persists, sometimes turning toward him or her silently, holding a pause, then continuing your talk will be sufficient. Sometimes a direct, calm reply—"Just give me a few more minutes and I'll be glad to take your questions"—will do.

Making humor your ally

On occasion, a heckler's comment will be so creative and well-timed that it will prompt laughter and even applause from the audience. How do you save face, and your command of the stage, when this happens? Go with the flow. Show you're a good sport. Laugh along with the audience. At times, such a line may spark you to think of an ingenious, humorous reply. If it works, the laughs and the audience are yours. But be sure to time your comeback well. Wait for the laughter to subside a bit so that you can be heard and so that you don't appear to be stepping on your would-be competitor's laughs.

If inspiration fails you, but you need to make the transition, a variation on the following will often suffice: "Well, humor has its place; but people like this audience know we can't afford to joke around if we're going to meet the challenge of . . ."

Great speakers take advantage of foul-ups and blunders: They make great setups for humor. Look for them—a faulty light, a server dropping a tray, microphone feedback—and make sure your audience notices them, too. If they prompt you to come up with a great aside or a self-effacing one-liner, go for it.

Handling crises

On occasion you will face the need to speak under crisis conditions. (See Chapter 4 for more discussion of effective communication during emergencies.) A crisis may require immediate summation. Often, when discussing a crisis, speakers scrap the structure of a formal talk.

Get the bad news out immediately. Explain the situation. Clarify what happened or did not happen, why, and how. Tell the audience what responses are under way or are being considered. Share with them what action is necessary, and when. You want to first generate feedback and support, and then motivate your audience to be involved in supporting the government's efforts.

Dealing with self-doubt

Many speakers worry themselves with self-doubt. Why does your audience want to hear from *you?* Why should they be interested? For several reasons. Because you are highly informed and have information they need. Because you have a special perspective vital to their full understanding of an issue, a condition, or a situation. Because they seek leadership and direction. And because they have questions or concerns that you can best address.

Be positive, uplifting, and in control. You are the master storyteller, the caring advocate, and the objective, highly informed specialist. Your job is to champion your city or county. Remember Virgil's advice: "Have the courage to be wise." You have the responsibility to share your wisdom.

Jitters are normal. When managed, they can add an undercurrent of energy to a talk. Take a few deep breaths, and believe—really believe—that you will do well. Don't strive for perfection. Your goal should be to deliver a dynamic and meaningful performance. If you can find some privacy before your talk, try a method some actors use to get "up" for a scene: Briefly stretch or shadow-box. You will feel energized and ready. When you walk up to the mike, immediately look for friendly faces in the audience, and speak directly to them to encourage yourself.

Speaking on television and radio

The presence of broadcasting technology adds new factors. When broadcast, your every gesture and sound can be magnified. The great secret here is to be both relaxed and attentive.

Television

At one time a television appearance was a special opportunity requiring special preparation. Now you need to be prepared for the camera and microphone at any time. Consider this a blessing. Understood and used effectively, television can enable you to project your clearest and most effective messages. It is your ultimate audiovisual aid.

Awareness and focus

Remember that in a public setting you may be on camera constantly. Be aware of your manner, your facial expression, and your actions. An innocent whisper to a colleague or constituent might be misinterpreted by viewers.

When you speak on TV—be it a response to a commissioner's question or a keynote address—focus your attention primarily on your live audience, addressing your key points to the camera occasionally. Also pay attention, in a relaxed way, to other speakers.

Dressing and positioning yourself

Dress conservatively, avoiding contrasting patterns and bright colors. Dense patterns, such as herringbone, pinpoint dots, and small checks, can create a distracting shimmer effect on camera. A brilliant white shirt or blouse will sometimes show "hot spots" under studio lighting.

It's said that everybody looks ten pounds heavier on film and video; the effect created by generously cut clothes and heavily padded shoulders will be compounded on TV. You will probably spend most of your time sitting under hot lights, so avoid heavy or constraining clothes. Women should be wary of short, tight dresses and narrow, unpleated skirts. Finally, a few miscellaneous tips. When you are seated and wearing a long jacket, sit up straight and sit on the tails, to avoid an ill-fitting appearance. Avoid shaded or tinted eyeglasses; you want to come across as open and honest to your viewing audience.

Your body language should communicate energy and enthusiasm. But remember that quick, jerky movements are distracting on the small screen. You are striving for a graceful, comfortable appearance that projects your sense of confidence.

On the radio

Call-in radio is increasingly offering opportunities to share your local government's message. But if you're scheduled to be a talk-radio guest, keep in mind that your distinguished profile, that dress or suit you look so good in, and all the body language in the world—things that serve you so well on TV or at the podium—will do you no good at all. The only things that matter are your wits and your voice.

On radio, take extra care to speak straightforwardly. Unless you are an experienced actor, efforts at evasion or glibness will be magnified in the ears of your undistracted listeners. You can protect yourself from being caught flatfooted by adopting a strategy of redirecting questions to areas that best serve your message: "You're absolutely right that the traffic jams being caused by subway construction are a problem, but what we really need to consider is the whole transportation picture." Always try to put a constructive spin on your remarks. (For more detailed guidance on the special requirements of radio and TV appearances, see Chapter 6.)

Self-evaluation afterward

Dale Carnegie once said, "A good speaker usually finds when he finished that there have been four versions of his speech: the one that he prepared, the one that he delivered, the one the newspapers said he delivered, and the one that he wishes, on his way home, that he had delivered."[9]

Think it over. Did you reach your goals? Share your key points? Develop a rapport with your audience? Feel energized by the experience? Were you convincing? If you are a bit disappointed, don't dwell on it, learn from it.

Listen to or view the tape of your talk. Ask trusted colleagues and family members to help you critique your performance. This may seem painful at first, but give it time. You will see or hear both strengths and weaknesses. Make notes and review them as you prepare your next talk.

Your leadership role in local government provides continuous media-presentation opportunities. Today the public and your team members want and need constant information. View your skill at public speaking as your most effective communication tool. Always be ready, and use it wisely.

Checklist

Presentation opportunities and responsibilities abound in the local government setting.

Most presentations fall into one of four categories: *impromptu, extemporaneous, from manuscript,* and *from memory.*

Look for speaking opportunities, but don't be afraid to decline if accepting an invitation would not serve your objectives as a local government manager. Share public-speaking opportunities with well-prepared members of your staff.

Always be on the lookout for presentation ideas. Be ready to tape or jot down your original ideas when they arise.

Set presentation goals. Keep them few and simple. Limit the points you wish to make, to enable your audience to focus on, understand, and remember your message.

Know your audience. Speak to its interests and sensibilities.

Every speech has at least three sections: an *introduction,* a *body,* and a *closing.*

Write and speak for the ear, the way you naturally speak.

There are many effective ways to begin your talk. Humor is effective when used appropriately. An anecdote or a shared experience can connect you with your audience. Or you may raise a question or challenge that prompts your audience to respond or ponder the situation. The important thing is to tailor your introductory remarks to the occasion.

The closing gives you an opportunity to summarize your talk by restating your main points.

Invigorating when appropriate and effectively presented, humor can chill or even alienate an audience if it misses the mark.

Many local governments require public addresses on policy-related matters to be cleared with the public information office or the office of the mayor or executive. Find out and make sure to follow your local government's policy on public speaking.

Location can make or break a talk. Assess and if possible manage your speech setting to gain an edge.

Use audiovisual (AV) equipment to enhance your presence and message.

At one time a television appearance was a special opportunity requiring special preparation. Now you must always be prepared for the camera and microphone.

Call-in radio increasingly offers opportunities to share your local government's message.

10 Local Government Publications

Every local government has to issue publications of one kind or another. A small city or county may limit its efforts to a simple audit report required by state law, typed by the mayor's or manager's secretary. Larger jurisdictions are likely to issue a newsletter and various other publications—on topics such as taxes, changes in recreation program schedules, new pet-control ordinances, and other subjects of current interest. The largest localities, including cities and counties central to metropolitan areas, are likely to prepare elaborate brochures and reports for a variety of purposes.

In larger cities and counties, many publications are the responsibility of a public information officer who has considerable experience and training in publications work. In smaller local governments, however, other employees may have regular assignments for publications, such as a brochure or flier.

If you work in a local government, and particularly if you are in a supervisory or managerial position, you probably spend a lot of your time writing, editing, possibly designing, reviewing, and distributing information to various people. So whether you realize it or not, you are both a reporter and an editor. That means you need to be able to analyze information and summarize it concisely and precisely, so that you can communicate effectively with your audience. You may also be responsible for choosing a means of delivery for your message as well as a format and design that help the reader understand your message.

By virtue of your position, you share the responsibility for creating an image of your local government. If you want that image to be positive, you need to know all you can about communicating effectively. To test your skills, think about how you like to receive information.

Do you enjoy reading reports that are overloaded with jargon or words that you don't understand because they are too technical? How do you feel when you receive a huge report that is all text—without pictures, graphs, lists, or charts? What you find uninteresting, irritating, or difficult to understand will be just as uninteresting, irritating, and difficult for your constituents to read. It's crucial to think carefully about putting together a message in a format and language that a broad readership will understand, appreciate, even enjoy.

Publications today are simpler, shorter, and easier to read than they used to be. The writing has become less formal. Despite the ridicule that is often heaped on government reports for stilted writing and impenetrable jargon, they have actually improved in recent years.

Publication design, too, has improved. It is more varied than it used to be. Layout has become less cluttered and more straightforward. Paper and ink are appearing in a variety of colors. Striking illustrations are adding variety to reports. Illustrations, especially photographs, have become far more personal and informal—and therefore more effective. Using computer-generated clip art, now available in numerous and relatively inexpensive computer programs, multiplies the options for designing a publication. These changes have made it possible to produce high-quality work that is attractive, easy to read, and inexpensive.

Your publications have two main objectives: they should communicate information about a particular subject and they should create a positive image of your organization and of you. If you have never had training in preparing publications, help is readily available. The most visible providers of classes in editing, writing, and production, such as four-year colleges and art institutes, may not meet your scheduling needs and cost limitations. So don't overlook community colleges, technical schools, noncredit continuing-education courses, vendor-sponsored classes, and the one-day training seminars offered by publishers' associations and editorial-services companies. Your local newspaper might also give you guidance.

This chapter will help you plan a publications program that puts your local government's best foot forward. It covers the following topics:

Planning a publication

Writing and editing

Design

Selecting appropriate technology

Producing the publication

Working with your printer.

Planning a publication

Effective communication requires that your message be clear and consistent. You would never want to have the Public Works Department send out information in a flier one week that was contradicted the next week in a Planning Department newsletter. Nor would you prepare a series of related informational brochures that failed to incorporate similar design characteristics or that failed to make reference to information to be found in other publications in the same series. Carefully planning a publications program can save you embarrassment, confusion, and extra work. So even if you can't predict all of the publications you may need to issue in a year's time, you should keep in mind what has already been printed and how it might complement—or conflict with—what you now intend to publish.

The first step in planning your publications program is to review the publications that are central to your local government's communications. Three publications are basic for many cities and counties: a general brochure about the government, a newsletter, and an annual report. Local governments are also likely to publish employee newsletters, an employee handbook, news releases, and technical material issued in standard formats (such as building regulations, reports of city council or county board meetings, and legal notices). There may also be newspaper advertisements, such as those announcing holiday-related closings of government offices or sign-up times for recreation programs. Utility-bill inserts, consumer-affairs bulletins, and other advisory materials may also be part of your publications program.

Assess effectiveness

After you have assembled overall information on publications, you can evaluate everything that has been proposed for one year and see how the pieces fit together. Now consider the objectives of the publications program you envision. Do the publications you have planned meet those objectives? Or are some of them no longer justifiable in light of what you now want to accomplish? This is also a good time to look at prior years' publications. Are some of them outdated? Did they reach the appropriate readership? Could some of the information now be consolidated in a new publication? The answers to these questions will help you set priorities for new and revised publications.

Needs vary with publics

Once you have determined your objectives and decided which publications you need to produce to meet those objectives, take the time to think about your readers. It is time well spent, because it will determine how successful the publications program will be in the end.

When you plan your publications program, bear in mind that not everyone in your community has similar capabilities in comprehending the written word. To communicate with readers who have certain physical disabilities or who speak a language other than English, you may need to broaden the range of information materials you develop.

Senior citizens

If you serve a community where large numbers of older people live, a significant portion of the population may find it difficult to read the type sizes that often are selected for publications. Use larger type sizes for some of your printed publications, especially those intended for this group of citizens. Or tape-record publications for duplication and distribution at senior centers and other places where older residents gather. Creative, thoughtful approaches to meeting your mandate to serve people of all ages and abilities will pay off in greater public appreciation and support of local government programs.

Linguistic subcommunities

Many communities face special distribution challenges as they attempt to reach residents for whom English is not the primary language. Unless the local government has demonstrated its interest in linguistic subcommunities in a positive way, their residents are likely to mistrust you. Neglecting or postponing communication of any kind until you have to send out tax statements or turn off a neighborhood's water will hardly build the kind of trusting relationship that will help you to gain access. It is never too soon to identify the leaders of linguistic subcommunities and to begin working with them to identify the informational needs of their constituents.

Your chances of reaching citizens who seldom or never use English will be improved if you make a serious, professional effort to provide them with printed materials that respect different cultures and use their languages accurately, idiomatically, and sensitively. If you need help in translating materials into the appropriate languages or dialects, try to find someone in the community—a member of a local cultural organization or business group, for example—to advise you. If that does not work

Figure 10–1   A flier distributed to Spanish-speaking residents of Pasadena, California.

PASADENA HEALTH DEPARTMENT

Clinica Para Vacunas

en

Jackie Robinson Center
1020 North Fair Oaks
Health Unit — Room 200
797-9883

días de atención

LUNES 8:30 a.m. – 11:00 a.m.
Solamente vacunas
(no pruebas del tuberculosis)

MARTES 1:30 p.m. – 4:00 p.m.
Vacunas y pruebas del tuberculosis

VIERNES 8:30 a.m. – 1:00 a.m. and 1:30 p.m. – 4:00 p.m.
Vacunas y pruebas del tuberculosis

Padres deben acompañar a niños menores de 8 años
Por favor traiga la tarjeta de vacunas anteriores

Effective 3/4/91

out, check with area colleges and universities. Students or faculty members are occasionally available to help at a low cost (some may even be willing to donate their time). Or try the local chapter of the American Translators Association or of the Translators Guild for referrals to accredited professional translators. If all else fails, inquire with the U.S. Department of State for the nearest embassy or consulate that can provide assistance.

Do not hesitate to recruit a panel of advisers from the community to tell you whether your translation reflects local usage. They can also advise you on the effectiveness of the illustrations you have chosen, considering the background and experiences of the people will be seeing them. (See Chapter 8 for more information on communication and culture.)

Distribution

Choosing the most appropriate method of distribution or delivery can make all the difference in whether a publication is read—and understood—or ignored (or else misunderstood). A professionally produced brochure might do a wonderful job of telling your message, but it cannot do so unless it reaches your target readership. The distribution system is sometimes overlooked until after the product has been prepared, which is often too late.

Good planning can give you maximum coverage of the intended readers. For example, if you plan to put a stack of brochures or fliers on counters in public places, think ahead of time about designing an eye-catching cover. You might also design a special "Take One" sign to draw attention to your informational item.

Cost-effective dissemination

Saving money on distribution is possible without sacrificing either quality or coverage of readerships. Using low-cost but appropriate media could make the difference between a publications program that is only mediocre and one that efficiently meets the local government's need to connect with the community. For example, a short reminder to citizens that tax bills will soon be arriving at their houses may be communicated more effectively on the back of local utility bills than in a special mailer or an expensive newspaper advertisement. Many citizens who would never take the time to read through an entire town budget will at least scan a brochure that summarizes the important changes—particularly if it is well illustrated with charts and graphs.

Citizens who would never read an entire town budget will scan a brochure that summarizes the important changes.

If you plan to mail out a brochure or flier, you might want to make it a "self-mailer." Reserve the back panel for a stamp and address, so that it can be mailed without using an envelope. That can net significant savings for your publications operation—and ultimately for the local government as a whole.

Informal distribution, or "piggybacking"

Another method of distribution for various publications is to convince interested civic associations, students, or volunteers to go door to door. Or you might set up a distribution system in cooperation with the chamber of commerce, the Welcome Wagon, or other groups that have regular contact with your intended readership. Such a group might even share the production costs—provided that the copy is particularly appropriate to their goals and takes into account their interests or needs.

Besides saving money, cooperative production and distribution has another advantage: it lends credibility to a publication. We all tend to be more trusting of people we know or those whom we consider our peers.

We are naturally more receptive when a message from local government is distributed by our peers or when it seems to carry the imprimatur of an organization with which we are comfortable.

Although familiarity with the group distributing the material can be an advantage, be aware that it could be detrimental in some cases. That is why it is especially important to be sensitive and attuned to your readership. If the organization you are thinking about working with is controversial or has a credibility problem, rethink your plans. Reputation, once lost, is hard to reclaim.

Study your organization's ethics code to be sure that you are not involving yourself in a conflict of interest by using any of the groups discussed above. If you are not certain of the legal ramifications, consult your city or county attorney.

Specific publications
Different types of publication can be distributed in a number of ways.

Newsletters
Newsletters can be distributed in several ways. Newsletters published for the entire community can be mailed separately, enclosed in other mailings such as utility bills, inserted in local newspapers, or delivered door to door if you have access to low-cost or volunteer labor. Always be sure to send copies to the media; even the best reporters occasionally miss stories, and they are always looking for feature ideas. Your newsletter can serve as a reminder or provide a tip on any number of subjects.

Make sure that every employee receives a copy of the newsletter at the same time, so that no one feels left out.

If your organization is small, distribution of in-house newsletters can be quick and simple. Larger organizations often distribute newsletters with paychecks, at staff meetings, or through interoffice mail. Regardless of the system you use, make sure that every employee receives a copy of the newsletter at the same time, so that no one feels overlooked or left out.

Annual reports
Distribution of annual reports can be expensive, particularly if you decide that the report should go to everyone in your community. If you mail it out, bulk rates will help reduce the cost. If you distribute it as a newspaper insert, the distribution can be figured into your total production cost. To help reduce expenses, consider asking volunteers or local civic groups to deliver the report door to door.

Utility-bill inserts
The utility bill is one of the items most frequently received by citizens from local government. Therefore it is one of the easiest and cheapest ways to communicate with a large number of citizens. Utility bills also provide a convenient way to send messages to selected neighborhoods or groups within the community.

Regardless of the readership or the message, a utility-bill insert is an almost certain way of getting attention, since almost everyone opens bills. But because renters and residents of group homes or senior centers may not receive a utility bill, you will need to find alternative means of communicating with them if it is important for all citizens to receive the information included as inserts in utility bills.

To control the quality, content, and frequency of utility-bill inserts, one person in the organization should be responsible for reviewing and scheduling all inserts. Inserts should be scheduled well in advance, and their frequency should be closely monitored, to avoid overwhelming citizens with a barrage of information. One advantage of this kind of oversight is that matters such as the weight of the inserts can be regulated to control mailing costs.

Mail your newsletters in utility bills

The City of Modesto inserts a city information letter within its monthly utility bills. The four-page 6½-by-7-inch mini-newsletter, which is mailed to 52,000 Modesto residences, allows the city to communicate frequently with residents about such items as rate changes, water conservation, council goals, and city services. Citizen response has been excellent. A recent newsletter survey generated 5,500 replies. The city includes such items as free bus passes and coupons to city-sponsored events in the newsletter to generate enthusiasm. "We wouldn't be able to publish the newsletters without the use of the utility bills. Without the bills, postage costs alone would be $10,000," said Cathy Gorham, public information officer.

Source: Elliot Wolf, "Eight Great Ideas for Communicating with Citizens on a Shoestring Budget," *Western City* (September 1992), pp. 20–21.

Your local government should have a policy on whether inserts are accepted from outside the organization—and if so, under what conditions. For example, would you allow an established community charity to run an insert during its annual campaign? If so, what about the local conservation group? May private groups, such as the organizers of a local cultural fair, include a registration insert? What criteria will apply for deciding what groups or organizations qualify to be allowed an insert? Is there a fee or charge to outside agencies for including their inserts? Finally, if you allow outside groups to schedule inserts, what happens if one of them must be dropped for lack of space or some other reason?

Cities and counties that have insert programs often find themselves inundated with requests from outside agencies and groups.

Cities and counties that have excellent insert programs often find themselves inundated with requests from outside agencies and groups. Some discussion and preparation at the outset can spare your local government some difficult decisions and frayed relations down the road.

You should at least have a written policy on the use of inserts that addresses whether outside groups may submit inserts, the submission procedure, length and format, due dates for submission, and fees. The policy should also include information on circumstances under which an outside group's insert may be eliminated.

Although you might please some local organizations by allowing them to use your mailings, you might also be running a risk of causing hard feelings or even legal difficulties when you are confronted by unexpected problems. For example, what if you have to omit the food pantry's insert because the city council wants you to send out information about a rate increase instead? Or what will you do if a racist organization sponsors a food pantry drive and meets your requirements for an insert?

If you have been allowing nongovernment organizations to "piggyback" inserts in governmental mailings, perhaps you should reevaluate your public-information program. You may find that the space you have given to other organizations could be better used for announcements and information that concern your city or county. For example, you might use the space to provide information on dog and cat licensing, to notify the public about changes in the refuse collection schedule or to list collection points for recyclables. Some communities even use the back of the return section of their utility bills for short citizen surveys and to communicate the results of those surveys.

Figure 10–2 A public information brochure sent to 300,000 Phoenix, Arizona, households with their monthly water bills.

notes

A Publication for the Citizens of the City of Phoenix | **August 1993**

PHOENIX STREETS NEED "PARENTS"

If you would like to become involved in the community and help keep Phoenix neighborhoods clean, contact the city's "Adopt-A-Street" Program.

You, your family, school, church, company or neighborhood organization can get involved in Adopt-A-Street. All you have to do is care for and improve the aesthetics on both sides of a one-mile section of street. The city places a sign at the beginning and end of the street to recognize your efforts.

To date, 122 sections of Phoenix streets have been adopted and Adopt-A-Street signs have been installed. The program was created in October 1991 to respond to corporations and civic groups who were interested in keeping Phoenix thoroughfares clean and attractive.

For more information about how you, your company or organization can adopt a street, call Bruce Varker, Street Transportation Department, 256-4334.

Newspaper inserts

A newspaper insert is a good way to reach a wide readership with a great deal of information at a relatively low cost per copy. Newspaper inserts have already been mentioned as an appropriate format for some annual reports. How you use newspaper inserts may depend on the format and interests of local or regional newspapers.

If you haven't worked with the local newspaper on using it as a vehicle for special inserts or publications, it is worth a visit to the newspaper's advertising manager to talk about opportunities, costs, and formats. Most newspaper inserts are considered advertising and are marked as such.

Spend some time with the circulation department at the newspaper to see how many people you are likely to reach.

You can even do a newspaper "insert" that isn't inserted anywhere. In that case, you might contract with the newspaper printing plant to prepare a tabloid on a specific issue and distribute it through your own means, such as bulk mailing.

Spend some time with the circulation department at the newspaper to see how many people you are likely to reach through a newspaper insert. If you want to reach a large readership, an insert may be the most cost-effective way. You should make sure, however, that the newspaper readership matches your own readership fairly closely. If you live in an area where the local newspaper serves a broad region, you might end up paying for a product that goes to subscribers who do not even live in your community.

A growing number of newspapers have the ability to vary inserts by zones, routes, or editions. For an extra charge, they may be willing to make special accommodations for you but be sure you know what the cost will be up front. After you calculate the expense of stuffing the inserts and the waste from those that go to households that are not part of your constituency, you may find that a bulk mailing is less expensive.

Use your community newspaper

The City of Santa Paula is publishing its quarterly city newsletter as an insert in the *Santa Paula Chronicle.* To ensure that all residents see the newsletter, it is inserted in the Wednesday newspaper edition, which is distributed to all residents. The city writes the copy, with the newspaper typesetting the text. The city pays a fee of $350 for the typesetting and printing of approximately 1,500 copies of each issue, an extremely affordable alternative. The city does not have to pay the cost of folding and inserting, or mailing costs.

Source: Elliot Wolf, "Eight Great Ideas for Communicating with Citizens on a Shoestring Budget," *Western City* (September 1992), p. 20.

Newspaper advertisements

Most local governments are required by law to use legal advertisements for certain special events such as public hearings, bid openings, and employment opportunities. Newspaper ads should not be overlooked for other purposes, though. They are often a good way of capturing attention. The old saying that it pays to advertise is true.

It is also true that the appearance and content of an ad influence its effectiveness. A classified ad may be all you need to publicize a job opening. A display ad is more appropriate if you want to attract the attention of a broad readership, such as those who would be interested in your summer recreation program or the schedule for neighborhood budget hearings.

Newspaper ads can also be used for public-service announcements. The local newspaper might be willing to prepare and run certain public-service ads at no cost, depending on the topic. But beware of one pitfall here. Public-service announcements are used to fill space only when regular advertising or news copy runs short, and unpaid ads usually aren't published according to a schedule. If the timing of your message is important, you might have to pay for the advertising to guarantee publication when you want it.

If you pay for a newspaper ad, expect to pay for the same information to be advertised on radio or television. It is unfair to expect the broadcast media to run public-service announcements if you paid for advertising in the print media. (See Chapters 6 and 7 for more information on advertising by local government.)

Figure 10–3 A display advertisement run in area newspapers by the Lancaster County (Pennsylvania) Planning Commission.

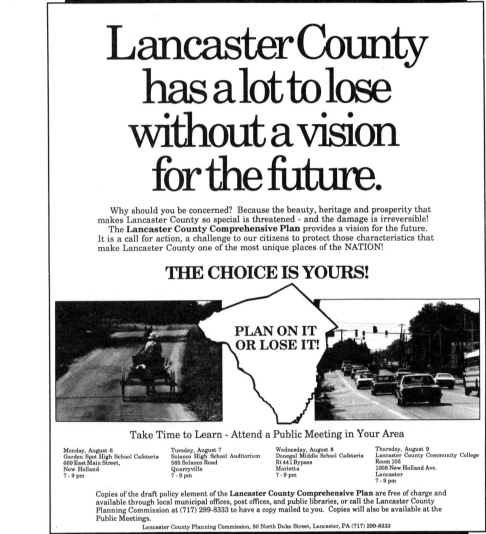

Miscellaneous media
Many other printed formats besides actual publications can be used to deliver brief messages or capture attention. They include door hangers; decals and stickers; posters; bus, taxi, and subway cards; calendars; and billboards (outdoor advertising). These formats are usually appropriate for short messages that have a long life. Posters, billboards, and public-transportation cards, for example, can be used to remind residents about hot line numbers, to encourage ride sharing or the use of public transportation, or to announce special events. Often you can prepare one message and reproduce it in several formats to draw attention to your message in different places.

Door hangers provide an opportunity to get messages to local residents quickly, cheaply, and imaginatively. A door hanger can be used to communicate timely information to a well-defined neighborhood. The

Door hangers get messages to local residents quickly, cheaply, and imaginatively.

primary advantage of a door hanger is that it allows you to leave an important message with the occupants of a home or business when you are unable to speak with them in person.

Depending on the nature of the announcement, you might need some help from volunteers to distribute the hangers. If the hanger is used for a specific local government function, such as inspections, the staff who will be doing the job can distribute the hanger. If the readership for the hanger is broad and volunteers are not readily available to help with distribution, newspaper ads or direct-mail brochures may be easier and less expensive to develop and disseminate.

Billboards are an often overlooked source of publicity for local governments. Although their numbers have diminished in recent years, they can be used effectively to convey terse but important public-service messages. Appropriate messages concern topics such as upcoming events or health and safety. Local governments can sometimes obtain advertising space on billboards at little or no charge. And many outdoor-advertising companies will assist with designing and producing the message for your government.

You need to use this medium very judiciously. Not all billboards are welcome in the communities where they are sited. So you need to lay the groundwork for good community relations. Try to make contact with the local neighborhood association before soliciting or accepting billboard space in a residential area.

For more guidance on how to reach the proper readerships for specific public-information products, see Chapters 1, 2, 6, and 7.

Publications in general

Some publications need not be distributed to everyone, but it is important to send copies to people and groups with a direct interest. Techni-

Contact the local neighborhood association before soliciting billboard space in a residential area.

Critical elements of planning a publication

When you think you are ready to prepare a publication, ask yourself these questions:

What types of people constitute the readership for this publication? Who are they? What are they looking for? What is the level of their interest? How deep is their knowledge (both in general and on this public issue)?

Do I understand the material I am trying to convey?

Why is the message being presented?

Am I certain that the facts are accurate?

How much time do I have to prepare the materials? How does the time available compare with the time it takes to prepare and produce the type of publication I am considering?

Have I decided on the most logical and effective means of communicating my message, rather than the easiest, the cheapest, or even the most impressive? Would my message come across more effectively with audiovisuals? Or could additional materials be developed to give the message broader dissemination?

What is the expected "shelf life" of the material I plan to prepare? Am I producing something that will be used once and then quickly become outdated? Or am I giving general information that will be used a long time without needing any updating?

Could the material be developed as a joint venture with some group in the private sector or with other public agencies? Are there others who might be interested in the message and willing to help finance the undertaking?

What publicity resources are available in my community, such as professional public relations agencies and professional print shops, that would help me select a medium or even help design my publication at little or no cost?

How many copies of the product am I likely to use? Can I save money by printing or producing beyond my immediate needs, thereby reducing the unit cost? Or would a large print run simply generate extra copies that would go unused?

How does this material fit in with other publications of my local government?

If you do not have answers to all of the above questions, you need to do more planning. If you feel comfortable with your answers, then you are ready to begin working on the specifics of your publication.

cal changes in subdivision regulations, for example, should be sent to the local real-estate board and the builders council.

Some groups should regularly receive everything—or almost everything—that your city or county publishes. Such groups include reporters from newspapers, television, and radio; the city council or county board; the local taxpayers' association and the chamber of commerce; and libraries. It is especially important to send these groups newsletters, the annual report, budget documents, and management reports on issues of the day.

Assign responsibility

Begin working on specifics by delegating responsibility for the various tasks involved in the production of your publication. Who will be assigned to write the material? Who will be responsible for the design? Who will coordinate the printing and distribution? Knowing the answers to these questions up front—and making the assignments early—can prevent delays in the production process.

Most local government publications are written by employees. When assigning the writing, remember to balance the need for clear writing with the need for accurate technical information. It may be helpful when you are publishing material on technical topics to ask a knowledgeable nonspecialist to read it and tell you whether he or she thinks the general public would understand it.

Budget

You will need to draft a budget and get estimates of the costs. For a periodical (such as a newsletter), you do not need a budget for every issue of the publication. In some instances, the costs may include the work of illustrators or photographers; outside typesetting and duplicating services; production costs, including printing and binding; and mailing or other methods of distribution. (Guidance on production schedules is given later in this chapter.)

Organize the process

It is indispensable to draw up a schedule for all the important steps in the production process. Major stages include (1) the preparation of the first draft; (2) review, revision (editing), and rewriting; (3) selection of the printer; (4) selection of photographs and other illustrations; and (5) preparation of specifications. Guidance on those tasks is given in some detail below.

The four steps involved in getting started can be summarized as follows:

1. Define objectives, identify the readership, and outline the components of the publication or publication program.
2. Assign component responsibilities.
3. Develop a budget.
4. Assign the responsibilities of writing, editing, and proofreading the publication—preferably to three different people.
5. Draw up a production schedule.

Schedule

A realistic, verifiable production schedule is essential to producing a publication on time and within budget—which is your goal. Having deadlines for each step pinpoints responsibilities and helps maintain control of the total production process. If the target date for delivery is to be met, each step must fall into place at predetermined times and in an orderly manner.

The production schedule should include checkpoints for copy preparation (writing and editing), design and layout, typesetting, proofreading, artwork, illustrations, final approval, printing, and delivery. Some steps can be done concurrently. Others must follow an inflexible sequence. Time intervals should be shown in business days and should allow for weekends and holidays.

It is best to prepare a schedule in chart form, with space to show planned and actual start dates and completion dates. The chart lets you know at a glance whether the production process is on schedule.

Writing and editing

People write to communicate. If the writing is clear and concise, they will be understood. Sometimes it is enough just to be understood. Usually, though, it is also important to create an image or a feeling about a message or about the organization. When you fail to consider what image you want to create, you may either unintentionally create a mistaken image or leave the reader unsure about what your organization is and does.

Get it right the first time

After it has been disseminated, the written word can never be withdrawn. A printed message may be seen by readerships far beyond those it was intended to reach. The less those readers know about the organization that prepared the message—and its goals—the more likely they are to draw conclusions only on the basis of what they see and read. Even when you take steps to correct an error or clarify a statement that was misunderstood, you can never be sure that the whole original readership will see the clarifications.

Therefore, every aspect of preparing the message is significant. The way you write, the method you use to disseminate what you write, and the graphics you use to accompany your written words all determine how effectively you communicate. Those elements will be covered in this chapter.

Figure 10–4 Publication production schedule.

Title: _____

Operation	Responsibility	Progress start/finish					Completion date		Cost	
							Scheduled	Actual	Est.	Actual
Publication plan										
Copy preparation										
Layout/design										
Illustrations										
Typesetting										
Artwork										
Printing										
Delivery										

Analyze your readers

Your assessment of your readership and the purpose for writing each publication should always guide you in deciding on the content and style of a publication. Good writers have the ability to use several styles. For each type of publication they find a style that is appropriate to its purposes and its readership.

The larger the potential readership, the harder it is to determine its limits. Nothing illustrates this problem better than the annual city or county report. The readership for such a report might include such disparate types as business owners, factory workers, homemakers, students, office workers, and teachers. The diversity of their interests, reading abilities, perceptions of their position in the community, and motivations makes it difficult to write for them all in one publication.

Analyzing the intended readership is the first step in planning any writing project. People are influenced by their past associations as well as by their present situations. Their backgrounds—their values and their experiences—determine their reactions to words and phrases. When your readership consists of people you know, you can develop a publication suited to what you know about them. When the readership consists of people you do not know, writing a publication to suit them becomes more difficult. Even so, two important types of information are often available: readers' education levels and the kinds of jobs they do.

Education is the key to gauging reading level. Census Bureau data are an excellent source of demographic information, including education levels. Orient your publications to what that information tells you about

---

How foggy is your writing?

When Rudolph Flesch published the first readability formula, he started a controversy that went on for decades. Part of the debate centered on the simplicity of the formula he developed in 1949. Another part centered on the desirability of reducing reading difficulty and the possible sacrifice of exact meaning or "adult" content that a reduced level of difficulty might entail. In response, other researchers added more sophisticated scales to Flesch's.

Robert Gunning's "Fog Index" provides an easy way of estimating the reading level of your writing. (It will not indicate whether you write in a style interesting enough to keep your readers awake, however.)

1. In a writing sample that is at least 100 words long, divide the total number of words by the number of sentences. This will give you the average sentence length.

2. Count the number of words three or more syllables long, omitting proper names; combinations of easy, shorter words, such as *teenager* and *bookkeeper*; and verbs that are three syllables long because they end in *ed* or *es*. This will give you the number of "difficult" words. Divide this number into the total number of words in the passage to get the percentage of difficult words.

3. Add the average sentence length (calculated in #1) to the percentage of difficult words (calculated in #2). Multiply the sum by 0.4. The result will be your readability score, expressed in terms of school-grade reading level.

A score of 17 indicates that people who have a college degree could read your writing easily. A score of 11 puts you in good company—with *Time* and the *Atlantic Monthly.* Most people in the United States would be able to understand what you write—a good position for any government official to be in.

A score of 9 may mean you should consider using longer words or longer, more complex sentences. But before you act too hastily, remember that John Steinbeck, the Pulitzer-Prize-winning author, often wrote on a ninth-grade reading level, and no one considers Steinbeck childish.

One lone sample, of course, will not give you an entirely accurate reading. Taking several samples provides better information. But even the use of several samples does not assure absolute accuracy. Many college juniors would be unable to define the word *tacit*—although it is two syllables long. But most fifth-graders know what *difference* means, although it does not fall into any of the "exception" classes for easy three-syllable words.

Given that such tests are not absolutely accurate, why should you bother? Because self-assessment of your writing is healthy. It keeps you alert for bad writing habits that (like crabgrass) tend to take over if left undetected.

the reading levels of residents of your locality. According to the Census Bureau, about three-quarters of Americans over age 25 have completed high school. So it is likely that your readership, whether they are employees or customers of your local government, will read more or less at the high-school level.

The key to successful writing is to make sure it is suited to the expectations and abilities of your readership. For example, a brochure on job training for adults who have not completed high school should read differently from a brochure on economic development that you distribute to local business leaders. This is not to say that any piece should be simplistic or that you should regard any readers as unintelligent. But the needs of various population groups do differ.

If you are not certain how to write for the general population, look at a mainstream national magazine for clues.

If you are not certain about how to write for the general population, look at your local newspaper or a mainstream national magazine for some clues. There are tests you can do yourself to gauge the readability of what you write. Most public school systems have reading teachers who could be helpful in analyzing the reading level of the writing you produce. Another way of finding out the reading level of your local residents is to include some questions about your publications and whether or not they are read in citizens surveys. Be sure to give those who say no the opportunity to indicate whether the problem is the content, the format, or the writing style.

Overcoming writer's block

Writing is a creative process requiring inspiration, and all writers "freeze" at times. Even professional writers find themselves without words now and then. But self-observation and writing exercises can help you face those crises.

One method of self-observation starts by making lists. Take a piece of paper and divide it down the middle. Mark one side "easy" and the other "difficult"—or one "good" and the other "bad." What you label them is not important, as long as the entries in one column include observations about your surroundings and state of mind when writing goes well, and the other lists observations about your surroundings and state of mind when writing proves difficult. The observations should include aspects like physical condition, location, ambient temperature, noise conditions, and mood.

Writers who observe themselves long enough to know the conditions under which they write well can sometimes break through what has become known as "writer's block" by purposely setting up the surroundings, emotions, stresses, or other conditions they need in order to write well. If this tactic fails, though, there are others.

One common method of beginning is simply to begin anywhere, by "mental dumping." Just write anything that comes to mind. You might include comments about the problem, about the difficulty of finding a solution, about anything. Writing about the project or problem—even when this writing seems disorganized—can be a psychological mechanism for thinking the problem through. Once your thoughts are on paper, you can rearrange them into something sensible and develop a structure. For writers who have completed their research but do not know how they wish to approach the subject, this method may constitute the vital link in the thinking process.

Another fruitful method for some writers is to talk about the project with others. The comments and questions of people who are not familiar with the project can help you identify what needs to be written.

Getting something onto paper is the most important thing. Even well-written, well-planned pieces need some fine-tuning afterward. The fear of writing an imperfect piece should not stop you from beginning. Perfection is really a goal of rewriting, not of writing. Find a process that works for you, and stay with it.

Write the way you speak

One style appropriate for almost all situations is the conversational style. It is the most natural style, and therefore the most readable.

A pompous, overblown style in which unnecessarily long words and stilted, noun-heavy syntax serve to obscure the meaning is counterproductive in any situation. Conversely, a conversational style improves communication, thus advancing the goal of your message.

Make your messages read and sound as if you were talking directly to someone. Sometimes that ability alone makes an experienced journalist stand out. You can do the same—whether you are preparing a report that will go to the county executive or developing a brochure about a new program. Be sure to watch out for reader-stoppers—words or phrases in your text that you would never use in a conversation.

Jargon lesson no. 1

Good ideas can be stated with simple wording. They have enough virtue to survive on their own. Success in local government employment does not depend on your ability to confuse citizens and co-workers. Frequent use of jargon does not impress those who know the subject and is guaranteed to offend those who are not insiders. Here are two of the most common kinds of jargon that you should avoid:

Bureaucratese. Bureaucratese uses big words for little ideas. People are "advised their entitlements have been suspended" instead of "told their checks have been stopped." When bureaucrats agree in bureaucratese, they "answer in the affirmative" instead of saying "yes." Programs are "implemented" rather than "begun," and information is "input for review and consideration" rather than "considered." They never "retire," but eventually we read that they "have terminated their employment after considerable tenure in office." When enough of these phrases are strung together, the effect is amazing, as in this example:

> "After assuring yourself that all pertinent procedures and preparations have been accomplished, permission is granted to initiate the overall implementation of combat operations."

Translation: *"You may fire when ready"* (Admiral George Dewey).

Legalese. Legalese relies upon using several words that mean the same thing, tied together with "whereas," "therein," "thereto," "thereof," and other words added to wills and contracts to make them confusing. Those who become adept at using legalese stop using three- and four-syllable words that come from Latin and Greek and begin using real Latin and Greek phrases.

The more formal the style, the more likely the reader will feel alienated from the source of the writing.

A conversational style involves simple wording, direct sentence structures, and appropriate pronouns. It does not require you to abandon conventional punctuation and format. Nor does it mean that you must "write down to" your readers.

A conversational style makes peers of writer and the reader. The more formal the style, the more likely it is that the reader will feel depersonalized and perhaps alienated from the source of the writing—in your case, the local government. When in doubt, go for simplicity. If you guess wrong and err on the side of informality, your readers will still appreciate how easy it was to read your writing.

Being able to use different styles increases your versatility as a writer. But with that ability comes an obligation to tailor your style to your readership and your purpose. If you use a breezy style and tone when writing about a crisis, you may face an angry constituency. Not only will you fail to communicate the original message effectively, you may also create a need for additional, explanatory communications at a time when other activities are keeping your hands full.

Tips for better writing

1. Choose a writing style appropriate to your audience, your purpose, and the situation.

2. Use concrete language.

3. Limit the use of jargon to occasions when it will be easily understood.

4. Avoid unnecessary words.

5. Use the active voice rather than the passive voice.

6. Write with variety in mind.

7. Keep most sentences simple.

8. Keep related words together in a sentence.

9. Be sure your writing has coherence.

10. Use positive rather than negative statements.

Accurate information, positive tone

Perhaps the most important reporting skill is accuracy. Inaccuracies, no matter how slight, are inexcusable. You are in the position of being the expert, and your readership will assume that what you write is correct. Whatever the format, purpose, focus, or readership of your message, you should check your facts carefully, and then recheck them. If you make an error, correct it as quickly as you can. Even the best reporters make errors. If you seem unconcerned about minor errors, however, you will find it hard to sustain your reputation as a reliable source of information.

Even when a message is negative, try to present it in the most positive way possible. You can do it without lying or even shading the truth. (The results of misleading the public are never positive.)

A business using this "positive tone" approach, for example, would not simply apologize to a customer for selling a defective machine and repair it free of charge. The smart business would return the machine along with a letter assuring the owner that, for example, "the repaired machine will give years of good service." A government using this approach would tout the improved services that would be made possible by a tax increase, or the fiscal stability that would result from a budget cut.

Another positive-tone tactic is to offer alternatives. Citizens who receive fliers announcing the interruption of water service are likely to be frustrated and angry. They may be mollified, though, if the same flier lets them know that bottled water is available at a parks and recreation facility, or that they may take a shower at the locker room of the municipal pool during periods of interrupted service.

If putting a positive spin on a basically bad-news message is not possible, appealing to the community's better judgment by offering substantive reasons for the local government's decisions or actions often soothes tempers. If your government makes a practice of communicating with local residents only when the news is bad, though, you would be justified in expecting a suspicious, cynical response regardless of what you were to say.

Types of local government publications

Your local government can generate numerous publications, depending on the needs of your locality. Different publics, different purposes, and different resources dictate the content and style of each publication you will produce. A few types that have been found to be most useful are discussed below.

Newsletters

Newsletters are often the most regular and comprehensive medium for disseminating local government publicity, whether in house or in the community. Although you might in some cases be able to produce one newsletter to serve both the internal *and* external readerships, usually the kinds of information needed by those two readerships may differ enough to warrant separate publications. In both cases, however, newsletters are more than simply a valuable source of current information. They are also a way to instill pride in the community, the activities of the local government, and the work of local government employees.

The success of your newsletter will depend on its regularity as well as its content.

To decide how lengthy to make a newsletter, you need to consider the time and other resources you have available. You may decide to produce a single page of quickly printed information. Or you might be able to put out a more elaborate multipage publication with photographs and graphics.

Once you have decided how frequently your publication will come out, try to stick with the schedule. That way, readers will become used to seeing the product at a certain time, and contributors will be able to plan far enough in advance to submit timely articles and announcements. The success of your newsletter as both an information resource and a public-relations tool will depend on its regularity as well as its content. Most newsletters are published either quarterly or monthly; some appear bimonthly.

Turning negatives into positives: The "pigging" of Delaware, Ohio

When the city of Delaware, Ohio, decided to "pig"—clean out—the large mains that brought water to the city from its water-treatment plant, the staff knew that residents would have many questions. Among the staff's concerns was that they had to shut off the water supply to various parts of the city during the late-night and early-morning hours. If any problems cropped up during the "pigging" process, water service would be interrupted during hours when residents would be preparing to go to work and school.

An intensive campaign to inform and prepare the community was begun several months before the project was to get under way. Included in newspaper advertisements and mailers to homeowners were cartoons of pigs popping out of or into water lines and faucets. By the time the cleaning of the lines began, the bristled (but hardly lifelike) brushes that were forced through the mains had become real little pigs in the community's collective imagination. Even the team of city workers who were to help the contractor had purchased special "Pig Team" t-shirts. On the damp fall night that the first pig was to pop out of a water main, a large, cheerful, cider-drinking crowd gathered during the post-midnight hours to celebrate the event.

The real test came several nights later, however, when problems came up. The pigs were stuck, and there was no hope of turning on the water in time for several thousand residents to take their morning showers. As the days dragged on, problems persisted, and water became a prized commodity in affected areas of the community. Unlike in earlier water emergencies caused by broken water mains, the public generally remained calm and sympathetic.

The only conclusion that could be drawn from the experience was that the public information campaign had been effective. First, city residents knew why the project was necessary, what the risks were, and what would happen if problems occurred. Second, they perceived that the city council had made a thoughtful decision to proceed and that steps had been taken to minimize the inconvenience to the residents.

The major factor, however, was the image that had been created of competent, lovable little pigs racing through the water lines—all for the good of the community. The only surprise to the government was the high degree of empathy and the sustained level of support from the public.

Figure 10–5 Employee and community newsletters produced by the city of Salina, Kansas.

E·s·p·r·i·t
CITY OF SALINA · EMPLOYEE NEWSLETTER

Volume 11, Number 1   January / February 1992

Food a highlight

Holidays at firehouse: different from most

As most of us sat down to our holiday meals, we probably never gave a thought that for some folks duty called, keeping them from joining family and friends around the holiday table.

For persons working a 24-hour shift, such as firefighters and emergency medical personnel, this means that they are away for the entire holiday.

It is an interesting, if somewhat unfair, quirk of a 3-shift rotation that the shift on duty on Thanksgiving Day will also be on duty on Christmas Day as well as New Year's Eve. Leap year throws in a double whammy with the same shift working the holiday schedule

HERE'S SANTA — Christmas eve at a nearly empty City-County Building is brightened by a surprise visit from the jolly, plump man in the red suit who took a break from his toy delivery to hand out Snickers to good City employees.

Peter Brown Photo

One Keepers' Place

Museum 'environment' draws well at opening

More than 150 visitors were on hand for the opening of One Keepers' Place at the Smoky Hill Museum on December 7.

Mary Douglass, Curator of Collections, led groups on collections tours in the Museum basement and explained more about the collection and preservation techniques used by modern museums. Visitors also got a chance to hear the Smoky Hill River Rascals, directed by **Colleen Jewell**, perform Christmas songs.

One Keepers' Place is an interactive environment for children and adults. Would-be gumshoes cracked the cases at the 1930s-era mock detective agency, learning about Great Plains history and the buffalo. Other cases touched Salina history, such as finding the oldest remaining building — the carpentry shop built by **Luke Parsons** and **Simeon Garlitz** in 1860 now located at 105 N. Front St. — and the town's oldest continuously operating business — Seitz Shoes at 108 S. Santa Fe.

Such history mysteries are the basis of the room, encouraging children to use a line-up, lab and wall safes to link together clues that solve stories about the history of Salina and the region.

Funded primarily by the Friends of the Smoky Hill Museum, One Keepers' Place took almost two years to complete from concept to opening. The theme was conceived by a committee of volunteers, and the room's floor plan is
(See MUSEUM on page 3)

Official Fire Department Photo

...tation #1 are (clockwise ...sley, Ron Householter, ...' Keith Teasley. Please

---

A report from your City government

The Salina Citizen
June 1991

June 7-9

It's Festival time again— what more can be said?

by Lana Jordan
Festival Coordinator

The Smoky Hill River Festival is fifteen years old. Hard to believe! Each year the Festival begins again — like a rhythmic, familiar tradition we can count on. Yet it's always new — with its special combination of different-old-new: a tricky balance maintained by a structure that is seasoned and flexible.

The Festival is a unique blend of music, food, children, visual arts, the challenge of competition and the excitement of celebration. The Festival experience offers each of us those wonderful feelings of expectation and surprise. That is what the Smoky Hill River Festival is all about!

The Thursday Night Festival Jam officially opens Festival '91 weekend on June 6. This 6:00 to 10:00 p.m. showcase of local and regional talent on the Gazebo features fifteen area groups performing a variety of music, followed by a half-hour final concert by the nationally known band, **Alias.** The first single produced by this group, "More Than Words Can Say," went to #1 on the R & R and *Billboard* charts.

Headline Entertainment

The Cones Sisters
Friday evening, June 7,
on the Gazebo

They really are sisters — Jan,
See Festival page 2

CATCH REGENCY at Festival '91. Please see story.

Internal Affairs

Complaints about police can be filed with unit

In January, James D. Hill was named Salina Chief of Police. Chief Hill comes to our city after eighteen years of law-enforcement service to the citizens of Lincoln, Nebraska. One of the departmental changes he has instituted is discussed in the following interview.

James D. Hill

An internal affairs unit is new to the Salina Police Department. Exactly what does it do?

JH: The Salina Police Department recently formed an Internal Affairs Unit, staffed by Lt. Jack Gallagher, who reports directly to me.

The Internal Affairs Unit is a fact-finding body charged with investigating complaints against the police department or any of its members. It is responsible for initiating and carrying out these investigations and for maintaining complete records of their activities. All of their findings will be forwarded to me for final disposition.

How do you define "complaint"?

JH: Formally, as a criticism of the delivery of police services which did not meet the complaining citizen's expectations, or as
See Internal Affairs page 6

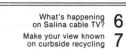

CITY OF SALINA

Internal newsletters

Newsletters designed primarily for staff members tend to be focused on life within the organization. Types of articles that work well in an employee newsletter include the following:

Information on changes in staffing, such as hirings, promotions, and retirements

Explanations of actions by the governing body that affect employees or would be of general interest to employees

Results of athletic events or information about special events for employees

General local government news that helps inform and involve employees.

An employee newsletter works best when it is informal and personal. The stories in it should both capture the flavor of the organization and provide a perspective on it.

Occasional short stories or photos about humorous events are popular. Remember, however, that humor should never be at someone else's expense. A good test of a story or picture is to think about how you might feel if it were you instead of another employee in the spotlight. If you would be uncomfortable, hurt, or angry—or even if you are unsure about how a particular employee might feel—it is best not to include an item.

In writing an employee newsletter it is also important to consider any cultural or other differences among employee groups that could result in misunderstandings because of either their inclusion in or exclusion from a story or picture. Just as you would seek ways to communicate with the diverse groups in the community, you should look for opportunities to ensure that all of your employees feel included in the local government family.

Although newsletters should always serve a motivational purpose, they must also address serious issues such as layoffs, race relations, and sexual-harassment cases in a responsible and reasonably forthright way. If an appeal to the employees' right to know does not impress your local government administration, a desire to protect the credibility of its own publications should. Any unflattering news about your local government will assuredly find its way into the local media, whether it appears in your newsletter or not. A substantive newsletter that respects employees' intelligence is one of local government's best weapons against the rumor mill. (See Chapter 8 for more information on internal communications.)

In writing a newsletter it is important to consider any cultural or other differences among employees that could result in misunderstanding.

Community newsletters

Appropriate items for a general community newsletter include the following:

Articles on new programs and services

Feature stories about citizens and employees who have made special contributions or who represent a specific element of the community

Notices and feature articles on special events, such as an annual Independence Day parade

General reminders about tax bills, leash laws, pool schedules, and seasonal events

Articles on the functions of various departments

Information on the local budget and how it will affect services and taxes

An events calendar.

Annual reports

The soaring costs of printing and mailing require you to evaluate the purpose, readership, content, and format of your published annual report. You may find that several mandated and optional reports can be combined into one multipurpose report, or that low-cost printing methods—one-color printing with photographs or quick-copy techniques—can be used without sacrificing the overall quality of the product.

Regardless of the report's specific form, the following information should be included:

Names of elected officials

Letters of greeting from the locality's top elected official and top appointed official (if your locality uses the manager form of government)

An organization chart

A directory of local services

Schedules for meetings of the governing body and important boards and commissions

Financial information

Highlights of department activities

Explanations of any changes in programs or policies since the last report

Highlights of important goals or plans for the coming year

Telephone numbers that citizens frequently ask for.

Short publications

In addition to newsletters and reports, you can also use a variety of short publications for communicating with the public.

Brochures and fliers

Brochures and fliers are an inexpensive yet effective way of communicating brief but important messages. Explanations of local government services, commemorations of special events, information about specific government procedures or requirements, and tips on matters such as fire safety and home security are typical topics for brochures and fliers. In any case, they should be kept short, simple, and to the point.

Fliers are especially useful in publicizing one-time-only events or when you need to get information out in a hurry. Some common uses for fliers are as follows:

Announcements of upcoming events such as public hearings, recreation programs, or neighborhood cleanups

Planting instructions for a neighborhood garden program

Announcements of short-term programs such as the distribution of free smoke detectors in certain neighborhoods.

Fact sheets

Copy for a fact sheet is not written like copy for fliers. As the name implies, a fact sheet is a straightforward, concise listing of significant facts associated with an issue or topic. Fact sheets tend to deal with such subjects as the following:

How to deal with hypertension

How to apply for a local grant to support a neighborhood project

How to identify residential fire hazards.

Fact sheets can be particularly useful for communicating information at public hearings or other special meetings so that everyone attending has the same basic information. They also can be prepared to supplement special reports for people who aren't likely to read the reports but are interested in the basic facts. Fact sheets are useful to the news media because they make some note taking unnecessary and ensure that names will be spelled correctly and figures will be accurate.

The purpose of a fact sheet is to present a series of ideas in an accessible format. Therefore it should be only one page long and have a standard format with a brief introduction or summary heading. Fact sheets are often effective when constructed in a question-and-answer format. If long or detailed explanations of the facts are needed, a fact sheet is probably not the best medium for your message. As a rule of thumb, if you can't make each point in a simple sentence, a fact sheet probably won't work.

Figure 10–6 The Baltimore County (Maryland) Public Schools make use of simple computer graphics to enliven a flier announcing adult-education offerings.

Dulaney High School, 255 Padonia Rd. 21093

DULANEY ADULT EDUCATION CENTER

BALTIMORE COUNTY PUBLIC SCHOOLS

Adult Education

makes the difference

887-4064

Thomas A. Boram, Center Principal

FALL 1993

COUNTY RESIDENT / NONRESIDENT
• County resident registration fee as listed.
• Nonresident registration fee is the fee listed plus $5.00 user fee.

SENIOR CITIZEN DISCOUNT (60 and Older)
• County resident senior citizen deduct $5.00 from registration fee listed.
• Nonresident senior citizen pays the registration fee as listed.
• No reduction for lab/material fees, tours, or community service courses.

Fees Refunds must be requested **before** the second class. Fees for materials/food/books vary and will be collected the first night of classes.
• *Make checks for registration and lab fees payable to: Dulaney High School.*

Schedule Classes begin the week of September 20 and meet from 7:30 to 9:30 P.M. unless otherwise indicated. Classes are closed for inclement weather when day schools are closed. Classes end the week of November 29. Holiday: November 24-28 - Thanksgiving Holiday.

Enrollment Classes with small enrollments may be cancelled (fees refunded) or run with a reduced number of sessions at the same fee.

Registration

BY MAIL
Registration forms in catalogs at county libraries or by phoning 887-4064.
Deadline August 27.

BY PHONE
887-4064
Mastercard or Visa charges only; begins July 19.
Deadline August 27.

BY FAX
887-4666
Mastercard or Visa charges only; begins July 19.
Deadline August 27.

BY WALK-IN
Tuesday & Wednesday, September 14 & 15:
7:30-9:30 P.M. at the center.

Utility-bill inserts

Inserts in utility bills are good for transmitting brief, time-sensitive information such as the following:

Notices of rate adjustments

Notices of changes in billing procedures

Brief newsletters

Information on special local services

Explanations of complaint procedures

Reminders about renewing permits or licenses

Hints on topics such as home safety

Requests for volunteers

Forms, questionnaires, and surveys.

Newspaper inserts

Newspaper inserts can be used for a variety of purposes, including the following:

Comprehensive descriptions of recreation programs

Annual reports to citizens

Announcements, such as those for the opening of new facilities

Descriptions of new or expanded services or programs.

Newspaper inserts provide a means of communicating more detailed information than could possibly be included in a brochure.

Newspaper advertisements

If you are not sure how to write advertising copy, talk to a local newspaper or advertising agency.

Newspaper ads should accomplish two simple goals. They should (1) catch the readers' attention and (2) provide basic information. An ad for a public hearing, for example, should cover the purpose of the hearing, the time, the place, and any special procedures for testifying at the hearing. You might also include the name and telephone number of a contact person. Ads for a special program should include eligibility requirements, how and where to apply, deadlines, the cost of participation, and where to go for further information.

If you are not certain about what types of information are appropriate for newspaper advertising, or you are not sure how to write advertising copy, talk to professional people at a local newspaper or an advertising agency. They will be experienced with what attracts readers. And they might be willing to help you augment your message with predesigned artwork.

Miscellaneous publicity pieces

The copy should be brief and snappy if it is to be used for eye-catching publicity pieces such as door hangers; decals and stickers; posters; bus, taxi, and subway cards; calendars; and billboards. Short sentences and single words work best, because your readers will often be on the move when they see the message.

Typical material for door hangers includes explanations and notifications about routine or nonroutine events such as the following:

The need for meter readers or inspectors to enter the building

Scheduled interruptions in utility service for repair or maintenance

Temporary street closings or changes in parking patterns.

Door hangers can also be used to advertise special events, such as a community cleanup program. Or they may give residents helpful information, such as directions on the care of saplings that the local government has planted near their homes.

More tips and ideas on various aspects of communicating with the public are given in Chapters 2, 3, 7, and 11. Extensive guidance on various types of writing for a wide range of publications is given in Chapter 9.

Design

Local government publications such as newsletters seldom require a complete redesign, because their general formats will have already been established. Occasionally, however, a new publication is initiated or an old one is given a new look. If you strive for simplicity, dignity, and consistent identification of your city or county, you will already be a long way toward achieving good publication design.

Typography

Perhaps the most important visual aspect of any publication is the type. When you select type for a printing job, a clear understanding of the purpose and readership of the publication will make it easier to choose from the hundreds of *typefaces* that are available. Type size and line length should be chosen so that the material can be read with little effort. Attractive type gives the reader a subliminal invitation to read further.

A comparison between a contemporary daily newspaper and one from forty years ago will show that the trend in publications design has been toward longer lines. Today's typical column of newsprint is about two inches wide, almost twice as wide as columns from decades past. Most newsprint is set in type six to nine *points* (a twelfth to an eighth of an inch) high.

The most readable type styles for large blocks of copy will have serifs (curls and cross lines at the ends of letters). The main text of this book is set in type that has serifs. Sans-serif ("without serif") typefaces are effective for side material, headlines, and publications containing only small amounts of copy (such as fliers, signs, and posters). Script-style typefaces are tiring to read at a distance or for more than a few words. If they are used at all, they should appear only on invitations, certificates, and other short, ceremonial documents intended primarily to be looked at rather than read.

Like the copy you write and other elements of design, the type you select should fit the occasion and the readership. If you can't make up your mind about an appropriate typeface for, say, a brochure informing teenagers about a new public ice-skating rink, look at the full range of publications that appeal to that age group—the magazines they read, the books they enjoy, the advertisements they respond to—even the packaging of their favorite music and foods. When you've narrowed your choices, have some sample paragraphs set and review them before you commit the entire publication to a *type family*.

Type of different faces and sizes should be combined only sparingly in one publication. Indiscriminate combinations of sizes, styles, and *weights* in one publication look amateurish and frivolous—and may confuse the reader. In general, a publication will be easier to read if you use a single type family.

Figure 10–7   A method of type classification with examples in each category.

Old Style Serif	Caslon
Modern Serif	Bodoni
Square Serif	**Clarendon**
Sans Serif	Univers
Modified Sans Serif	Optima
Connecting Script	*Brush Script*
Non-Connecting Script	*Zapf Chancery*
Miscellaneous	**STENCIL**

Figure 10–8   One type size, ten-point type, in five typefaces: Lucida, Imago Extrabold, Times Roman, Helvetica Light, and Century Expanded.

Communication

Communication

Communication

Communication

Communication

Figure 10–9   The New Century Schoolbook
family of typefaces.

ABCDEFGHIJKLMNOPQRSTUVWXYZ   (Roman, all caps)

ABCDEFGHIJKLMNOPQRSTUVWXYZ   (Roman, small caps)

abcdefghijklmnopqrstuvwxyz   (Roman, lowercase)

ABCDEFGHIJKLMNOPQRSTUVWXYZ   (Italic, all caps)

abcdefghijklmnopqrstuvwxyz   (Italic, lowercase)

ABCDEFGHIJKLMNOPQRSTUVWXYZ   (Bold, all caps)

abcdefghijklmnopqrstuvwxyz   (Bold, lowercase)

One type face, New Century Schoolbook, in five type sizes:

For every publication, ask yourself what it is supposed to do
and who is going to read it   6pt

For every publication, ask yourself what it is supposed to do
and who is going to read it.   8pt

For every publication, ask yourself what it is supposed
to do and who is going to read it.   10pt

For every publication, ask yourself what it is
supposed to do and who is going to read it.   12pt

For every publication, ask yourself what it
is supposed to do and who is going to read   14pt

Illustrations   Government publications primarily use informative illustrations, especially photographs, that tell a story. For many purposes, nothing is better than a photograph of government activities and people against the background of government buildings and equipment.

A great deal of illustrative material—line drawings as well as photographs—is in the public domain and can be used without charge. Libraries, historical societies, and even local newspapers and museums are excellent sources.

Good photographs, like good writing, should be simple, clear, and concise—and they should say something. If the mayor and the city council are presiding at a ceremony, for example, they might be shown in animated conversation. They should not simply stand with hands at their sides, looking at the camera. Even if the subject is good, a photograph can usually be improved by *cropping* to eliminate unwanted detail and to give visual emphasis to the point of the picture. Various conversion techniques, including the creation of silhouettes, can enhance visual effectiveness. Your printer or photo shop should be able (and is probably eager) to give you ideas about effective ways to present your photographs.

Color   An attractive color combination can be achieved at little additional cost by using combinations such as dark brown ink on ivory paper or dark green ink on pale green paper. Although this method of using color is economical, you should still expect to pay somewhat more for the colored paper and for setting up the color run.

Judicious use of a second color (black usually being the first color) often gives a publication style. Some colors are naturally associated with certain local government activities—such as red for the fire department, blue for the police department, or green and brown for parks and recreation. Using those colors as memory hooks will trigger those mental associations in the mind of the reader.

When considering adding color to a publication, keep these guidelines in mind:

1. *Limit the selection.* Two colors, black and one other, are usually enough.
2. *Exercise restraint.* The second color should provide emphasis and should complement rather than compete with the first color.
3. *Use familiar colors.* Unless you are designing a quickly disposable publication aimed at teenagers (such as that skating rink flier), avoid faddish, offbeat shades. Regardless of the second color you use, make sure it is dark enough to contrast crisply with your paper stock and to appear legible alongside copy set in black type.

If you plan to do the job in house, make sure you have good equipment for this kind of work. A clean, professional-looking black-and-white publication is more attractive than one that has color but is hard to read. Take advantage of your printer's experience and get his or her professional opinions.

Tips for good design

Publications may be designed by you, by a co-worker, or by an outside professional. Regardless of the role you assume in a publication project, you will be well served by following a few simple guidelines.

1. *Keep it simple.* If the text, photographs, appendices, and other content elements are poorly organized, don't expect the design to create order out of chaos. Get editorial help before that stage.
2. *Keep it clear.* Someone picking up a publication should know immediately what it is, what it is intended to do, and who its readership is supposed to be.
3. *Make it complete.* Design not only for visual appeal but also for coverage of the subject: names of appropriate people—the city council or county board, for example; the date (always include at least the year of publication); any legally required information, such as postal indicia; illustrations; technical information such as tables and legal citations; and the seal or symbol of your city or county.
4. *Make it identifiable.* Someone picking up a publication should know right away that it was issued by your city or county.
5. *Make it cost effective.* Cost often is the first thing local government managers think about. And for many publications, the least expensive way is best. For some items, however, it pays to spend more. Weigh the trade-offs between the importance of the publication and the cost. If the cost of the publication becomes a public issue, its original purpose may be lost.

Typical publications and formats

The design that suits one publication will not work for another. Each type of publication has, so to speak, a personality, and its design should reflect that. A combination of layout, typeface, illustrations, color, and other design considerations ought to visually support what the words say, so that the reader is subconsciously aware of the harmonization of the form with the content.

Newsletters

An unpretentious design is usually the most accessible and able to draw in readers. A gaudy newsletter head that tries to look like an advertising piece distracts the reader by promising more than it can deliver. It is usually a mistake to crowd reference information (title of newsletter, name of the city or county, *logotype,* volume and issue number, date, address, telephone number, and names of local officials) at the top of the first page. A practical way to present all the information is to divide it into blocks. Keep the newsletter *masthead* at the top with the name, organization, and seal, symbol, or logotype of your locality. Show the other identifying information—volume and issue number, date, etc.—elsewhere on the first page. The name of the editor, authorization to

Figure 10–10 An excerpt from Phoenix, Arizona's annual report—a 40-page booklet with an unusual but convenient 5-by-9-inch format.

"Quality is not an act. It is a habit."

-Aristotle

Quality. At the City of Phoenix quality means serving you the best way we know how. It means continually improving the way we do our jobs. It means excellent results. It means giving city employees a role in providing and improving services. It means taking leadership roles in our community. And, it means building our future today.

These are all elements of Phoenix's quality program, a program that focuses on the bottom line – serving our customers.

To find out how well we're doing, we regularly conduct random telephone surveys of our residents. These surveys help us assess our strengths and our weaknesses. We ask your opinions about city services, city workers, quality of life, neighborhoods, transportation and environmental issues.

In 1991, almost 80 percent of the 1,600 Phoenicians surveyed in our biannual community attitude poll said they were somewhat or very satisfied with our performance. And, more than two-thirds of the respondents said the city's work force is productive.

As part of the Neighborhood Fight Back Program, residents clean up an empty lot. Our biannual community attitude survey lets us know how well we are serving our customers.

publish (if that is required by law), and other information can appear in a masthead on the second or third page.

Regardless of how you design the opening pages of your newsletter, make sure that the name of your locality is easily visible on the upper half of the front page.

Annual reports

Annual reports highlight the work of a local government during the preceding year. Some, such as annual financial reports, may be required by state law, others by the covenants of a municipal bond. Or a local government may decide that a well-designed, carefully produced annual report is a desirable public-relations tool.

If your local government decides that an annual report is a necessary and appropriate way to communicate important information about the community, give careful consideration to the format and design as well as the content.

Annual reports can be produced in many sizes and formats—including booklets, folders, and newspaper supplements. Some communities have found that a tabloid or news magazine inserted into the local newspaper is an attractive, effective, and inexpensive way of distributing an annual report. Many annual reports are issued as booklets, either 6 by 9 inches or $8\frac{1}{2}$ by 11 inches. Other formats include oversized brochures, booklets with plastic ring binders, calendars, and folded posters. Some communities—Arlington, Texas, and Phoenix, Arizona, to name two—produce ten- to fifteen-minute video annual reports. (See Chapter 11 for more information on the public-information applications of video.)

If your local government decides that an annual report is appropriate, give careful consideration to the format and design as well as the content.

Figure 10–11 Littleton, Colorado, incorporates its annual report into an 11$\frac{1}{2}$-by-11-inch full-color city events wall calendar.

The approach you choose will depend on the purpose of the report, the amount of information you want to get across, and the amount of money available for the project. Do not get carried away with designing an annual report. The careful blending of suitable size, a few typographic elements, well-written text, and photographs and line drawings of good quality produces a pleasing overall effect.

Brochures and fliers

The format for a brochure can range from several folded, stapled pages to one small sheet, perhaps folded only once. The most effective brochure copy is limited to the most important facts, carefully organized and presented in clear language. If possible, the text should be supplemented with pictures, graphics, or headlines that will capture attention and clarify important points.

Beneficial brochure

To acquaint the public with city services, Dallas, Oregon (9,560), published a brochure that serves as a directory and resource guide. The 8¾-by-6-inch folder contains a directory of city services, a letter from the mayor detailing eight goals for the year, a listing of each department and its function and phone number, and information on permits, licenses, and approvals. Information on the council-manager form of government, city council meeting schedules, money-saving tips for utilities, and frequently requested telephone numbers are also included. The city printed 5,000 copies and mailed one to each of the 3,800 households. The cost to develop and print the brochure was $7,500, or $1.50 per brochure. The brochure has received praise from citizens, and local real-estate agents have requested extra copies to distribute to new residents.

Source: ICMA, *The Guide to Management Improvement Projects in Local Government,* vol. 16, no. 4 (Washington, DC: ICMA, 1992) CCR-24.

It is better to say less or increase the size of your brochure than to reduce the type size.

The shorter the message, the more you can enhance its readability by using larger type. If you have more to say than fits your preliminary design, it is often better to say less or to increase the size of your brochure rather than to reduce the type size. The physical size of your brochure is important not only in relation to the copy you want to reproduce but also in terms of printing costs.

Paper is sold to printers in standard sizes, so preparing a brochure without thinking about stock paper sizes can cause a waste of paper at the print shop and a higher bill to the local government. You are required to pay for all the paper your print job requires—whether it ends up in your brochure or on the floor. Your printer can help you decide on proper dimensions.

Fliers are like brochures, only less expensive. They are generally printed on a single, unfolded sheet of paper, often using straight typed copy. The beauty of the flier is that, with a little extra effort, it can be written, edited, designed, printed, and multicopied all in one day. The type should be as large as possible, for maximum legibility.

Fact sheets

Fact sheets are similar in format to fliers, but they are more likely to be taken up with issues and to have less visual appeal.

A fact sheet should have a standard format and simple design and should be limited to one page (on both sides, for economy, if copy runs over one page). Make sure it is printed on the letterhead of the issuing local government or local government agency, to dispel any questions about the source of the information and to provide a point of contact for anyone who wants further information.

Newspaper inserts

The length of a newspaper insert can range from a single sheet printed on both sides to a full tabloid. Inserts can be printed on regular newsprint in black and white or on higher-grade paper with more than one color (depending on the printing facilities that are available and the amount of money you have to spend). They can be preprinted and delivered to the local newspaper for insertion into a specific edition. Or they can be printed by the newspaper itself.

Newspaper advertisements

The design of a newspaper advertisement, whether free or paid, must be visually compelling. When you decide to place an advertisement in a particular newspaper, look at advertisements that have appeared in previous issues and try to design something that will stand out from the rest. Typically, areas of black with headline type reversed to white, as well as large areas of white space, draw attention to an advertisement.

Miscellaneous media

The purpose of media such as door hangers; decals and stickers; posters; bus, taxi, and subway cards; calendars; and billboards is usually to promote an idea or opportunity. Therefore the design should be as attractive and catchy as the message. Bright colors and large type work well to capture attention for the fleeting minute that the local resident has to look at these publicity items while he or she is on the move.

The government budget

The annual budget and the capital budget usually do not present any design problems. These publications should be straightforward presentations of financial information for the city council or county board and other interested people. The information should be organized in a clear, consistent, and readable format. Budget summaries, either as brochures or fliers, allow more latitude in their design. The goal of these publications is to make sure that the general public has an opportunity to learn about and understand the key points of the budget.

Good visual appeal can make the difference in whether or not information about the budget is disseminated effectively. A minimal investment in graphics software can make it possible for you to produce your illustrations with the same computer on which your budget is created. Pie charts and graphs are especially effective in the presentation of budgets.

For this document, however, you might vary from the more traditional types of graphs and charts. For example, if you are illustrating the trend in the fire and police budgets, the trend lines might be represented by rows of fire trucks or police cars. The increase in flows at the water treatment plant might be illustrated by showing different sizes of water drops.

The possibilities for design are endless. Beware of getting so caught up in the design that you lose the clarity of the message you are trying to communicate. Sometimes less is more.

The Government Finance Officers Association presents awards to governments that present budget information in an accessible way. For information, contact the association at 1750 K Street, NW, Suite 650, Washington, DC 20006.

Figure 10–12   Part of the section entitled "Citizens' Insight into the Budget" from the annual budget document for 1993–1994, City of Abilene, Texas.

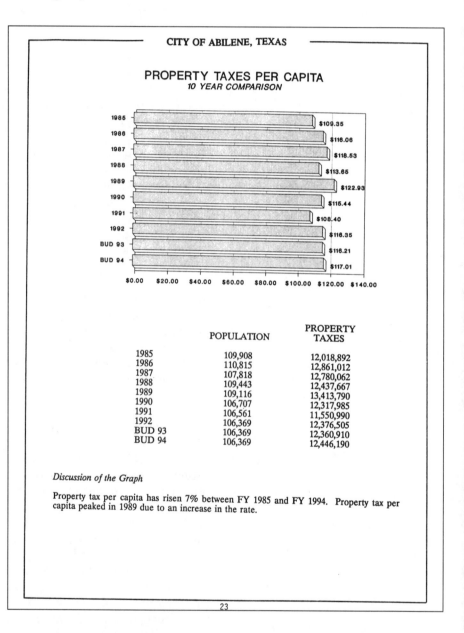

CITY OF ABILENE, TEXAS

PROPERTY TAXES PER CAPITA
10 YEAR COMPARISON

			POPULATION	PROPERTY TAXES
	1985		109,908	12,018,892
	1986		110,815	12,861,012
	1987		107,818	12,780,062
	1988		109,443	12,437,667
	1989		109,116	13,413,790
	1990		106,707	12,317,985
	1991		106,561	11,550,990
	1992		106,369	12,376,505
	BUD 93		106,369	12,360,910
	BUD 94		106,369	12,446,190

Discussion of the Graph

Property tax per capita has risen 7% between FY 1985 and FY 1994. Property tax per capita peaked in 1989 due to an increase in the rate.

23

Selecting appropriate technology

Although the types of publications that cities and counties produce have not changed significantly, the production technology has undergone a revolution. Even the early word-processing machines seem primitive when compared to current technology. The new technologies have created opportunities for a level of quality and variety in publications that most cities and counties previously could only dream about. The problems for most local governments will continue to be (1) evaluating which technology to get—and how much of it makes the most sense for their needs and (2) ensuring that its value—once it is purchased—is maximized.

If you spend several thousand dollars a year in outside contracts, it might be worthwhile to consider buying a desktop publishing system.

Computer vendors make it look and sound easy—"Buy a desktop publishing unit and you can do anything!" The reality is not nearly so simple.

The first question you should ask yourself in considering the acquisition of a desktop publishing system is whether you really need one. If you produce just an annual budget, an annual report that is distributed in the local newspaper, and a few newspaper notices and fliers each year, you will probably find it more cost effective to produce the raw copy on a computer using word-processing software. If, however, you find that you are spending several thousands of dollars a year in outside contracts to design, set up, and lay out your publications, it might be worthwhile to consider buying a desktop publishing system.

One way to determine whether you are ready to buy one is to compare your annual publications costs for setup and design to the cost of the system you plan to buy and the personnel you would need on staff to operate it. You can then begin to get a sense of your average project cost—or if you want to get very specific, your per-page cost—by either method.

At least for the first year or so, it is likely that you will continue to need some outside assistance on more complex projects, or projects that require a significant amount of graphic design. Many public relations firms that have sophisticated desktop publishing capabilities evaluate each

---

Self-testing your need for DTP

There are several questions to ask yourself if you are thinking about getting a desktop publishing system:

1. *Do you plan to hire additional staff to operate the system, or will you reassign incumbent personnel?* Unless you hire someone who has experience in desktop publishing, you should plan to provide extensive training and opportunities for practice. In addition to off-site study with experts in the use of your system, you may want to arrange some on-site training. A competent operator should be able to create simple newsletters and other publications in three to six months. Expect to give him or her a year or more to become competent in designing and producing more complex documents.

2. *What do you expect the system to do, and how will you allocate its usage?* The dangers in introducing desktop publishing to your organization are similar to those experienced when microcomputers became popular.

Just as information is power, the ability to create publications can be even more powerful. Before you buy anything, you should determine how it will be used and who will decide when it is used.

3. *Is it better to buy a desktop publishing setup that is basically a turnkey system, or should you get desktop publishing software that can be used with hardware you already have?* The advantages to adding the software to your current hardware are system compatibility and the ability to get maximum use out of your hardware. The drawbacks include getting a system that is less user-friendly and the creation of scheduling problems when the need to produce publications conflicts with other demands for computer time.

4. *How much hardware is enough?* If you have already evaluated desktop publishing alternatives, you know that almost anything is possible. If after talking to a salesperson you don't understand what a device is used for or how it might help you, don't buy it.

Beyond that basic guideline, before you seriously consider the purchase of desktop publishing hardware or software, you should decide how sophisticated you want your organization to become. Unless you already have someone on staff who has been trained and is knowledgeable, initially you may want to stick with basic software and hardware, including a high-quality laser printer. This basic setup will provide you the ability to create simple newsletters, brochures, and fliers.

5. *Could a computer consultant help you with the procurement decision?* You can always add to a system. It is much harder, however, to justify having spent thousands of dollars for a system that is underused. The cost of hiring a consultant to help you make this purchasing decision may be a good investment. If no consultant is available, talk to someone at a local university or institute who trains students in this field. You may also be able to obtain advice from a local business that uses desktop publishing.

project to determine whether it would be more cost effective for the firm to do a job in house or to contract it out, either partially or entirely, to specialty shops. Nowadays, typesetting and printing houses often offer design capabilities, in addition to binding and mailing services.

If you do get a desktop publishing system, be realistic about its capabilities. For example, if you believe that your current printer does not produce print of sufficient quality for certain documents, a desktop publishing system is not going to solve your problem unless you buy a better printer.

Your investment in a desktop system should buy you greater flexibility, a reduction in the time it takes to produce a document, and greater latitude in experimenting with graphics and other features of design. You will have to determine whether those advantages outweigh the financial investment and the management coordination and negotiation of adding the system.

Producing the publication

After the tasks of the planning, writing, editing, and design phases have been completed, the physical process of production can begin. Clear specifications for the printer (often called "specs") are essential to orderly, timely production. The specifications must (1) include all pertinent details and physical requirements and (2) be set forth in a well-organized memorandum. The more comprehensive the specifications, the less likelihood there is that you will be disappointed with the appearance of the finished publication or surprised by extra charges.

The specifications are integral to the process of selecting the printer, who is responsible for more than just the printing alone. Each prospective printer, or "bidder," needs to have identical information to base a realistic price on. Otherwise the quotations or bids from different printers will not be comparable and the differences in price among the bids will be misleading. Accurate, detailed comparisons are especially important if you are considering whether to do part of the work in house.

Preparing the specifications

To be complete, the specifications should be organized into the following six sections:

Overall specifications

Composition, layout, preparation of illustrations, and pagination

Paper

Printing

Binding

Distribution.

The overall specifications include the name of the publication, the quantity, the *trim size,* the number of pages, the type of paper, the number of ink colors, and whether the publication will be "self-covered" or have a separate cover.

If the quantity has not been set, request an estimate of the cost of a hypothetical quantity and the cost of any hundreds or thousands of copies beyond the base quantity. The additional cost rate can then be applied, within limits, to the cost of the base quantity. Ordering a few hundred extra copies in the beginning, which should add little to your costs, would be wise.

After the overall specifications have been determined, the physical materials of the publication must be prepared for printing.

Composition

The composition specifications include methods of typesetting, typeface, type size, dimensions of the type page, column width, and number of pages of composition.

The introduction of word processing and computers has had a significant impact on composition. In-house employees can now input their own work, check it, correct it and produce a final version of the manuscript or copy on disk. This disk can then be given to an in-house or external desktop publishing service, which will use page layout software to produce *page proofs*; these will show the typeset copy as it will appear in final page form. Alternatively, the disk can be sent to a typesetting company or—in some cases—the material on the disk can be transmitted to the company electronically by modem. The typesetting

Figure 10–13 A bid form with specifications used by the city of Lenexa, Kansas.

LENEXA CITY NEWSLETTER/PARKS BROCHURE SPRING/SUMMER QUOTE SPECIFICATIONS

*All Quotes Will Be Considered Valid For Two Issues of This Material (or six months)

January 27, 1992

The specifications for Lenexa's City newsletter are as follows:

<u>CITY NEWSLETTER</u> (1 example enclosed)

1. Eight pages (8 1/2" x 11")

2. Two-colored, recycled paper

3. Soybean based ink (both documents)

4. Stapled, folded (including the Parks brochure)

5. Approximately 16 pictures

6. Type set or pagemaker (include costs for both Parks Brochure and Town Talk documents in quote)

7. Similar structure as attached Winter "Town Talk"

8. Require two week turnaround for printing both documents. Must be delivered by printer to Lenexa Senior Center on _____.

9. 14,000 copies (no overrun charges will be accepted).

<u>PARKS BROCHURE</u> (1 example enclosed)

1. Eight page (8 1/2" x 11") Parks insert stapled/folded as a part of "Town Talk".

2. Similar structure as attached Parks brochure.

3. One color, recycled paper (70 lb. offset).

4. 15,000 copies (1,000 unattached to "Town Talk" and no overrun charges will be accepted).

5. Some camera-ready art included. Some clip art might be needed from printer.

All quotes shall be completed fully and returned by 5 p.m. on _____.

All proposed prices will be considered valid for two (2) issues of the City newsletter for Spring and Summer, 1992.

City reserves the right to accept or reject any or all quotes.

All negatives/art work used in preparation of material shall be considered the property of the City of Lenexa, and should be returned upon completion of order.

If you have any questions, please call Art Davis at 492-8800.

QUOTE $_____ for one (1) issue.

I agree to and understand the conditions set forth:

Please return quote to:
  Art Davis
  Asst. to the City Administrator
  City of Lenexa
  P. O. Box 14888
  Lenexa, KS 66215

_____
Signature   Date

_____
Business Name

company will format the copy according to your specifications and provide you with *galley proofs*. Even if your office has fairly simple computer equipment, you should be able to hand the typesetter a diskette of your raw copy that can then be formatted and readied for printing without having to be keyed into another system. If you work with a single typesetter on a regular basis, you may want to buy compatible software.

Preparation of illustrations

From the standpoint of printing, illustrations are of two types: *line* and *continuous-tone,* in either black and white or color. Line illustrations are formed by lines suitable for reproduction without further processing. Pen-and-ink drawings and cartoons are common examples. Continuous-tone illustrations consist of a broad range of tones requiring reproduction by the *halftone screen* process, which converts the picture into tiny dots and ensures clarity of the image when it is printed in your publication.

Photographs are nearly always reproduced by "shooting a halftone." This routine process is necessary if you want a professional appearance for your publication.

The preparation of artwork often poses technical problems that are best left to an experienced graphic designer. The overriding considerations are neatness, accuracy, and a complete understanding of the printing process. When you release the artwork to the printer, nothing should be left to be changed or adjusted later. Revisions after the publication has been photographically transferred to film for printing are very expensive. After you have processed a picture or other artwork, save the halftone if you think you might have occasion to use it again (if, for example, it's a head-and-shoulders shot of the county manager or a good drawing of city hall). This thinking ahead will reduce your future production costs.

Pagination

The final step is putting the illustrations and copy together in pages ready for printing. Until desktop publishing became common, this was generally done through the production of *camera-ready art* or *mechanicals.* In this process, which may still be used by organizations that do not have desktop publishing equipment, reproduction-quality proofs of the type and art are pasted up exactly in position on art boards. Spaces are left for any halftones that will be stripped in (inserted in the correct position) later by the printer. The art boards are then photographed by the printer to produce the film negatives from which the printing plates will be made.

If you are using desktop publishing equipment or have hired an outside designer or desktop publisher, the final pages, which may contain electronic art and desktop scanned photographs, are output to reproduction-quality proofs or negatives and then given to the printer, who will make the printing plates. In either case, save the art boards or your computer files if you think you may need to reprint a publication. It is less costly and time-consuming to make a few corrections or updates than to start over.

Choice of paper

Specifying paper can be confusing. Considerations include color, thickness, bulk, opacity, surface (glossy, matte, ribbed, and so on), availability, and cost. The difference in papers often can be seen only by direct comparison. Papers of the same *basis weight*, for example, vary in bulk, opacity, and finish.

If the choice of paper is important to the character of the publication, you can refer to sample books of the various papers available. Then the printer or paper dealer can make up *dummies* of sample blank pages. If in the course of your daily activities you come across a paper that you think will suit your publication, show it to your printer.

The nature of the publication will often suggest paper possibilities. An annual report with many photographs and illustrations might lend itself to a coated paper for good reproduction of halftones. If the detail of the illustrations is less important than the tone and atmosphere of the publication, you might prefer a softer paper that has a textured surface or a colored paper. Colors are limited in coated papers, but a wide range of colors is available in uncoated papers. They always cost more than white paper.

Although some of the early recycled papers did not work well for a number of publications—particularly those requiring high-quality photo reproduction—the situation has changed. Communities that are required to use environmentally sensitive paper generally can find one that meets their needs.

The paper specification must be exact as to color, finish, and weight, and whether it must be made from recycled papers or must be recyclable. Otherwise, the printers' bids may not be comparable.

Printing

The printing requirements of the publication usually dictate which process is used. Advances in photocopier and computer printer technology—particularly the addition of color capability and high-speed printing—have made it possible to print many local government publications in house. Many quick-copy businesses have the capability to produce small to medium-size runs of single-color or multi-color copies at a reasonable price. For large print runs or those that require superior quality, you still are likely to be working with a local print shop.

If color is used in the printing process, you must clearly state the color specifications. Color printing requires additional presswork, even if only one color in addition to black is used. Also, colored inks cost more than black. As a general practice, the color selection should be made from standard colors available from the printer, who will have an ink book of sample swatches identified by number. Otherwise it will be necessary to formulate and mix the color, thereby increasing the cost.

The paper, its surface characteristics, and its color may influence the selection of a colored ink. Consult with the artist or designer and the printer if color is critical to the publication in order to minimize the chances for disappointment.

If you are concerned about the environmental impact of your publication, many printers offer soy-based inks. Lenexa City, Kansas, indicates its preference for soy-based ink on its standard specifications sheet. (See Figure 10–13.)

Binding

The next step in production of a publication is some form of bindery operation. Consider the different types of fold and the limitations of mechanical folding equipment at the design and planning level. If you fail to think ahead of time about how your publication will be folded and bound, folding could become a costly manual operation.

For smaller publications, the two most common binding styles are saddle-stitch and side-stitch binding. In saddle stitching, staples are forced through the centerfold of the publication. This type of binding is the simplest and most inexpensive. The publication lies flat and stays open for ease of reading. Saddle stitching is used to bind most magazines and catalogues.

If the publication is too thick for saddle stitching, then side stitching is often specified. The pages are collated, by machine or by hand, and placed flat under a stitcher. The stitches are inserted about a quarter of an inch from the binding edge. The inside margin must be wider than that of a saddle-stitched publication in order to accommodate the stitches. Side-stitched publications cannot be opened flat, but the style does offer the characteristic of a square back, which is sometimes preferred. A separate, glued-on cover can be used to give a more finished appearance. Hardcover books are often bound in this way.

Two other frequently used binding styles are mechanical binding and perfect binding.

When a publication is mechanically bound, the pages are punched with a series of round or slotted holes on the binding edge. Then spiraled wire, a plastic comb, or rings are inserted through the holes. Room must be allocated in the inner margin for the holes.

In perfect binding, adhesive is applied to the edges of the assembled sheets of the publication and a cover is glued into place. Telephone books often are bound that way. Modern adhesives usually ensure that perfect-bound books last a long time.

Some common design and printing terms

Alley   The space between columns of type.

Art boards   Clean flat sheets often made of thin white cardboard, on which *camera-ready copy* (see below) is positioned for printing.

Artwork   Any image prepared for printing, except type. Some printers, however, include type when they speak of artwork.

Basis weight (weight)   A term printers use to indicate relative thickness of paper, on the basis of its weight in pounds per ream. "Sixty-pound" is a common weight of paper used in bound books.

Camera-ready copy   Reproduction proofs, line art, and halftones pasted in position on pages to be photographed for printing plates; also known as *mechanicals* or *paste-ups*.

Caption   Identifying or explanatory text that accompanies a picture or other illustration. Captions should not be confused with *headlines* (see below). Also known as *cutlines*.

Clip art   Illustrations that may legally and freely be cut from books or taken from a computer program for use in a publication. Permission to use clip art does not have to be obtained, as it would for a picture from another source that had been copyrighted.

Color key   A proof used in the process of four-color printing before printing plates are made. It consists of four sheets of acetate (one for each color) made from the artwork's film separations.

Column-inch   A space one column wide and one inch high. For example, a story that measures twelve column inches is one column wide and twelve inches long.

Composition   The transformation of manuscript, usually by some type of keyboard input, into a form suitable for making plates for printing.

Computer graphics   Illustrative material produced by means of a computer using software created for that purpose.

Continuous-tone copy   Images (usually photographs but also pencil or charcoal drawings) that have a range of tones of various values from black to white, resulting in gray tones that have no clear line of demarcation between them.

Crop   To eliminate parts of a photograph to improve it as a composition or fit it into a particular space.

Desktop publishing   The creation of documents or publications using personal computer software to position text and graphics as they will appear on the printed page. The actual printing of the final document may be done with a printer attached to a computer or by other means.

Dummy   A layout sheet for magazines, newsletters, and other publications on which rough proofs, sketches, and other materials are placed to show the general position of elements for preparing camera-ready copy.

Font   A complete assortment of type in one face and one size—including capitals, small capitals, and lower case, together with figures, punctuation marks, and other commonly used signs and accents. The italic and bold of a given face and size are generally considered separate fonts.

Galley proof   A trial print or sheet of typeset copy as it will appear when printed.

Halftone   A photomechanical reproduction in which continuous-tone copy is reproduced by photographing the original copy through a fine screen, thus creating dot or line patterns.

Distribution

The final specifications for your publication should cover packaging, shipping, and delivery. Although often overlooked in the first stages of production, instructions for these tasks should be incorporated into the original specifications. That enables the printer to order any boxes or special packaging that may be necessary and to arrange for unusual delivery or mailing requirements. These instructions also eliminate time-consuming repackaging and extra handling.

Working with your printer

Finding the right printer to meet your needs is a challenge. The objective is to choose one who will complete the job on time, whose work quality is acceptable, and who will quote prices that can be forecast with accuracy and on a competitive basis. It is important to set standards, so that price alone is not the overriding consideration. Keeping a file of printers can make this process easier. This file can also include useful information on sources of design, artwork, photography, typesetting, and mailing services. You can evaluate each source by talking with printers' representatives, examining samples of work, checking references, and maintaining performance records.

Because the cost of printing is usually the largest single item in the

---

Jump   The point at which a story stops on one page and is continued on another page. The word is used by printers and editors as a verb ("Jump this to page_") and as a noun ("Put the jump on page_").

Justified composition   Lines of type that align vertically at both ends.

Layout   Plan showing position of text and visuals on a page, often following a previously designed grid.

Leading   The space between lines of type. The greater the leading (pronounced "ledding"), the more space there is between lines.

Line copy   Camera-ready copy (type or artwork) that is solid black with no intermediate shades of gray between black and white. Every mark is solid; everything in the background is eliminated, to provide maximum contrast. An unshaded pen-and-ink sketch is an example of line copy.

Logotype   A visual corporate or organizational identifier made up of a symbol and the name or initials of the organization in a uniform format. The bell symbol with the name of a local telephone company is a familiar example. (See Chapter 2 for information on local government logos.)

Mark-up   The process by which proofs are marked with corrections and instructions.

Masthead   The printed matter in a newspaper, magazine, or other periodical that usually gives the title, publisher, date, volume, issue, and pertinent details of ownership, advertising rates, and subscription rates; names of editors and other staff may also be included. The term also applies to the name of the periodical displayed at the top of the first page.

Mechanical   A piece of camera-ready copy containing all type and design elements, arranged in exact position and marked with accurate printing instructions. (See *camera-ready copy*, above.)

Optical Character Recognition (OCR)   A mechanism that uses a scanner to "read" information from a printed document into a computer.

Pica   A unit of typographic measurement equal to twelve points. (See *Point* below.) Six picas constitute one inch.

Pixels   The tiny dots generated by a computer, scanner, or other device to make up a graphic of various tones. The arrangement of the pixels determines the image that is produced.

Point   The basic unit of typographic measurement (0.01384). Twelve points make up one *pica* (see above); seventy-two points make up one inch.

Ragged right   Composition in which the right-hand margin is unjustified—that is, not vertically aligned.

Sidebar   Related information set beside or near the primary story or article in a newsletter or other publication.

Trim size   The final size of publication pages after being trimmed at the printing plant; usually expressed in inches, with the horizontal dimension given first.

Typeface   The particular design of alphabets, numbers, and other elements in a type font that distinguishes each face from thousands of others.

Type family   All the variations of one typeface, including capitals, small capitals, lowercase, italic capitals, italic lowercase, boldface capitals, and boldface lowercase. Roman, italic, and boldface fonts are separate members of a type family.

Weight   The variations in thickness of a typeface, ranging from light to bold; some typefaces have as many as six weights.

publication budget, you need to take special care in that purchasing decision. Narrow the choice to printers with adequate facilities to do the work on time. If you see a locally produced publication that you like, find out who printed it.

When the printer's proposal has been accepted, instructions should be brought into sharp focus and loose ends tied down. All production requirements should be reviewed at the time the publication is turned over to the printer. Changes to the specifications may affect both cost and service.

If the publication is at least a two-color job, ask the printer for *color keys*. Color keys are an inexpensive way of ensuring that the right colors are in the right place. For critical color work demanding precise color reproduction, the artist and printer should be consulted. Work of this character may require the printing of some type of color proof, which will add to the cost.

Cooperation at every stage of the production will keep the publication moving toward completion. Although it is the printer's responsibility to keep the customer informed of the progress of the publication, to be able to justly blame the printer for missing a critical delivery date is cold comfort. Telephone calls between you and the printer during production give evidence of your interest in the publication and keep both you and the printer alert to possible problems.

You and the printer are partners in executing your publications program. The more, and the sooner, you communicate, the more successful your program will be. For those city and county governments in communities with only one printer, this relationship becomes especially important. It is to your advantage to know when the print shop must deliver the high-school football programs, or the inserts for the local supermarket. If you can anticipate when the printer is especially busy, you may be able to schedule more of your local government's jobs during his or her slow times. Not only will this ensure that your deadlines are met, it also will build a more positive relationship with the printer.

Checklist

For every publication, first ask yourself what it is intended to achieve and who is going to read it.

Suit the format, medium, and design to the audience and to the system you expect to use for distributing the publication.

Use clear, concise syntax that is oriented toward your particular audience. Try to avoid jargon and technical "in-group" language.

If you plan to prepare or print your publication in house, make sure you will have appropriate equipment available and in good working order. Before you invest in equipment—including desktop publishing systems—carefully evaluate its cost-effectiveness.

Assign clear responsibility for every step in the publication, from its planning to its delivery. Set realistic deadlines and communicate them early.

Design your publication with an eye to simplicity, clarity, and identifiability.

Photographs and other illustrations should inform, not merely embellish.

Be sure your specifications are complete, including the method of composition;

responsibility for proofing and for checking photographs and layout; types of binding; envelopes, self-mailers, mailing bags, and other kinds of carriers; and delivery dates.

Prepare specifications so that all competitive bidders have complete, identical information for competitive bids.

To save money on composition, prepare copy so that it is clean and complete.

When you have chosen the compositor and the printer, work closely with them to ensure that their work is of good quality and is completed on time. Communication is the key to good working relationships.

11 The Role of Cable Television

"Three—two—one. Cue talent. 'Hello, and welcome to this edition of City Beat, your weekly update from city hall. Today we'll be talking with the mayor and the city manager about key local issues, and you'll be able to call in live with your questions and comments. This program is brought to you by the public affairs department of the city government on its cable-access channel. And now to our guests.'"

Where have you heard this type of introduction? Well, maybe you haven't heard it yet, but more and more local governments are tuning in to the burgeoning possibilities of using electronic means for external as well as internal communications. Electronic communication could be helping your local government stay in contact with its own work force, with elected officials, and with the public. Using electronic media makes administration more efficient and keeps decisionmakers at every level up to date with technical information and news that they need in the judgment calls they make each working day.

This might mean equipping an area or a room in which members of the electronic press corps are briefed. Or it might mean equipping a room in which employees are trained in the techniques of effective interviewing. It might involve using public service time on radio and television stations to promote a local government program. Or the government might get into the television business itself, by operating a cable-access channel and producing its own programming.

In days gone by, a simple notice posted on the bulletin board at city hall or in the county government building might serve to inform the public; along with announcements carried by the local newspaper, that was all that was needed for a public information program. But not in this electronically advanced era. Today, the simple old methods of publicity are inadequate. The daily onslaught on your citizens includes not only various newspapers but also brochures, magazines, indiscriminate direct mail, billboards, radio, and television—not to mention films, videos, and information from computer bulletin boards, on-line services, and the like. The public, bombarded daily with multiple messages in various media, will seldom stop to read a piece of paper on a bulletin board or notice a small announcement in a local newspaper.

Why have cities and counties been turning to new electronic technologies, and why have they been developing programs to work with the news media? Simple— because they work. How else could a government get into the living rooms of its constituents on a regular basis with coverage of meetings on issues important to them, information on a new local service, or notification of an upcoming critical referendum? Whereas few localities can afford expensive advertising or promotion campaigns, many are finding out that a good cable franchise can reap them long-term benefits. Those benefits include training channels, government-access channels, video support equip-

ment, and an invaluable electronic doorway into thousands of homes.

What are the main advantages of cable TV for local government communications? It's instantaneous. It's open. And it's accessible. Via radio, people found they could join a forum of fellow citizens and government officials hashing out a critical political issue without leaving the comfort of home (especially advantageous to disabled residents). Now, via cable TV, citizens can gain access to gavel-to-gavel, live coverage of council meetings.

Of course, the new technologies do not come without their attendant problems and costs. Once a local government has committed funds to sophisticated communications equipment and programs, it must follow up with a long-term commitment to (1) hiring and training people for set-up, operations, and maintenance as well as (2) maintaining and replacing equipment as it wears out or becomes outdated. It is not enough simply to order video equipment from a catalog, for example; you have to have competent people to write the script, be the talent, edit the tapes, promote the show, and air the program.

Then what about evaluating the costs in terms of the benefits? It is not always easy to measure the satisfaction of employees or citizens with the various communications products. You will need to make ongoing efforts to monitor whether the advantages are continuing to justify the investments you are making. It is essential to (1) conduct research, (2) solicit feedback, and (3) keep track of the amount and quality of the coverage you are getting. Communication programs have to be able to stand up under the same level of scrutiny as other enterprises of your local government. An investment in communications has to cover all the costs of equipment, training, programming, and personnel. To allocate that investment wisely, you need to establish (1) goals, (2) objectives, and (3) a communication plan.

The purpose of this chapter is to outline and describe the capabilities of cable television—how cable might enhance your locality's communication with residents of the local community. The chapter deals with the advantages of government-access TV and the importance of the cable franchise. It emphasizes the importance of planning in establishing any video program. You will also find tips on operating an access channel; staffing your operation; setting up, choosing the content of, and maintaining your programming; doing the actual work of production; and getting the kind of publicity you want and need. Specifically, the topics you will be reading about are as follows:

Developing a video plan

Getting started with a good cable franchise

Points for negotiation

Managing video operations

Using volunteers, interns, and free-lancers

Filling the "programming hole"

Publicizing the programming

Gauging the viewership

Keeping up the quality

Using videotape

How to get production work done

What's in the future?

Developing a video plan

More and more communities are learning that if they have a good cable-television franchise, they have a clear channel of access for broadcasting TV programs into the homes of the local residents. Locally important information and stories can be transmitted onto residents' screens via government-access television. Complete video coverage of live meetings gives citizens an exceptional opportunity to make informed choices on important community issues. Live call-in programs put the public in touch with elected officials and other leaders of the community.

If it is to work for you, local government television demands full commitment—of funds, staff, equipment, and facilities. The video production has to be good, too, because today's television watchers are discriminating viewers of scores of channels that offer well-financed and professionally produced programs.

Originating high-quality television programming is a tall order. But unfortunately some communities have acquired access channels and equipment through a cable-television franchise without having developed and put in place a video plan to use those assets. Because of that, channels are remaining unused, equipment is inoperable, and the video products, if any, are substandard. Using cable-access television effectively requires both short-term and long-term planning.

To expect to have success in video programming, you need to develop and establish a framework ahead of time. Judicious planning before actually making any purchases will give you a guide that you can use for directing the allocation of resources, staff members, facilities, and programming to meet the goals of your local government and the expectations of your public. Most communities have discovered that a phased-in approach is the best way to get into television.

Having a video plan that phases in staff members, equipment, and programming over the course of a number of years offers two advantages. First, it lets a local government test the enterprise step by step and that way be able to fine-tune the whole operation. Second, phasing in a video program incrementally makes it much easier to convince elected officials and members of the community of the advantages it has to offer than if you tried to impose a full-blown program on them all at once.

A comprehensive plan for the use of video should address five main issues:

Funding

Management and staffing

Facilities

Capabilities

Programming.

Funding Where will the money come from? Will the operation be a part of the general fund? Will cable-franchise fees, production revenues, grants, and other similar sources pay for it? Or will you institute a charge-back system to recover the costs from user agencies? Many local governments use general-fund revenues or a portion of franchise fees (if available) through the public information or communications office of the local government. Some communities apply to local, state, and federal organizations for grants to produce their programs—in those cases, the programs are often on topics in the arts and humanities, or on public safety, emergency management, or the environment.

Management and staffing How will the video program be managed? What levels of staffing are necessary to meet expectations for the program? When are additions to the staff scheduled? What specific technical and creative skills should they have? Is your local government willing to create new, unique job classifications (descriptions of positions probably do not exist in the table of organization)? Will the pay be competitive enough to secure qualified and experienced employees?

What does it cost to get into government TV?

The amount you spend on setting up a local government-access channel will depend on variables such as the monetary participation and franchise requirements of the cable operator; the size of the local government and its cable subscriber base; the level of sophistication of the local government's public information and video programs; the level of management and political support; and the constant changes in video technology.

As in most things, you get what you pay or plan for in government-access television. As you plan, you need to consider several points. First, what franchise obligations does the cable operator have to assist local government in getting on the air? A good franchise agreement spells out detailed require-

ments for the cable operator to support government-access programming on the cable system. Support may include microwave and/or cable networks, videotape playback systems, character generator or videotext equipment, satellite downlinks, production equipment, and even in some cases studio facilities. Depending upon the technical sophistication of the operation, equipment to support government-access programming may cost from several thousands to millions of dollars.

Second, who writes, edits, produces, and hosts the programs? If local government already has a communications office, then the staff may be qualified to start a video program. In most cases, however, dedicated video production personnel are needed to supplement current staff, volunteers, and interns if the program is to grow and be successful. You should plan to pay video staff salaries that are at par with

similar positions in local public or commercial television stations.

Third, do not forget that government-access television requires an annual operating budget for salaries, utilities, tape stock, equipment maintenance and replacement, supplies, printing, advertising, postage, program acquisition, and so forth.

Local government may get into television at little or no cost, depending upon the cooperation of the cable operator and the franchise in place. However, as the program grows, dedicated funding will be needed to support a meaningful video operation. It is advisable to check with other communities already in government television for recommendations and advice on funding, equipment, staff, facilities, franchise requirements, programming, and promotion.

Facilities   Where will the operation be housed? Are facilities available that have the necessary studio ceiling heights, access to cable and microwave, heavy air conditioning, and support space? Would it be better to start with an interim studio and expand later? Should your local government build and equip the operation or involve the cable operator as a partner? Are any plans in place for depreciation, maintenance, and upgrades to the equipment?

Capabilities   What levels of technical capabilities is it reasonable for you to expect? When should you expect to achieve them? Does the agency plan to be a "full-service" cable broadcaster operating government-access video, training video, and other video channels? Or are simple bulletin-board announcements and televised meetings all that are planned?

Programming   What level and diversity of programming do you plan to have? What are reasonable programming objectives? How and when will they be met? What program sources will be available to provide live, taped, and satellite-fed material?

Getting started with a good cable franchise   Government-access television is only as good as the franchise with the local cable company. Without a strong franchise agreement that spells out the cable operator's obligations to provide services such as channel capacity and equipment, your local government is not assured of the ability to direct programming into local residents' homes. That is why a good cable franchise should be at the heart of any comprehensive video plan. Because most agreements run ten to fifteen years, it is critical that you get long-term commitments from the cable company in writing before starting government-access television.

Federal cable regulations

In 1992, Congress reversed its position that local governments should not be able to regulate cable television rates and customer service standards. It passed the Cable Television Consumer Protection and Competition Act, which gives local and state governments the option to regulate cable television's rates and to impose new, strict customer service standards.

Local governments have to decide whether it is in the interest of their community to enter this regulatory arena and, if so, what it will cost them in time and money.

The Federal Communications Commission (FCC) set some initial deadlines in 1993 for local governments wishing to file notice with the FCC of their intent to impose the new customer service standards and to regulate cable television rates. However, as of April 1994, only 20 percent of communities had filed to be certified to regulate cable rates.

Communities decide whether to enter the regulatory arena after considering a number of factors, including the quality and price of the cable service offered in their community. Many communities are using these regulation initiatives as an opportunity to open a dialogue with the local cable system to pursue plans for providing the latest in communications technology.

Source: Adapted from John Kenny, "The Telecommunications Revolution and Your Community," *MicroSoftware News* (October 1993): 1, 2.

Few communities have the luxury of having experienced cable administrators, technical experts, and communications counsel on staff to help design and negotiate a cable franchise. Many jurisdictions hire a cable-television consultant to be a partner at the negotiating table. A good consultant will know the status of federal cable legislation and the outcomes of recent court cases. He or she will be up to date on what communities have been asking for—and getting—in recently approved franchises. (A sidebar later in this chapter includes a list of national organizations that may be helpful in providing information about cable consultants, the cable law, program sources, and successful government-access video operations.)

A competent cable consultant will prepare an analysis of the present cable operation (if there is one). He or she conducts an on-site review of the cable plant to evaluate its condition, its capacity, its maintenance, and its adherence to technical standards. The consultant will scrutinize the company's current customer service, staffing, resources, and program offerings. He or she will ascertain what the community needs in terms of cable services as well as public, educational, and government access.

After reviewing the cable system and assessing the needs of the community, the consultant will prepare a cable "blueprint" that will help guide your local government in the negotiation process. You should also be given recommendations on upgrades to the cable plant, program services, calculation of franchise fees, standards of customer service, information on subscribers, reporting requirements for operators, support for community-access programming, and more.

Points for negotiation

When representatives of local government sit down at the negotiating table, they should know exactly what is necessary to meet the long-term needs of the community in the areas of *public*, *educational*, and *government* (PEG) access. A video plan should already be in place that spells out what local government is going to do to operate these video assets. Key points for negotiation include access channels, interconnection, equipment and upgrades, signal links and facilities, institutional networks, and government training support.

The 1992 Cable Television Act's impact on local governments

Prevents the granting of exclusive franchises, as has so far been customary, and encourages the awarding of competitive franchises.

Allows municipal authorities to operate their own cable systems.

Provides the authority to enforce the various "consumer protection and customer service" provisions of the act.

Allows states and/or franchising authorities to regulate the ownership or control of a cable system.

Allows enforcement of the newly legislated provisions on "children's protection from indecent programming on leased access channels."

Gives the local franchising authority additional powers over the cable system's ability to change channel assignments.

Sets up procedures by which franchising authorities can deal with franchise renewals.

Limits the monetary liability of a state, county, city, or town if it is sued by a cable operator for carrying out the provisions of the act.

Source: *Public Management* (October 1993): 7.

Access channels

You need to know what channel capacity is needed to meet program expectations. Sometimes one composite channel for PEG access is sufficient, with a provision that when the channel reaches a certain level of use it will split into three or more separate channels. Some communities need multiple-channel capacity immediately, with additional channels programmed for activation during the term of the agreement.

Interconnection

Many communities have more than one cable operator. It is critical that PEG access programming be simulcast to all cable subscribers so that complete coverage will be obtained. It can be done by requiring that the systems be interconnected so that access programming is shared and available to all cable locations.

Equipment and upgrades

How will the video programming be produced? What equipment will be used—the government's, the cable system's, or both? Be sure that specific equipment is requested from the cable operator to support access operations. Details that should be spelled out include requirements for maintenance, replacement, and upgrade over the life of the franchise agreement.

Signal links and facilities

How will video programming get onto the cable system? The cable company should provide the necessary cable or microwave links with the system. The operator should provide all equipment, towers, antennas, and quality-control measures. And what about studios? The government may provide a video production center for its own programming. Or there may be community studios operated by the cable company, or perhaps a non-profit group. These issues should be covered in the local cable agreement.

Institutional networks

A cable system is in effect a pipe through which video, data, voice, and other electronic services can be shipped. Your cable franchise should consider linking government facilities, police/fire/emergency-management centers, training locations, arts and cultural buildings, community video production studios, the convention center, libraries, and schools, among other facilities. That will make it possible for public affairs programs, training sessions, teleconferences, interactive video, and a multitude of government support services to be originated from remote locations and provided to cable customers or selected facilities. With many cable operators converting their systems to fiber-optics technology, channel capacity and capabilities have mushroomed.

Videoconferencing saves police patrol time

New York police officers, driving on Staten Island to the Richmond County District Attorney's Office, used to dread traffic jams and the concomitant one and a half hour commute for court-related meetings. But thanks to a videoconferencing system serving New York City's judicial system, the officers aren't stuck in gridlock anymore.

According to police estimates, officers are saving approximately 700 patrol hours (per month) by attending district attorney's meetings and some informal hearings on TV.

Much of the equipment and many of the facilities for the New York videoconferencing project are being provided at little or no cost by equipment vendors and the city's cable companies, which must provide an institutional cable network as part of their cable-franchise agreements.

Source: Len Strazewski, "Video Conferencing Saves Police Patrol Time," *City and State* (April 6, 1992), p. GM6.

Government training support

What if a fire-department trainer could look into a TV camera and be live to all fire stations? Or if the town manager could explain the new budget to employees and take phoned-in questions over a closed video network? It's possible, with discrete channels on the community cable system. Be sure to consider this capability in your franchise discussions. The cable operator should provide the channel capacity, signal links, playback equipment, and other facilities necessary to support training.

Managing video operations

Once you have a franchise that provides equipment and channels, how do you manage a community video program? First, it is important to decide whether the PEG access operation is going to be combined or separate. In other words, will everyone use the same facilities, or will public, educational, and government institutions be responsible for their own operations? Local governments have taken different approaches to this critical decision, including *separate management, cable-operator management,* and the *nonprofit corporation.*

Separate management

Each programming entity (public, educational institutions, and local governments) originates its own programming and operates separate channels. This approach helps avoid competition for air time and disagreements over programming. Management guidelines should be developed for all video operations. If one studio and joint equipment are used, then an allocation system must be in place to manage those assets equitably.

Cable-operator management

Sometimes the cable company is charged with managing some or all of the PEG access channels. Often the cable system will direct the public-access channel, including operation of the studio and the allocation of air time. This management keeps government from having to handle the day-to-day decisions on public access that can quickly become management and political problems.

Non-profit corporation

Some communities have a nonprofit corporation that manages access channels, schedules studios, loans equipment, and provides oversight of video operations. Often these organizations are funded by a portion of the franchise fee collected from the cable operator. This method may be used only for the public channel, or it may include educational and governmental entities.

Using volunteers, interns, and free-lancers

Producing good government television requires talented staff members: people who are experienced in writing, producing, shooting, and editing video. There never seem to be enough qualified people to do the job. But help may be as near as your local technical school, college, university, or civic club. Many government video operations make use of volunteers, interns, and free-lancers to supplement their permanent staffs.

These individuals often work for free just to be able to operate a television camera or to be part of a video production. Others will work as part of an internship between the government and a local educational institution. Many schools have radio and television courses, and students are delighted to get hands-on experience in a real video operation. Most students work for nothing; the school usually requires you to supply a student evaluation when the work is over. With proper training, community volunteers can operate cameras at council meetings or help produce a government public affairs show.

The use of paid free-lance technicians, camera operators, and other personnel is a moneysaver. Instead of carrying a large video production staff on the payroll, you can bring in hourly contract employees when you need to, to complete a production crew. Potential free-lancers can be found at public, educational, and commercial broadcast stations, as well as in the local cable company.

Local government workers can also supplement the permanent video staff. Employees can be trained in a video workshop so that a pool of qualified persons will always be available to support your productions. The local government video staff, a local technical college with video-production instructors, or consultants can present the training.

Filling the "programming hole"

Television has a big appetite. Filling the "programming hole" on a government-access channel is a big job, especially if you're running a twenty-four-hour operation. Because of its nonprofit basis, government-access channels can repeat programs frequently to pick up additional viewers. Effective video scheduling should include program blocks at convenient times in the morning, afternoon, and evenings. The programs should be directed at the audiences most likely to be watching television at those times. Viewer surveys will help direct scheduling and the programming mix. Government programming falls into several categories.

Character-generated information

When taped, live, or satellite-fed programming is not on the channel, most stations use character-generated information (CG) or videotext. This material can feature a calendar of government meetings, public service announcements, job offerings, schedules of events in recreation centers, news announcements, and other need-to-know information about local government. It is important to keep CG copy current, so that viewers see change on the channel. The audio is also important. Educational radio, satellite music services, or even police and fire calls are used as an audio "bed" for government video.

"Name that tune"

The city of Des Moines, Iowa (190,000), has teamed up with a local FM radio station to promote its government-access cable-television channel and programming. The FM station, referred to as "The Official Color Radio Station of the City of Des Moines," airs daily announcements promoting city services and activities. The city writes the announcements for the show, while the station provides the talent to record them. In return, the city's television channel will carry the broadcast audio signal of the radio station during alphanumeric message displays and will also broadcast promotional announcements for the radio station. The city estimates that the air time given by the station is worth $110,000 a year. The agreement between the city and the FM station, selected through a bidding process, is effective for one year, and can be renewed by mutual consent for two one-year periods. To promote the agreement, bumper stickers were printed at a minimal cost and placed on all city vehicles.

Source: *The Guide to Management Improvement Projects in Local Government*, vol. 14, no. 1 (Washington, DC: ICMA, 1990) CCR-4.

Coverage of meetings

One advantage of government-access television is that it can provide gavel-to-gavel live coverage of meetings, while commercial broadcasters have to be content with a ninety-second story on the evening news. Cablecasts of meetings of councils, commissions, authorities, and boards make up most government video programs. Coverage of meetings should use the same quality of production standards as other programming. Multiple camera views and quality presentation of charts, slides, videotapes, and other graphic materials will present a professional image of local government. Retransmission of televised meetings on different days and times will extend the audience beyond that of the original broadcast.

News and information

What citizens need to know about programs, services, fees, and events is as near as their television set and the government channel. Regular features that keep the public up to date with important customer information are popular. News about recreation programs, human services, crime and fire prevention, solid waste services, transportation alternatives, job training, pet ownership, and many other topics makes excellent program material. Remember, your edge is that the news media give only limited coverage to these topics.

> **Focus on Dunedin**
> Dunedin, Florida (37,000), is providing accurate and timely information about city government and community-service events through its weekly cable-television program. "Focus on Dunedin" is hosted by the chairman of the volunteer city commission's Public Relations Advisory Committee. The program covers issues such as budget proposals, tax rates, growth management, downtown redevelopment, city departments' functions, and volunteer boards and committees. Taped in advance, the program airs on the government-access channel four times weekly, including the half-hour immediately preceding each commission meeting. Guests have included city commissioners; the city manager; city attorney; city clerk; city staff heads; and county, state, and federal officials. Periodically special live telecasts entitled "Call City Hall" invite citizens' telephone calls with answers provided on the air by elected officials and staff. Technicians, equipment, and facilities are donated by cable franchisees. Local newspapers publicize the show.
>
> Source: *The Guide to Management Improvement Projects in Local Government*, vol. 14, no. 3 (Washington, DC: ICMA, 1990) CCR-20.

Public affairs programs

Discussion of important community issues is a natural for government television. A moderator with knowledgeable guests can explore all sides of a subject—and even take viewers' live telephone calls. Information may also be presented in documentary fashion, such as a video annual report. Phoenix, Arizona, and Arlington, Texas, are just two of the growing number of cities producing video versions of their annual report. These reports, which usually run about ten minutes, provide informative, high-quality programming for the local cable-access channel that can be run throughout the year. Videotaped features can help frame issues and stimulate discussion on televised public affairs programs.

Community forums

The reach of public hearings, community meetings, and forums can be greatly extended by cable-access coverage. Many citizens do not attend public meetings. But they may watch from the comfort of their homes if the event is on television. And with a telephone bank, local government can receive questions and comments from these viewers during the program; these can be presented live "on the air" or written down and presented during the meeting. Regardless of the approach, government is seen as willing to receive input from citizens.

Dade County presents the "human side"

The guests on today's show are two female crack addicts, one of whom is HIV-positive, and both of whom are pregnant. They discuss the cycles of their addictions—how they have led to prostitution, pregnancy, AIDS, and lives of misery. They want assistance from the county human-services department.

This would be heavy stuff even for Oprah Winfrey, but the host of this show, which runs on a nonprofit cable channel operated by Dade County, Florida, is an assistant human-services director whose original job description never included being on TV.

"At first it was scary," says Carmen Morrina, who has hosted "Human Side" since its inception in 1985. "But it's really a great opportunity, because once a week I get to listen to our clients one-on-one. It gives me an opportunity to hear their stories and how we've helped them."

Morrina says the show is a "great outreach tool. It brings us very cost-effectively into the homes of people who might need our services.

People have a wonderful way of identifying with someone they see on TV and responding, and calling and getting help if they need it, much more than they would if they just saw something on paper."

Source: Nichole Achs, "Late Night with Local Government," *American City and County* (March 1992), p. 54.

Arts and entertainment

"Soft" programming will help balance meetings and public affairs coverage. All communities have historic, arts, cultural, and entertainment assets. These make splendid cable programming and help inform citizens about these resources, many of which are supported by local government funds and facilities. People affiliated with these programs will be eager to help produce, host, and support video programming.

Other sources of programming

Filling the program hole may require tapping outside sources. Videotapes are available from a variety of agencies and nonprofit groups. These groups are always seeking air time for their messages. A video combined with discussion can make a good program segment. In some cases, these groups can be trained to produce their own programming and contribute shows on a regular basis.

Some national associations have video lending libraries and information about government-access television. Videotapes are available on many topics—some subjects are so generic that they may make good programming on access television in other communities. Consider checking the sources given in the accompanying sidebar for program material and reference information on government-access television.

Video programming is also available via satellite. With a satellite dish, public-domain programs can be taped or aired live. Teleconferences from national groups may be used for public or employee education. Some shows are without cost; others may require a fee. Programming may be transmitted either occasionally or daily (such as training for fire and police personnel). Satellite program directories and schedules are available at your local library or by subscription.

Other governments may help with material for video programs. Nearby communities may have already produced a show on a subject common to your area. Why do it again if it is already on tape? Sometimes councils of governments or state league associations are willing to serve as tape exchanges for their member jurisdictions.

Finally, most communities are home to independent video producers who create high-quality productions. Consider a film and video festival to honor good productions, and then air the winners on the access channel. The activity could be sponsored by a local arts group, museum, or film and video association. Or establish a policy encouraging the regular screening of locally produced video products.

Figure 11–1   A production specialist in the city of Raleigh, North Carolina, prepares to shoot a city cable program.

Sources of information about government-access TV

City-County Communications and
    Marketing Association (3CMA)
409 Third Street SW
Washington, DC 20024-4414

International City/County Management Association (ICMA)
777 North Capitol Street NE
Washington, DC 20002-4201

National Association of Counties
440 First Street NW
Washington, DC 20001-2080

National Association of State Telecommunications Directors
c/o Council of State Governments
Iron Works Pike
P.O. Box 11910
Lexington, KY 40578

National Association of Telecommunications Officers and Administrators
1301 Pennsylvania Avenue NW
Washington, DC 20004-1793

National Federation of Local Cable
    Programmers
P.O. Box 27290
Washington, DC 20038

National League of Cities
1301 Pennsylvania Avenue NW
Washington, DC 20004-1793

Public Technology, Inc.
1301 Pennsylvania Avenue NW
Washington, DC 20004-1793

U.S. Conference of Mayors
1620 I Street NW
Washington, DC 20006

Publicizing the programming

Attracting viewers to a government access channel takes a lot of work. The channel itself should be used to list choices of programs on a daily basis. Promotional videos highlighting upcoming programs are also effective. But first check with your local cable company, because these videos may also be getting used as inserts during breaks on other channels.

Unfortunately, many daily newspapers will not list government-access programming in the television grid, on account of limited space. Weekly papers may. Sometimes both will publicize special programs, televised meetings, or other unique events scheduled for the channel. News releases and public service announcements are helpful to get the word out. Utility-bill inserts are a good way to list channel offerings; making these up will require that program schedules be developed far in advance to meet publication deadlines. (See Chapter 10 for more information on utility-bill inserts.)

Voice mail and recorded messages are inexpensive ways to provide a TV schedule for government programming twenty-four hours per day. Some communities use paid advertising to publish the schedule. Channel highlights, especially televised meetings and hearings, are of interest to neighborhood and business groups. You will reach many citizens if you provide TV schedules to the newsletters published by these organizations. Be sure to place schedules in brochure racks, reception areas, and other public places. (See Chapter 10 for information on producing publications of these kinds.)

Gauging the viewership

Few government-access programs are listed in the viewership ratings prepared by the national research firms. To judge the TV audience, therefore, local governments must do research of their own. Formal research is best—but also expensive. A good idea is to "piggyback" questions on an existing survey. The cost is kept low, but the information will be statistically accurate and data will be available on viewers' demographics as well as program choices.

How Vancouver, Washington, measures viewership

While viewership is often hard to measure, there are several key indicators of the special bond the community has formed with the city/county government channel. These include

A weekly mailing (upon request) of program listings for the channel to over 350 people;

Regular listing of programs in the Sunday TV guide in the local newspaper;

Mailback surveys distributed by the cable company, which indicate that more than 10 percent of the 40,000 subscribers watch the channel at least once a week; and

Direct feedback received by the city council members and the mayor from the community indicating that city council is a regular part of the Monday-night agenda in many Vancouver homes.

Cable-TV office staff average ten "dubs" or copies a week of programming for people in the community (done free of charge as long as citizens provide a blank tape).

Source: Donna M. Mason, "Vancouver, Washington, on Camera!: How One City Made Public-Access TV Big Time for Citizens," *Nation's Cities Weekly* (August 27, 1990), p. 4.

Another way to obtain viewership information is to query the public via questionnaires. They can be placed in utility-bill inserts, advertisements, or appeals on the cable channel. Keep in mind that this method is not scientifically precise but is rather a "snapshot" in time of opinion about government video. Random telephone surveys can also be conducted to sample viewer feedback. Or live call-in shows can gauge public sentiment about new program offerings or the current line-up.

Keeping up the quality

Cable television today offers scores of channels—from local broadcasts to sophisticated programming imported via satellite. Viewers expect to see high quality. If the government channel has inferior production values and a poor signal, viewership will suffer. Adequate equipment and funds must be available to provide a high-quality image to the cable company. The company in turn must transmit a clear picture to all cable customers.

The government video plan and cable franchise should address needs for equipment and standards for quality. Maintenance, replacement, and upgrade of production and transmission equipment are vital to keep the quality of programs high. Preventive maintenance guidelines should be in place to direct timely service of vital components.

Using videotape

Beyond airing programs on the broadcast media or cable television, there are many uses for videotape. First of all, it can serve as a part of the record for meetings that are televised and videotaped. Tapes can assist clerks responsible for producing official minutes by identifying speakers by sight; this is especially helpful when more than one person is talking. Videotaped meetings may be rebroadcast to a broader television audience.

The documentation of important local government projects is a task made for video. If you need a record of construction progress for legal and other reasons, then consider videotaping regularly. Stationary cameras may be used to provide a continuous record on a time-lapse basis; the image may be referenced with a date and time code and then played back at regular speed so that the project appears as it comes out of the ground. These tapes may also be used to give elected officials and the news media an armchair tour of capital construction without leaving the government center.

Chapters 6, 7, and 9 offer more information on the uses of videotape.

"Evidence" for the versatility of government-access video

In Beverly Hills, California, safety, noise, and traffic violations committed by tour buses driving through residential areas were documented by the government-access video crew. The videotape was successfully used as evidence in a court action that banned the large buses from residential streets.

Source: Robert Havlick and Cheryl Farr, "Video Technology: Programs and Uses," *MIS Report* (January 1987), Washington, DC: ICMA, p. 15.

How to get production work done

As emphasized above, producing high-quality video requires equipment and a creative staff. The use of video workshops to train employees, interns, and interested volunteers will build a pool of qualified technicians to supplement the permanent video staff. But there are other ways to get video production work done as well.

Local institutions, corporations, and nonprofit groups may have video-production facilities. Many colleges, technical schools, school systems, utilities, and arts and cultural groups produce video programming. Can local government use these video assets? Ask. These organizations may be willing to produce programming as a public service, if they get appropriate credit and recognition. Perhaps they can loan a writer, producer, or videographer to a project; they may offer their studio or editing equipment.

Educational and public broadcasting stations are always looking for community programming ideas. Talk to them and suggest topics for talk shows, specials, documentaries, and forums and see whether they are willing to coproduce a show. What happens when their editing equipment and studios are not in use? Are the facilities available for other users? Might they provide production services at no cost, or at a public service rate?

Your cable operator may have public-access studios, equipment, and independent producers available to do government production work.

Your cable operator may have public-access studios, equipment, and independent producers available to do government production work. It is not uncommon for the cable company to coproduce programming or originate shows from its studios for the government-access channel. A good relationship between the cable operator and local government can result in cooperative productions.

Commercial production houses are in the business to make money on video, so don't expect them to offer many free services. Some do, however, take on occasional pro bono projects for community public service programs; it's good corporate public relations. Consider pitching your program idea to local production houses. Just keep in mind that the subject should have broad community appeal and that there should be adequate recognition planned for the production company.

If you plan to bid video services, know what you need. It takes a person knowledgeable about the industry to write and interpret video bid proposals. Video production is highly technical, and the quality of work can vary widely. Ask to see samples of video work produced by companies submitting proposals. Check references. Make sure that bids all include the services needed, such as writing, direction, videography, editing, equipment rental, music, sound effects, narration, audio mix, talent, and tape duplication. Video production is a professional service. In creative-services proposals, the low bid is not always the best.

Need help in developing and evaluating video-service proposals? Ask a local college with a video-production department, or a service group such as a professional public relations society for advice. They know the industry, reasonable production prices, and the track record of local video companies.

What's in the future?

Communications technology is changing daily. It's reasonable to envision cable television including "one-stop shopping" for local government. Request information about a government service; pay a water bill; register to vote; or express an opinion on a community issue—all this could be done via an interactive keyboard linked to local government via the cable system. With more cable systems increasing their channel capacity and switching to fiber optics, the use of this utility for government purposes is increasing dramatically. That's why long-range plans must be a part of cable-franchise discussions.

Two-way communications from city hall to citizens is not an unreasonable goal for local government TV. With today's emphasis on customer service, a home cable connection has the potential to become a government's "drive-in window." Cable technology has the potential to change the way government does business—with automatic water meter readings, direct billing of government services, personalized viewing of video programming, instant feedback on community issues, home fire and burglar alarm systems, interactive training for local government employees at remote locations, and much more.

The Information Age is here

The cable-television government-access channel in Iowa City, Iowa (50,000), provides a twenty-four-hour, information-services interactive television feature. Citizens tune in to the channel, call the information-services number using a touch-tone phone, and request any information in the system via a touch-tone code menu. The information appears on the television sets of all subscribers watching the channel. Offerings include council agendas, bus maps, tax and recycling information, job opportunities, wanted posters, missing children's photos, and polls and surveys. One viewer may access the service at any given time. Each user has a variable three-minute time-frame to use the system once he or she has called. The system is monitored to determine what information is most useful and most frequently accessed by users.

Source: *The Guide to Management Improvement Projects in Local Government*, vol. 14, no. 3 (Washington, DC: ICMA, 1990) CCR-21.

Home personal computers (PCs) can become ports to a variety of customer services, including those of local government. It may soon be routine for citizens to request a service, file a complaint, obtain information, or make a suggestion from their PC via the cable without ever talking to a live person. Home adult education, specialized communications for people with disabilities, and at-home work capability are all feasible. Cities and counties that plan their cable communications future today will enjoy the benefits tomorrow.

Summary

More and more jurisdictions are using government-access cable television to supplement traditional public information programs. With cable television, meetings and public hearings can be telecast live, gavel to gavel, the ultimate in open government. Citizens may call talk shows and query local officials. Programs on services and departments can provide important customer-service information. And government acquires a direct and immediate means to inform and receive feedback from its customers, the taxpayers.

But becoming a cable broadcaster requires long-range planning, a strong cable franchise, and a commitment to high-quality programming. A video plan should address key issues such as funding, staffing, facilities, equipment, capabilities, and programming. Volunteers, interns, freelancers, and trained local government staff can supplement paid production personnel.

Programming must be good, because the public is used to seeing high-quality video. Filling the "programming hole" requires a creative blend of character-generated information, coverage of key meetings, news and information, public affairs programs, community forums, arts and entertainment, and much more. Programs are also available from other jurisdictions, associations, and satellite services.

Publicizing programming and gauging viewership are important in sustaining a high-quality government-access operation.

It's not unrealistic to imagine widespread use of two-way communication via cable television in the near future. From reading water meters, to paying utility bills, to registering an opinion during a public hearing, it may all be done over wire cable or fiber optics. A relationship between citizens and local government based on instant access may be just around the corner.

Checklist

Effective local government television requires a commitment of funds, staff, equipment, and resources if it is to compete with commercial programming for the attention of increasingly selective viewers.

A *video plan* is the framework in which a local government's video program operates. It should address funding, management and staff, facilities, capabilities, and programming.

The scope and success of a video plan depend largely on the kind of agreement the local government obtains with the local cable operator.

From the perspective of local government, the most important community need in establishing a video plan is ensuring public, educational, and government (PEG) access.

Local government video can be operated either by separate management (with public, educational, and government functions having distinct operations and channels), by the cable operator, or by a nonprofit corporation.

Consider using volunteers, interns, and free-lancers to supplement local government's permanent staff as necessary.

The types of programming that appear on local government television include character-generated information, meetings coverage, news and information, public affairs programming, community forums, and arts and entertainment.

Publicity, readership surveys, and comprehensive plans to upgrade production and transmission equipment will help sustain the quality of local government television in a competitive TV environment.

Besides serving as a means of telecasting programming, videotape has many uses as a means of creating and preserving documentary information for internal use.

The local private sector, including nonprofit organizations, is a potential source of assistance with video-production work.

Cable television is gradually becoming a medium of instant contact between citizens and local government.

Notes

1 Effective Management Means Effective Communication

[1] Amy Cohen Paul, *Future Challenges, Future Opportunities: The Final Report of the ICMA FutureVisions Consortium* (Washington, D.C.: ICMA, 1991).

2 The Identity and Image of Local Government

[1] Robert Townsend, *Up the Organization: How to Stop the Corporation from Stifling People and Strangling Profits* (Greenwich, Conn.: Fawcett, 1970), p. 13.

[2] Robert Levering and Milton Mokowitz, *The 100 Best Companies to Work For in America* (New York: Doubleday, 1993), p. 231.

[3] Douglas J. Watson, Robert J. Juster, and Gerald W. Johnson, "Institutionalized Use of Citizen Surveys in the Budgetary and Policy-Making Processes: A Small City Case Study," *Public Administration Review,* May–June 1991, pp. 232–39.

3 The Local Citizen: Voter, Taxpayer, and Customer

[1] Jim Duffy, "Streetwise," [Baltimore] *City Paper,* August 27–September 2, 1993), pp. 7–8.

[2] Jonathan Walters, "The Cult of Total Quality," *Governing* (May 1992), pp. 38–42.

[3] W. Edwards Deming, *Out of the Crisis* (Cambridge, Mass.: Massachusetts Institute of Technology, Center for Advanced Engineering Study, 1986), pp. 23–24.

[4] Jeffrey E. Disend, *How to Provide Excellent Service in Any Organization* (Radnor, Pa.: Chilton Book Co., 1991), p. 16.

[5] Tod Newcombe, "Multimedia: Will Government Communicate Better?" *Government Technology* (October 1991), 1, pp. 44–47.

[6] Diane Roth, "Breaking the Language Barrier," *Colorado Municipalities* (November/December 1992), pp. 13–15.

4 Communicating with Elected Officials

[1] James Griesemer, *Future Challenges, Future Opportunities: The Final Report of the ICMA FutureVisions Consortium* (Washington, D.C.: ICMA, 1991).

[2] Wayne F. Anderson, Chester A. Newland, and Richard J. Stillman II, *The Effective Local Government Manager* (Washington, D.C.: ICMA, 1983), p. 6.

[3] G. Curtis Branscome, "A City Manager's View," *Partnerships in Local Governance: Handbook* (Washington, D.C.: ICMA, 1989), pp. 3–5.

[4] James Banovetz, "The Role of the City Manager in Effectiveness Team Building," *The National Civic Review* (July/August 1990), p. 351.

[5] Charldean Newell, *The Effective Local Government Manager* (Washington, D.C.: ICMA, 1993), p. 59.

[6] James H. Svara, "Understanding the Mayor's Office in Council-Manager Cities," *Popular Government* (1985), p. 102.

[7] Ronald O. Loveridge, *City Managers in Legislative Politics* (Indianapolis and New York: The Bobbs-Merrill Company, 1971), p. 78.

[8] Richard C. Wilson, *The Loma Prieta Quake: What One City Learned* (Washington, D.C.: ICMA, 1991), p. 12.

[9] Judith A. Rambeau, "Automated Message System To Aid Commerce Disaster Response," *Western City* (January 1992), 12–13.

[10] Wilson, *The Loma Prieta Quake*, p. 62.

5 Employees: The Local Government Team

[1] Remarks by Brigadier General (Ret.) H.J. (Jerry) Dalton Jr. to the annual Air Force Worldwide Public Affairs Conference, October 8, 1991, Homestead Air Force Base, Florida.

[2] Alvie L. Smith, *Innovative Employee Communication: New Approaches to Improving Trust, Teamwork, and Performance* (Englewood Cliffs, N.J.: Prentice Hall, 1991), p. 80.

[3] Smith, pp. 229–30.

[4] Julie Foehrenbach and Steve Goldfarb, "Employee Communication in the '90s: Great(er) Expectations," *Communication World,* International Association of Business Communicators, May–June 1990, pp. 101–6.

[5] Elizabeth Hollander and Jean Franczyk, "The Need to Value Our Government Workers," *Governing,* September 1991, p. 10.

[6] "Restoring Communications," an entry submitted by the Communications Department of Pratt and Whitney, East Hartford, Connecticut, in the 1990 Silver Anvil awards competition sponsored by the Public Relations Society of America, pp. 1–2.

[7] Geoffrey Perkins, ed., *Employee Communications in the Public Sector* (London: Institute of Personnel Management, 1986), pp. 8–11, 20.

[8] Smith, p. 21.

9 Patrick Jackson, "Federal Express Trains Managers to Communicate with Front Line," *pr reporter,* March 25, 1991, pp. 2–3.

10 Smith, p. 110.

11 Perkins, p. 8.

12 "Winning Agreement on Job Responsibilities, Goals, and Priorities," in *The Guide to Employee Communication* (Pitman, N.J.: Communication Publications and Resources, 1990), p. 34.

13 Laurey Berk and Phillip G. Clampett, "Finding the Right Path in the Communication Maze," *Communication World,* International Association of Business Communicators, October 1991, p. 30.

14 "Restoring Communications," p. 2.

15 Berk and Clampett, p. 31.

16 Ibid.

17 Perkins, p. 37.

18 "Confronting Employees You'd Rather Avoid," *Practical Supervision,* May 15, 1992, pp. 6–7.

19 "Plain Speaking With Employees," *Practical Supervision,* November 15, 1991.

20 Jonathan Walters, "The Cult of Total Quality," *Governing,* May 1992, pp. 38–42.

21 Patrick Jackson, ed., "PMI: PR Staff Must Let Managers Communicate," *pr reporter,* March 25, 1991, pp. 1–2.

6 Working with the News Media

1 Michele Frisby, "Public Information: Educating and Communicating" (*MIS Report,* March 1991), p. 3.

2 Scott M. Cutlip, Allen H. Center, and Glen M. Broom, *Effective Public Relations,* 6th ed. (Englewood Cliffs, N.J.: Prentice-Hall, 1985), p. 431.

7 Communication Planning and Staffing

1 City of Chesapeake, Virginia, *City of Chesapeake Public Relations Program* (Chesapeake, Va.: City of Chesapeake, 1991), p. 1.

8 Interpersonal Communication

1 Genie Z. Laborde, *Influencing with Integrity* (Palo Alto, CA: Syntony Publishing, 1984), pp. 1–3. See also *The Structure of Magic: A Book about Language and Therapy* (Palo Alto, CA: Science and Behavior Books, 1975), and *Frogs into Princes: Neuro Linguistic Programming* (Moab, UT: Real People Press, 1979), both by Richard Bandler, for information on neurolinguistics.

2 David Keirsey and Marilyn Bates, *Please Understand Me: Character and Temperament Types* (Del Mar, CA: Prometheus Nemesis Books, 1978), pp. 1–4. See also Isabel Briggs Myers and Mary H. McCaulley, *A Guide to the Development and Use of the Myers-Briggs Type Indicator* (Palo Alto, CA: Consulting Psychologists Press, 1985).

3 Herbert A. Simon, *Administrative Behavior* (New York: Macmillan, 1947), p. 154.

4 For examples of such programs in the public sector, see David Osborne and Ted Gaebler, *Reinventing Government: How the Entrepreneurial Spirit is Transforming the Public Sector* (Reading, MA: Addison-Wesley, 1992). See especially Chapter 9, "Decentralized Government: From Hierarchy to Participation and Teamwork," pp. 250–79.

5 Terrence E. Deal and Allan A. Kennedy, *Corporate Cultures: The Rites and Rituals of Corporate Life* (Reading, MA: Addison-Wesley, 1982), pp. 85–103.

6 Jerome B. McKinney and Lawrence Howard, *Public Administration: Balancing Power and Accountability* (Oak Park, IL: Moore Publishing, 1979), 241.

7 Christine Becker, *So Now You're a Trainer: A Practical Guide for Practical Trainers* (Washington, DC: International City/County Management Association, 1991). See pp. 3–7 for an overview of human resources development programs.

8 Lennie Copeland, "Learning to Manage a Multicultural Workforce," *TRAINING: The Magazine of Human Resources Development* (May 1988), pp. 49–53.

9 Equal Employment Opportunity Commission, *Guidelines on Discrimination Because of Sex* (29 CFR 1604.11(c)).

10 Bobby R. Patton and Kim Griffin, *Decision-Making in Group Interaction* (New York: Harper & Row, 1978).

11 John Ingalls, *Human Energy: The Critical Factor for Individuals and Organizations* (Reading, MA: Addison-Wesley, 1976), p. 93.

9 Effective Presentations

1 Scott M. Cutlip, Allen H. Center, and Glen M. Broom, *Effective Public Relations,* 6th ed. (Englewood Cliffs, N.J.: Prentice-Hall, 1985). Quoted in Michele Frisby, "Public Information: Educating and Communicating," *MIS Report* (March 1991), p. 5.

2 Charles "Chic" Thompson, *What a Great Idea!* (New York: Harper Perennials, 1992).

3 James C. Humes, *Standing Ovation* (New York: Harper and Row, 1988).

4 Dale Carnegie, *Quick and Easy Ways to Effective Speaking* (New York: Pocket Books, 1990).

5 Warren Bennis, *On Becoming a Leader* (Reading, MA: Addison-Wesley, 1989).

6 Gene Perret, *How to Hold Your Audience with Humor* (Cincinnati, Ohio: Writer's Digest Books, 1984). Mel Helitzer, *Comedy Writing Secrets* (Cincinnati, Ohio: Writer's Digest Books, 1988).

8 Joan Detz, *How to Write and Give a Speech* (New York: St. Martin's Press, 1984).

9 Carnegie, *Effective Speaking,* p. 46.

For Further Reference

1 Effective Management Means Effective Communication

Cutlip, Scott M.; Center, Allen H.; and Broom, Glen M. *Effective Public Relations*. 6th ed., Englewood Cliffs, N.J.: Prentice Hall, 1985. The bible of organizational communication since 1952, the sixth edition includes chapters aimed at employees in government, public schools, and higher education.

Dunn, S. Watson. *Public Relations: A Contemporary Approach*. Homewood, Ill.: Irwin, 1986. A thorough overview of communication as done by institutions, with a practical approach to various techniques of communication. Includes a chapter on communication in the public sector.

Garnett, James L. *Communicating for Results in Government: A Strategic Approach for Government Managers*. San Francisco: Jossey-Bass, 1992. See especially Chapter 1, "Why Communication Is So Crucial to Government Success," pp. 3–19.

Gunter, Barrie. *Consumer Profiles: An Introduction to Psychographics*. New York: Routledge, 1992. Scholarly but accessible overview of psychographics.

Hamilton, Seymour. *A Communication Audit Handbook: Helping Organizations Communicate*. New York: Longman, 1987. Describes a how-to process that organizations can use to assess their communications and set goals for improvement.

Newsom, Doug, and Scott, Alan. *This Is PR: The Realities of Public Relations*. 3d ed. Belmont, Calif.: Wadsworth, 1981. Offers a practical approach to organizational communication, with plenty of illustrative material.

Stoner, Randall C. *Practical Promotion: Strategies for Improving Services and Image*. Washington, DC: ICMA, 1992. Includes dozens of case histories on local government communication programs throughout the United States, on a variety of topics from customer service to crisis communication.

2 The Identity and Image of Local Government

City Seal Committee, City of Kansas City, Missouri. *City Loop Style Book: A User's Guide*. Kansas City, Mo.: City of Kansas City, n.d. A combination mini-manual and case study of how one city has adopted and popularized its city logo. Also available as an appendix in *Practical Promotion: Strategies for Improving Services and Image*, by Randall C. Stoner (cited above).

Desky, Joanne, "Public Administrators Hook Up to Technology." *PA Times*, May 1, 1993, pp. 3, 13. Documents the spread of voice mail and other computer-based automated telephone systems.

Hodges, John C., et al. *The Harbrace College Handbook*. 11th ed. San Diego: Harcourt Brace Jovanovich, 1990. The thick little manual that—despite its title—everyone first got to know in high school. Unlike some of our high school acquaintances, it has aged well and still has good advice to offer. Its chapter on business writing includes good examples of effective letters.

Janowitz, Morris, and Hirsch, Paul, eds. *Reader in Public Opinion and Mass Communication*. 3d ed. New York: Free Press, 1981. Articles on formation of public opinion, the effects of public opinion on public policy, communications, media and audiences, and public opinion and democratic objectives.

Lesikar, Raymond V. *Basic Business Communication*. 4th ed. Homewood, Ill.: Irwin, 1988. Offers detailed guidance on writing letters; includes a section on communication in management.

Lippmann, Walter. *Public Opinion*. 1922. Reprint. New York: Free Press, 1966. Still widely read and quoted. Valuable for discussions of barriers to communication.

Miller, Thomas I, and Miller, Michelle A. *Citizen Surveys: How to Do Them, How to Use Them, What They Mean*. Washington, D.C.: ICMA, 1991. Developed by two employees of the Division of Research and Evaluation of the City of Boulder, Colorado, this ICMA Special Report provides practical guidance on measuring citizens' opinions of local government.

Morgan, David L., ed. *Successful Focus Groups: Advancing the State of the Art*. Thousand Oaks, Calif.: Sage, 1993. Tells when and how to use focus groups, how to integrate focus-group interviews with other types of survey research, and how to avoid problems in applying focus-group techniques to various populations and settings.

Townsend, Robert. *Up the Organization: How to Stop the Corporation from Stifling People and Strangling*

Profits. Greenwich, Conn.: Fact, 1970. A best seller soon after its publication, this classic of management literature was in many ways a generation ahead of its time, with its emphasis on creativity and its irreverence toward venerated orthodox premises and practices.

Zagoria, Sam. *The Ombudsman: How Good Governments Handle Citizens' Grievances*. Cabin John, Md.: Seven Locks Press, 1988. An explanation of the concept by a former ombudsman for the *Washington Post*.

3 The Local Citizen: Voter, Taxpayer, and Customer

Bass, Bernard M., and Avolio, Bruce J., eds. *Improving Organizational Effectiveness through Transformational Leadership*. Thousand Oaks, Calif.: Sage, forthcoming. See especially Chapter 9, "Corporate Reorganization and Transformations in Human Resource Management," by K. Galen Kroeck.

Garnett, James L. *Communicating for Results in Government*. San Francisco: Jossey-Bass, 1992. See especially Chapter 7, "Communicating with Government's Publics," pp. 165–200.

Gurwitt, Rob. "A Government That Runs on Citizen Power." *Governing*, December 1992, pp. 48–54. A look at Dayton, Ohio, the "state of the art" in participation by citizens in local government.

Miller, Thomas I, and Miller, Michelle A. "Standards of Excellence: U.S. Residents' Evaluations of Local Government Services." *Public Administration Review*, November-December 1991, pp. 503–13. A helpful source for local government officials looking for comparative benchmarks for assessing the delivery of services.

Osborne, David, and Gaebler, Ted. *Reinventing Government: How the Entrepreneurial Spirit Is Transforming the Public Sector*. Reading, Mass.: Addison-Wesley, 1992. See especially Chapter 6, "Meeting the Needs of the Customer, Not the Bureaucracy," pp. 166–94.

Potapchuk, William R. "New Approaches to Citizen Participation: Building Consent." *National Civic Review*, Spring 1991, pp. 158–68. Argues that "a positive, open, and collaborative civic culture will help promote constructive community decision making and trust between citizens and [local government] staff." Cites towns and cities where such planning has been successful.

Thompson, Stephanie. "Plugging into Constituencies." *American City and County*, August 1991, pp. 67–70. Describes how cities and counties are using new technologies to improve communications with local residents.

Wagenheim, George D., and Reurink, John H. "Customer Service in Public Administration," *Public Administration Review*, May-June 1991, pp. 263–70. The authors explain the citizen-as-customer concept and offer tactical and strategic approaches to applying it.

4 Communicating with Elected Officials

Denton, E. H., and Pisciotte, Joe P. "Enhancing the Governing Body's Effectiveness." In *The Effective Local Government Manager*, 2d ed., edited by Charldean Newell, pp. 53–79. Washington, D.C.: ICMA, 1993. Discusses the changing role of the governing body, the manager's responsibilities, barriers to effective manager/council relations, and how to strengthen policymaking capabilities.

Gordon, Gerald L. *Strategic Planning for Local Government*, Washington, D.C.: ICMA, 1993. Provides step-by-step guidance for developing reliable strategic plans that can help communities establish future goals and objectives. Includes examples of city and county environmental scans and internal analyses, goals, strategies, implementation plans, and update procedures.

Groves, Sanford M., and Valente, Maureen Godsey, *Evaluating Financial Condition: A Handbook for Local Government*, 3d ed. Washington, D.C.: ICMA, 1994. Shows how to develop easy to understand graphs to convey financial information. Helps managers assess how internal management practices, legislative policies, and demographic and economic forces affect their local government's financial health.

National Civic League. *Handbook for Council Members in Council-Manager Cities*. 4th ed. New York: National Civic League, 1989. Covers organization and conduct of council meetings and the relationship of the council to the manager.

Svara, James H. "Understanding the Mayor's Office in Council-Manager Cities." *Popular Government*. Institute of Government, University of North Carolina at Chapel Hill, North Carolina, 1985. Focuses on the unique communication role of the mayor as educator, liaison with the manager, and team leader for the council.

Tobin, Thomas. "The Budget as a Communication Tool." *MIS Report*. Washington, D.C.: ICMA, February 1988. Describes elements of effectively managing a budget process and presenting it in a way that will help elected officials understand the policy implications of their decisions.

Wilson, Richard C. *Loma Prieta Quake: What One City Learned*. Washington, D.C.: ICMA, 1991. A vivid account of how Santa Cruz, California, planned for, responded to, and recovered from the Loma Prieta earthquake in 1989. Describes the roles and responsibilities of top officials; covers communications issues.

5 Employees: The Local Government Team

Banovetz, James. "The Role of the City Manager in Effectiveness Team Building." *National Civic Review*, July/August 1990, pp. 350–53. The author suggests that the modern manager in local government must transcend old roles as agent of the elected council and director of his or her staff, and become a team builder.

Communication Publications and Resources. *The Guide to Employee Communication*. Pitman, N.J.: Communication Publications and Resources, 1990. Includes samples of "real-life" communication policies.

Frank, Stanley D. *Remember Everything You Read: The Evelyn Wood 7-Day Speed Reading and Learning Program*. New York: Avon, 1992. An updated version of the classic guide to reading rapidly while retaining comprehension.

Fruehling, Rosemary T. *Write to the Point: Letters, Memos, and Reports That Get Results*. New York: McGraw-Hill, 1992. A popular and widely available guide for the professional audience.

Garnett, James L. *Communicating for Results in Government: A Strategic Approach for Public Managers*. San Francisco: Jossey-Bass, 1992. See especially Chapter 5, "Strengthening Exchanges with Subordinates," pp. 99–138.

Katzenbach, Jon R., and Smith, Douglas K. *The Wisdom of Teams: Creating the High-Performance Organization*. New York: Harper, 1993. Offers guidance to effective teamwork among both staff and management.

Osborne, David, and Gaebler, Ted. *Reinventing Government: How the Entrepreneurial Spirit Is Transforming the Public Sector*. Reading, Mass.: Addison-Wesley, 1992. See especially Chapter 3, "Competitive Government: Injecting Competition into Service Delivery," pp. 76–107.

Perkins, Geoffrey, ed. *Employee Communications in the Public Sector*. London: Institute of Personnel Management, 1986. Recommends dividing the information you wish to communicate into five categories—*progress*, *profitability*, *plans*, *policies*, and *people*.

Sensenbrenner, Joseph. "Quality Comes to City Hall." *Harvard Business Review*, March/April 1991, pp. 4–10. The former mayor of Madison, Wisconsin, relates his experiences implementing total quality management and offers practical advice.

Smith, Alvie L. *Innovative Employee Communication: New Approaches to Improving Trust, Teamwork, and Performance*. Englewood Cliffs, N.J.: Prentice-Hall, 1991. Although he urges managers to trust their instincts when communicating with staff members, the author also

espouses careful planning of efforts to build teamwork.

6 Working with the News Media

Alvarez, Maribel. "Working with Multi-Ethnic Media." *Western City*, September 1991, pp. 29–30. The author, who is the press secretary to the mayor of San Jose, California, notes that in spite of their "nontraditional characteristics," "ethnic media have the unique advantage of penetrating important sectors of the public otherwise isolated from mainstream information sources."

Cutlip, Scott M.; Center, Allen H.; and Broom, Glen M. *Effective Public Relations*. 6th ed. Englewood Cliffs, N.J.: Prentice-Hall, 1985. A comprehensive, basic text containing practical information on the use of public relations techniques.

City of Claremont, California. *Media Relations Policy Manual*. Claremont, Calif.: City of Claremont, 1991. Outlines a comprehensive policy governing dissemination of official city information. Includes guidelines on responding to media queries, what to do when contacted by the media, and how to clarify inaccurate information released by the media. Also available as an ICMA Clearinghouse Report: Order no. 40562.

Frisby, Michele. "Public Information: Educating and Communicating." *MIS Report*, March 1991, entire issue. Discusses the history and evolution of government public relations, the responsibilities of the modern public information officer, and the ways in which local governments use information tools.

George, Karen A.; Summerfield, Scott; and Erlewine, Sheri. "Establishing a Public Information Program." *Western City*, September 1991, pp. 26–28, 55. Provides a brief, step-by-step guide to developing a public-information program. Aimed primarily at city governments, although the advice provided is widely applicable.

"Working Toward Good Media Relations." *Texas Town and City*, September 1992, pp. 40–41, 59. Offers thirteen terse pieces of advice to public officials whose duties include media relations.

7 Communication Planning and Staffing

Anderson, Desmond L., ed. *Municipal Public Relations*. Chicago: ICMA, 1966. Helps put the public-information function in context by providing a comprehensive history of "government publicity."

City of Chesapeake, Virginia. *City of Chesapeake Public Relations Program*. Chesapeake, Va.: City of Chesapeake, updated annually. Running more than fifty pages, this document is one of the relatively few examples of a comprehensive communication plan for a local government.

Frisby, Michele. "Public Information: Educating and Communicating." *MIS Report*, March 1991. In addition to a history of the public-information function in government, includes brief case studies of communication programs developed by several small U.S. cities.

Garnett, James L. *Communicating for Results in Government*. San Francisco: Jossey-Bass, 1992. See especially Chapter 3, "Applying a Strategic Model to Government Communication," pp. 34–67.

George, Karen A.; Summerfield, Scott; and Erlewine, Sheri. "Establishing a Public Information Program." *Western City*, September 1991, pp. 26–28, 55. Provides a brief, step-by-step guide to developing a public-information program. Aimed primarily at city governments, although the advice provided is widely applicable.

Stoner, Randall C. *Practical Promotion: Strategies for Improving Services and Image*. Washington, D.C.: ICMA, 1992. Chapter 3, "Structuring for Promotion," pp. 18–29, is especially helpful, with descriptions of how different cities have organized people and departments for public-information purposes.

8 Interpersonal Communication

Bandler, Richard. *The Structure of Magic: A Book about Language and Therapy*. Palo Alto, Calif.: Science and Behavior Books, 1975. A practical introduction to concepts of neurolinguistic programming and its applications for interpersonal communication.

Bandler, Richard. *Frogs into Princes: Neuro Linguistic Programming*. Moab, Utah: Real People Press, 1979. An update on NLP, including basic concepts and practical applications.

Deal, Terrence E., and Kennedy, Allan A. *Corporate Cultures: The Rites and Rituals of Corporate Life*. Reading, Mass.: Addison-Wesley, 1982. An early discussion of the importance of nonrational factors, such as ritual and culture, in organizational life.

Janis, Irving L., *Victims of Groupthink: A Psychological Study of Foreign-Policy Decisions and Fiascoes*. Boston: Houghton Mifflin, 1972. Cases studies include the Bay of Pigs, Pearl Harbor, and the Vietnam War. Skillful use of history to make points that are applicable in all organizations.

Kiersey, David, and Bates, Marilyn. *Please Understand Me: Character and Temperament Types*. Del Mar, Calif.: Prometheus Nemesis Books, 1978. An overview of the development and use of the Myers-Briggs Type Indicator, its relationship to C.G. Jung's theory of personality types, and its applications in organizations.

Laborde, Genie Z., *Influencing with Integrity*. Palo Alto, Calif.: Syntony Publishing, 1984. Background information on communication theory as it relates to human behavior, as well as practical advice and exercises to improve skills in communicating.

Briggs Myers, Isabel, and McCaulley, Mary H. *A Guide to the Development and Use of the Myers-Briggs Type Indicator*. Palo Alto, Calif.: Consulting Psychologists Press, 1985. A user's guide to clarify how the theory of personality types as evaluated through the Myers-Briggs Type Indicator can be translated into practice.

Patton, Bobby R., and Giffin, Kim. *Decision-Making in Group Interaction*. New York: Harper and Row, 1978. A primer on theory of groups, with discussion of the dynamics, the decision making, and the effectiveness of groups.

Thiederman, Sondra B. *Bridging Cultural Barriers for Corporate Success: How to Manage the Multicultural Work Force*. Lexington, Mass.: Lexington Books, 1991. Practical ideas for improving communication with workers whose English is limited.

9 Effective Presentations

Bennis, Warren. *On Becoming a Leader* (audiocassette). : Nightingale-Conant. Leadership guru Warren Bennis advises, "The art of leadership is the art of being human."

Carnegie, Dale. *Public Speaking*. New York: Pocket Books, 1956. Another of the communication classics by the late author of *How to Win Friends and Influence People*. Dale Carnegie and Associates, Inc., also offers seminars in communication and "people skills."

Cook, Jeff Scott. *The Elements of Speechwriting and Public Speaking*. New York: Macmillan, 1989.

Decker, Bert. *You've Got to Be Believed to Be Heard*. New York: St. Martin's Press, 1992. Communication consultant Decker suggests ways to streamline complex information into simple yet informative presentations.

Detz, Joan. *How to Write and Give A Speech*. New York: St. Martin's Press, 1984. Hands-on advice from a practicing speechwriter.

Dutton, John L. *How To Be an Outstanding Speaker*. 2d ed. Appleton, Wisc.: Life Skills, 1987.

Garnett, James L. *Communicating for Results in Government*. San Francisco: Jossey-Bass, 1992. See especially Chapter 9, "Improving Communication Skills," pp. 249–75.

Graivier, Pauline. "How to Speak So People Will Listen: Tips for Better Verbal Presentations." *Planning*, December 1992, pp. 15–18. Communication consultant Graivier, whose clients have included the city of Dallas, offers advice on everything from visual aids to when to wear your jacket unbuttoned and when not to.

Helitzer, Mel. *Comedy Writing Secrets*. Cincinnati, Ohio: Writer's Digest Books, 1988. Humor-writing guru Mel Helitzer explains how to develop gags by "associative brainstorming"; he also offers other suggestions to take some of the mystery out of writing comedy.

Humes, James C. *Standing Ovation*. New York: Harper and Row, 1988. Guidance from a one-time presidential speechwriter.

Perret, Gene. *How to Hold Your Audience with Humor*. Cincinnati, Ohio: Writer's Digest Books, 1984. A humorist, Perret nonetheless aims his guidance at speakers interested in humor as a means, not an end.

Platt, Suzy, ed. *Respectfully Quoted*. Washington, D.C.: Library of Congress, 1989. A collection of quotations that members of Congress most frequently ask the research specialist at the Library of Congress to provide, arranged by speaker and category. Especially handy for subjects in the realm of government and public service.

Quick, John. *Dog and Pony Shows: How to Make Winning Presentations when the Stakes Are High*. New York: McGraw-Hill, 1992.

Thompson, Charles "Chic." *What A Great Idea!* New York: Harper, 1992. Creative and unorthodox approaches to problem solving.

Recommended Periodicals
The Executive Speaker
P.O. Box 292437
Dayton, Ohio 45429
Vital Speeches of the Day
City News Publishing Company
P.O. Box 1247
Mount Pleasant, S.C. 29465

10 Local Government Publications

Baker, Kim, and Baker, Sunny. *Color Publishing on the PC: From Desktop to Printshop*. New York: Random House, 1993. Probably not required reading for the beginning desktop publisher, but well-written and informative nonetheless.

Bernstein, Theodore. *The Careful Writer: A Modern Guide to English Usage*. New York: Atheneum, 1965. Essential reading for writers and editors. Includes a surprisingly entertaining list of usage issues, arranged alphabetically.

Chicago Manual of Style. 14th ed. Chicago: University of Chicago Press, 1993. A standard reference on English style, oriented toward scholarly (as opposed to journalistic or governmental) publications, for authors, editors, copywriters, and proofreaders. Includes a lengthy bibliography of reference works.

Glover, Gary. *Image Scanning for Desktop Publishers*. Blue Ridge Summit, Pa.: Windcrest Books, 1990. An excellent resource for anyone interested in or committed to a more sophisticated desktop publishing operation. Easy to read and understand, even for novices.

Goldstein, Norm, ed. *The Associated Press Stylebook and Libel Manual*. Reading, Mass.: Addison-Wesley, 1992. Generations of reporters and writers have relied on this classic.

Judd, Karen. *Copyediting: A Practical Guide*. Los Altos, Calif.: William Kaufmann, 1982. Explains the copyediting process. Provides guidance on commonly accepted practices in copy editing and the use of style sheets. A good guide to the use of grammar and punctuation.

Miller, Casey, and Swift, Kate. *The Handbook of Nonsexist Writing*. 2d ed. New York: Harper and Row, 1988. A guide to graceful and sensible writing that is also nonsexist. Provides particularly helpful advice on how to avoid disagreement of subject and verb.

Nadler, James. *The Dover Clip Art Library (PC Edition)*. New York: Bantam Books, 1993. A reasonably priced collection of clip art for the computer.

Strunk, William, Jr., and White, E. B. *The Elements of Style*. 3d ed. New York: Macmillan, 1979. A "little book"—as Strunk called it— offering terse practical advice by the Cornell University professor and amusing but instructive mini-essays by his most famous pupil.

Tobin, Thomas. "The Budget as a Communication Tool." *MIS Report*. Washington, D.C.: ICMA, February 1988. Includes successful examples of the increasingly important task of devising a city or county budget that makes sense to the customers of local government.

Williams, Patricia A. *Creating and Producing the Perfect Newsletter*. Glenview, Ill.: Scott, Foresman, 1990. Everything from the selection of a name for your newsletter to distribution methods. A good desktop reference.

11 The Role of Cable Television

Achs, Nicole. "Late Night with Local Government." *American City and County*, March 1992, pp. 54–57. Includes suggestions on how local government can make the most of its relationship with the local cable franchiser.

City of Arlington. *1991–92 Annual Report Video*. Arlington, Texas: City of Arlington, 1992. Representative of the increasingly common practice of producing an annual report in video as well as print formats. In an effective touch, the narrator introduces herself as a city resident at the opening of the video. Running time about 10 minutes.

City of Phoenix. *1991–92 Annual Report*. Phoenix, Arizona: City of Phoenix, 1992. Another annual report in video form, this one notable for the inclusion of frank discussion of the city's problems as well as its successes. Running time about 10 minutes.

Finucan, Karen. "Roll 'Em: Getting the Most for Your Video Dollar." *Planning*, August 1990, pp. 12–16. Case studies and practical advice about generating and using video for public-information purposes.

Havlick, Robert, and Farr, Cheryl. "Video Technology: Programs and Uses." *MIS Report*, January 1987. A lively and helpful history of the early days (i.e., the late 1970s and early 1980s) of local government cable TV. Also includes a lot of practical advice that remains relevant.

Kupfer, Andrew. "Prime Time for Videoconferences." *Fortune*, December 28, 1992, pp. 90–95. Explains the problems and prospects of "meetings via video." Focuses on the increasing affordability of the technology.

Mason, Donna M. "Vancouver, Wash., on Camera: How One City Made Public Access TV Big Time for Citizens." *Nation's Cities Weekly*, August 27, 1990, pp. 3–4. A short, vivid, and informative case study of what one city has done to implement and popularize local government cable TV.

Stoner, Randall C. *Practical Promotion: Strategies for Improving Services and Image*. Washington, D.C.: ICMA, 1992. See especially Chapter 5, "Promoting Existing Programs to Citizens," pp. 46–73, which includes sections on interactive cable TV and videotext.

Thompson, Stephanie. "Plugging into Constituencies." *American City and County*, August 1991, pp. 67–70. Highlights different means local governments are using to introduce interactive communication technology.

Illustration Credits

About the Authors

Christine Becker is deputy executive director of the National League of Cities, a position she has held since December 1990. She has previously served as chief of staff in the Washington, D.C., Department of Corrections, chief of human resource development in the D.C. Office of Personnel, and director of education services at the International City/County Management Association. Ms. Becker holds a bachelor's degree in English literature from Boston College and an MPA from the University of Southern California Washington Public Affairs Center.

Del D. Borgsdorf is an assistant city manager in Charlotte, North Carolina. He is responsible for economic and neighborhood development activities. He has served as city administrator of Ann Arbor and Southfield, Michigan, and of Davenport, Iowa. Mr. Borgsdorf spent several years as a director of state and local government consulting for Coopers & Lybrand, with assignments from Newark, New Jersey, to Los Angeles, California. Mr. Borgsdorf holds a bachelor's and master's degree from the University of Michigan, Ann Arbor.

William H. Guerrant is director of the Public Service and Information Department of the city of Charlotte, North Carolina, a position he has held since 1971. He administers the internal and external public information programs for the city and directs video services, including an institutional network and government access and training channels. He is a presenter for many state and national organizations and is a founding member, past president, and board member of the City-County Communications and Marketing Association. Mr. Guerrant has also worked as a military journalist, photographer, and broadcaster and has served as public relations specialist for private industry.

Mark Hughes has served since 1979 as public information director for the city of Phoenix, Arizona. Previously, he worked for eleven years as director of Information Services at the University of Nevada, Las Vegas, and before that as an assistant in the News Bureau at Arizona State University. He began his career in journalism as a reporter for *The Arizona Republic*, the morning newspaper in Phoenix. He is the former president of the Phoenix Press Club and the Phoenix chapter of the Public Relations Society of America (PRSA). Mr. Hughes currently serves on PRSA's national accreditation board. He holds a master's in English from the University of Nevada, Las Vegas, and an bachelor's in journalism from Arizona State University.

Elizabeth K. Kellar is deputy executive director of the International City/County Management Association. She is the author of "The Ethics Factor" and editor of *Ethical Insight, Ethical Action*, *Managing with Less*, and *Effective Communication: Getting the Message Across*. She has also served as managing editor of *Public Management* magazine. In addition, she has made numerous presentations on ethics at state and national meetings. Ms. Kellar was previously the community relations officer, Sunnyvale, California, instructor for the National Training and Development Service,

and member of the Montgomery County, Maryland, Commission on the Future. She has a master's degree in journalism and political science from Ohio State University.

Jewel D. Scott is executive director of the Civic Council of Greater Kansas City, Kansas City, Missouri, a civic group made up of the chief executive officers of the Kansas City area's major business enterprises. She was formerly city manager of Delaware, Ohio, and prior to that was director of convention facilities and assistant to the city manager in Kansas City, Missouri. She also served as administrative aide/public information officer for the city of Lawrence, Kansas, and covered local government as a newspaper reporter for four years. Ms. Scott holds a bachelor's degree in journalism and a master's degree in public administration, both from the University of Kansas. She is active on several public boards and commissions in Missouri and was recently appointed by Missouri Governor Mel Carnahan to the Education Commission of the States.

Frederick Talbott has taught professional communications at Old Dominion University, at the Owen Graduate School of Management of Vanderbilt University, and at Midlands Technical College. He is an active speaker and leadership communications consultant, serving corporations, professional associations, and federal, state, and local government groups. He is also an active humorist whose work has included contributions to a humor writing workshop with the White House speechwriting team in 1991 and to NBC's *Saturday Night Live*. Mr.

Talbott holds a bachelor's degree in journalism from Florida Southern College and a master's in journalism and a Juris Doctor degree from the University of South Carolina.

Kenneth M. Wheeler is president of MDC Counselors, a communication counseling firm in Virginia Beach, Virginia. He has worked with more than seventy businesses, associations, and government agencies on various aspects of communication and marketing. He is a frequent contributor to magazines and newsletters and has conducted workshops and seminars throughout the country. Mr. Wheeler was director of Communications and Marketing for the city of Norfolk, Virginia, from 1971 to 1984 and was an urban affairs reporter with *The Virginian-Pilot* newspaper in Norfolk. A Phi Beta Kappa graduate of the University of North Carolina, he teaches graduate courses in public relations, marketing, and research at Regent University. ■

Index

Municipal Management Series

Effective Communication

Text Type
New Century Schoolbook and
Helvetica Condensed

Printing and Binding
McNaughton & Gunn
Saline, Michigan

Paper
Champion Pinehurst
Publishers Offset 60#